Languages in Contact

Introducing new findings from popular culture, the globalised new economy and computer-mediated communication, this is a fascinating study of contact between languages of pre-modern and modern societies. Lim and Ansaldo bring together research on multilingualism, code switching, language endangerment and globalisation into a comprehensive overview of world Englishes, creoles and other contact languages. Illustrated with a wide range of original examples from typologically diverse languages, including Sinitic, Austronesian, Dravidian and other non-Indo-European varieties, the book focuses on social and structural analyses of Asian ecologies and their relevance for current theories of contact phenomena. Full of new insights, it is essential reading for students and researchers across linguistics, culture and communication.

- Features numerous original examples and case studies, with a particular focus on Asia
- Critically evaluates the key issues and debates
- Analyses language contact in the context of globalisation and computer-mediated communication

LISA LIM is Associate Professor and Coordinator of the Language and Communication Programme in the School of English at the University of Hong Kong. She co-edited *The Typology of Asian Englishes* (English World-Wide 2009) and *English in Multilingual, Globalising Asia* (2009). She has developed the online resource *Linguisticminorities.hk*, for which she won the Faculty Knowledge Exchange Award 2014.

UMBERTO ANSALDO is Professor in Linguistics at the University of Hong Kong. His book *Contact Languages: Ecology and Evolution* (Cambridge University Press, 2009) garnered the Faculty Research Output Award 2010. He is co-editor of the Creole Language Library, and founding editor of the new journal *Language Ecology*.

KEY TOPICS IN SOCIOLINGUISTICS

Series editor: Rajend Mesthrie

This new series focuses on the main topics of study in sociolinguistics today. It consists of accessible yet challenging accounts of the most important issues to consider when examining the relationship between language and society. Some topics have been the subject of sociolinguistic study for many years, and are here re-examined in the light of new developments in the field; others are issues of growing importance that have not so far been given a sustained treatment. Written by leading experts, the books in the series are designed to be used on courses and in seminars, and include useful suggestions for further reading.

Already published in the series:

Languages in Contact

LISA LIM AND UMBERTO ANSALDO

CAMBRIDGE
UNIVERSITY PRESS

CAMBRIDGE
UNIVERSITY PRESS

University Printing House, Cambridge CB2 8BS, United Kingdom

Cambridge University Press is part of the University of Cambridge.

It furthers the University's mission by disseminating knowledge in the pursuit of education, learning and research at the highest international levels of excellence.

www.cambridge.org
Information on this title: www.cambridge.org/9780521149259

First published 2016

Printed in the United Kingdom by Clays, St Ives plc

A catalogue record for this publication is available from the British Library

Library of Congress Cataloguing in Publication data
Lisa Lim and Umberto Ansaldo, authors.
Languages in contact / Lisa Lim and Umberto Ansaldo.
    pages   cm. – (Key Topics in Sociolinguistics)
Includes bibliographical references and index.
ISBN 978-0-521-76795-8 (Hardback) – ISBN 978-0-521-14925-9 (Paperback)
1. Languages in contact.   I. Lim, Lisa, author.   II. Title.
P130.5.A64   2015
306.44 – dc23   2015012530

ISBN 978-0-521-76795-8 Hardback
ISBN 978-0-521-14925-9 Paperback

Contents

Figures

Tables

Preface

On a little dot of a tropical island in Southeast Asia just above the equator, a decade and a half ago, the Department of English Language and Literature of the National University of Singapore witnessed an encounter between two colleagues, one newly hired. Neither imagined that that contact would lead to any output of substance or significance, for the simple reason that they came from very different academic backgrounds and had, at that point, minimal knowledge or interest in the other's fields. One had trained as a phonetician and was working on a New English in the World Englishes paradigm. The other was a creolist and typologist specialising in Sinitic varieties. A standing joke was that we would never be talking about work when we got together outside office hours, so distinct and compartmentalised were our interests and expertise.

This ontological anecdote underlines the essence of this book. The studies of pidgin and creole languages on the one hand and World Englishes on the other are almost always written about as separate animals; an exception is John Platt, whose writing in the 1970s and 1980s did integrate the study of New Englishes with pidgin and creole studies, as is, more recently, Bao Zhiming. One primary aim of this book was indeed to bring our collective expertise in our respective fields together in an integrated view, such that what is common and comparable in the sociolinguistic factors and structural processes involved in the evolution of contact varieties – whether creoles, New Englishes or mixed codes – might be recognised. Our discussions in the early years planted the seed. Half a dozen years at the University of Amsterdam and the Amsterdam Centre for Language and Communication – in particular our engagement with colleagues in the Language Creation and the Sociolinguistics and Multilingualism groups and other scholars in Europe and the US, who were doing critical, cutting-edge research – profoundly influenced our thinking, especially in developing an analysis of New Englishes from a contact perspective. That being said, it might still appear surprising to the reader that it is a mere two chapters that appear to be dedicated to pidgin and creole languages and linguistics, these being the cornerstone of the study of languages in contact, when the majority of books in the field usually devote themselves entirely to them. However, the goal of this book was not to try to encompass what other colleagues have much more comprehensively and magnificently covered in other books on pidgins and creoles. Rather – as but one facet of the book – we aimed to distil the main topics in creole studies and provide a critical account for the reader to be able to better evaluate the significant issues and major debates in the field. Above all, what we wanted to do with this book was to integrate perspectives and research from the fields of multilingualism and code switching, language shift and endangerment, and language and globalisation – fields we have also been engaged in actively in our research and which are all significant in a consideration of languages in contact. To this end, a chapter is devoted to each of these. With the burgeoning in the past decade of language and globalisation studies, in particular, we felt it imperative that this book should also consider the new sites of contact that globalisation affords, including those arising in computer-mediated communication, popular culture and the globalised new economy. The phenomena of contact, its processes and products are manifested in myriad forms, beyond pidgin and creole languages, and extend beyond past scenarios into contemporary contexts.

Our remit, in the conceptualisation of this book, was also to bring to bear our research and expertise in contact scenarios of Asia. Thus, while we have endeavoured to give a sense of the central issues and classic examples of the various topics covered, we have foregrounded research and illustrations from Asia. These involve typologically diverse languages in contact, including Sinitic, Austronesian, Dravidian and other non-Indo-European varieties – many of them presented for the first time – from our own work and the work of others, and we discuss their relevance for current theories of contact phenomena.

This book, then, is one that is for students and scholars not only of creole studies but also of World Englishes, language endangerment, language and globalisation, language and communication, and policy and education. It is for anyone interested in considering the outcome of contact of all kinds – New Englishes, mixed codes, endangered languages – that have occurred and continue to occur in diverse ecologies. It is for the reader who is keen on exploring this field with fresh eyes, and on considering current and future research areas of promise for a deeper and renewed understanding of language contact in modern societies.

Acknowledgements

Contact begets outcomes. In a serendipitous encounter at a conference in Cape Town in 2007, Rajend Methrie, over a sublime Pinotage on a beautiful South African evening, invited us to contribute a volume on contact linguistics to his series, reflecting our unique perspective. As things happen in life, numerous events occurred and our trajectory evolved in the years that followed. We traversed continents to relocate from North Sea climes to the subtropical zone, back to the region we hold so dear: Asia. We both took up positions at the University of Hong Kong, involving critical administrative responsibilities. We became besotted parents. The pause all this brought to the writing of this book notwithstanding, we believe that our more recent years in Hong Kong, involving teaching on diverse courses related to contact linguistics and new research projects based in the region, collude to make this a much richer book than it would have been had we written it more quickly a few years earlier. We are grateful that Raj never got too impatient with us; on the contrary, he has been a source of unstinting support and encouragement. We are also extremely grateful for his pointed and constructive comments on the content and style of our drafts, which have been invaluable for shaping the manuscript for the Key Topics in Sociolinguistics series. His thoroughness, thoughtfulness and good humour are much appreciated.

We have had the privilege and pleasure over the years to share our views and engage in discussion over issues in contact linguistics, language endangerment and emergent varieties with numerous colleagues, and we are grateful for how our thinking and research have been shaped and sharpened by them: Enoch Aboh, Jacques Arends, Peter Austin, Dik Bakker, Peter Bakker, Bao Zhiming, Walter Bisang, Kingsley Bolton, Ariane Borlongan, Adrienne Bruyn, Hugo Cardoso, Jasone Cenoz, Katherine Chen, Michel DeGraff, Hans den Besten, Ana Deumert, David Gil, Durk Gorter, Ulrike Gut, Bernd Kortmann, Nicholas Evans, Nicholas Faraclas, Nikolas Gisborne, Martin Haspelmath, Bernd Heine, Raymond Hickey, Wolfram Hinzen, John Holm, Magnus Huber, Randy LaPolla,

Lee Cher Leng, Sarah Lee, Claire Lefebvre, Jakob Leimgruber, Li Wei, Ee-Ling Low, Christian Mair, Stephen Matthews, Rajend Mesthrie, Miriam Meyerhoff, Susanne Michaelis, Salikoko Mufwene, Pieter Muysken, Sebastian Nordhoff, Anne Pakir, Martin Pütz, Edgar Schneider, Armin Schwegler, Devyani Sharma, Geoff Smith, Larry Smith, Norval Smith, Rajendra Singh, Christopher Stroud, Uri Tadmor, Tan Ying Ying, Lionel Wee, Kofi Yakpo, as well as other colleagues in the Language Creation and the Sociolinguistics and Multilingualism groups of the Amsterdam Centre for Language and Communication during our years there.

Significant portions of the material in this book stem from courses we have been teaching at the University of Hong Kong: CCGL9024 *The life and death of languages: Diversity, identity and globalisation*, CCGL9038 *English as a global language in Asian contexts*, ENGL2030 *World Englishes*, LCOM1002 *Language, communication, society, field*, LCOM2005 *Language, communication and globalisation*, LCOM3001 *Cultural dimensions of language and communication*, LING2056 *Sociolinguistics* and LING2040 *Languages in contact*. Were it not for our students, we would not have developed some of the topics in this book, such as Chapter 6 on shift and endangerment, and Chapter 7 on contact and globalisation, and would not have expressed them in the way that we do. We have also drawn from our previous and ongoing research. The sections on Sri Lanka Malay are based on some of Umberto Ansaldo's and our joint articles and chapters, including: 'Identity alignment in the multilingual space: The Malays of Sri Lanka', in E. Anchimbe (ed.), *Linguistic Identity in Postcolonial Multilingual Spaces* (2007); 'Revisiting Sri Lanka Malay: Genesis and classification', in K.D. Harrison, D. Rood and A. Dwyer (eds.), *A World of Many Voices: Lessons from Documenting Endangered Languages* (2008); 'Contact language formation in evolutionary terms', in E.O. Aboh and N. Smith (eds.), *Complex Processes in New Languages* (2009); 'Identity alignment and language creation in multilingual communities', *Language Science* 32(6); 'Metatypy in Sri Lanka Malay', in R. Singh and G. Sharma (eds.), *Annual Review of South Asian Languages and Linguistics 2011* (2011); 'The lifecycle of Sri Lanka Malay' in *Language Documentation and Conservation* 7 (2014); 'Citizenship theory and fieldwork practice in Sri Lanka Malay communities', in L. Lim, C. Stroud and L. Wee (eds.), *The Multilingual Citizen: Towards a Politics of Language for Agency and Change* (forthcoming). Much of Chapter 5 on contact and ecology is based on and developed from Lisa Lim's work on particles and on tone, principally 'Mergers and acquisitions: On the ages and origins of Singapore English particles', *World Englishes* 26(4): 446–73 (2007); 'Revisiting English prosody: (Some) New Englishes as tone languages?', *English World-Wide* 30(2): 218–39 (2009); and the chapter on 'Southeast Asia' in M. Filppula, J. Klemola and D. Sharma (eds.), *The Oxford Handbook of World Englishes* (2014).

Lisa Lim's grant for her project on *The ecology and evolution of Asian Englishes*, from the Hong Kong Research Grants Council (RGC) General Research Fund (GRF) 2011/12 Exercise, provided her with two precious semesters with little or no teaching in the autumns of 2012 and 2013, which afforded her time to ponder and compose. Several locations around Hong Kong – cafés in Central en route to yoga practice, and cha chaan tengs in Wah Fu while waiting for playgroup to be over – provided conducive atmospheres to write with a purpose.

For discussions and comments on parts of this manuscript and other work that contributed to this book we are especially grateful to Hugo Cardoso, Stephen Matthews, Christopher Stroud and Viveka Velupillai. We are also grateful to our research assistants at various points of the compilation: Bonnie Wong and Vesela Dimitrova for background research and Jackie Lai for the most diligent, meticulous and swift assistance with the bibliography and the Chinese and Japanese scripts in the examples.

At Cambridge University Press we thank Andrew Winnard, Executive Publisher in Social Sciences, for his interest in and support of this project from the outset and his advice and patience throughout the writing of this book; Bethany Gaunt (who took over from Helena Dowson), Assistant Editor for Language and Linguistics, for her efficiency, support and good cheer, and especially for expediting things to the production process; production editors Ed Robinson and Chloé Harries for their clarity and competence; and Lydia Wanstall for her impeccably meticulous and thoughtful copy-editing.

We dedicate this book to our own most dazzling, inspiring and precious creation of contact, Kiran Jun Tito Ansaldo.

Abbreviations

APiCS	*Atlas of Pidgin and Creole Language Structures*
CLF	contact language formation
CMC	computer-mediated communication
CP	Creole Prototype
eWAVE	*Electronic World Atlas of Varieties of English*
H	'high' variety of a language; or high-level tone
HC	Haitian Creole
HCE	Hawai'i Creole English
HKE	Hong Kong English
IIUM	International Islamic University Malaysia
JC	Jamaican Creole
L	'low' variety of a language; or low-level tone
L1	first language
L2	second language
LBH	Language Bioprogram Hypothesis
M	'middle' variety of a language; or mid-level tone
MalE	Malaysian English
MOEI	Migrant Outreach Education Initiative
NHCSLV	non-hybrid conventionalised second-language varieties
NigE	Nigerian English
OED	*Oxford English Dictionary*
PerE	Peranakan English
SgE	Singapore English
SLA	second language acquisition
SLM	Sri Lanka Malay
SOV	Subject-Object-Verb
StdM	Standard Malay
SVO	Subject-Verb-Object
TMA	tense, mood and aspect
UNESCO	United Nations Educational, Scientific and Cultural Organisation

1 Perspectives on contact

1.1 INTRODUCTION

On 26 December 2004, an undersea earthquake occurred in the Indian Ocean with an epicentre off the west coast of Sumatra, Indonesia. At 9.0 on the Richter scale, it triggered a series of tsunamis along the coasts of most landmasses bordering the Indian Ocean, which inundated coastal communities with waves up to thirty metres, and killed more than 230,000 people in fourteen countries. Close to the epicentre, most of the Andaman and Nicobar Islands – an archipelago of 572 islands in the Bay of Bengal between Myanmar and Indonesia – were devastated. As it was feared that North Sentinel Island, one of the Andaman Islands, would also have been swamped, an Indian Coast Guard rescue helicopter was sent to check on casualties. A single naked bowman emerged from the forest and fired arrows to drive the helicopter away. This made the news, not only for the fact that the Sentinelese had survived the tsunami. What piqued the world's interest then – and continues to do so – was the existence of a 'Stone Age' tribe (as it came to be dubbed), numbering about 250, thought to be directly descended from the first human populations to emerge from Africa. The tribespeople were estimated to have lived on the Andaman Islands for up to 60,000 years, but with very little contact with the outside world for thousands of years. That their language is so different even from other Andaman Islanders suggests this lack of contact; that they continue to actively and violently reject any form of outside incursion or contact suggests they prefer it this way.

News of 'uncontacted peoples' such as the Sentinelese – that is, communities who live, or have lived, either by choice or by circumstance, without significant contact with globalised civilisation – never fails to garner the world's attention. The idea of having no contact with any other community, especially in today's global world, strikes most as incredible, in all respects. After all, contact between communities, and their languages, is such a fundamental human experience, one which

1

has been occurring since almost the beginning of humanity – an experience which by the very nature of human beings involves communication. It is of small wonder, then, that the study of languages in contact is of interest to many.

1.1.1 Speakers in contact

The study of language contact is an integral and important part of linguistics for a number of reasons that will become clear below. But before we even step into the realm of linguistics, it is important to appreciate that the study of language contact is really, as pre-empted above, the study of speakers in contact. In other words, it involves analysing and understanding what speakers of different languages do when they need to communicate across linguistic barriers imposed by their different languages. As such, language contact is the study of human societies, their histories, cultures and ideologies, and how these impact on human behaviour. In this sense, language is but a window on human nature, a documentable and describable domain, thanks to the analytical tools developed in linguistics, which can lead to deep insights into the way in which humans, as individuals as well as social networks, negotiate identity, power, ideology and ethnicity through linguistic acts. Language contact is therefore one of the fields of linguistics most likely to hold relevance for other traditional fields of humanities, such as history and philosophy, as well as education and the social sciences. Its importance cannot be underestimated; we live in a globalising world in which the economic tension between centre and periphery, the developmental challenges between North and South, and the scientific and technological competition between East and West exacerbate the necessity and urgency of cross-cultural communication and interethnic admixture. In this world, understanding how to manage the power of language, as a mediating tool as well as a site of struggle, is fundamental for a more enlightened and just society.

Since the publication some sixty years ago of Uriel Weinreich's renowned monograph *Languages in Contact* (1953), which, most scholars concur, marked the beginning of modern contact linguistics, work in the field has burgeoned. It has become one of the fastest growing areas of linguistics, with scholarship also drawing from diverse fields such as sociolinguistics, historical linguistics, dialectology and second language acquisition (SLA). A seminal introduction to the field is Appel and Muysken's (1987) textbook, while Thomason and Kaufman's (1988) widely cited book lays the foundation of language contact from a historical and genetic perspective. Pidgin and creole languages are given thorough treatment in the works of Holm (1988, 1989), as well as

Arends, Muysken and Smith (1994). The phenomenon of code switching is captured in studies such as Myers-Scotton (1993), Milroy and Muysken (1995), and Muysken (2000). Influential work in SLA and language contact can be found in Andersen (1983).

What do we look at when we study languages in contact? In this book, we will suggest that the most powerful approach to language contact is a sociolinguistic one. Six decades ago, Weinreich (1953: 83–110) demonstrated that the linguistic outcomes of language contact are in large part conditioned by sociocultural variables, including extent and degree of bilingualism; length of contact; geographical and demographic distribution; social factors such as religion, race, gender and age; use in different social functions such as education, government, media and literature; and political and ideological factors, including those of prestige and language loyalty. Indeed, it has thereafter been repeatedly argued, in other influential work such as Le Page and Tabouret-Keller (1985) and Thomason and Kaufman (1988), that speakers' agency is an important, possibly crucial factor behind language change. Thus, although it is at times useful to abstract the study of language away from speakers, we should not forget that it is ultimately in the speaker's actions, conscious or unaware though they may be, that the key to the processes of language contact lies.

A sociolinguistic approach is also important if we are prepared to acknowledge the limitations of structuralist approaches to language contact. Despite the intense search for constraints that might lead to a deeper understanding of universal aspects of language structure, the field of contact linguistics has time and again proven that no constraints hold when speakers of different grammars come into contact. Language admixture can be as varied and creative as the sociocultural contexts allow it to be. This, to be fair, is in line with latest developments in Chomskyan linguistics, which acknowledge that universal or hard-wired aspects of language structure might have to be confined to a few elementary operations of generic cognitive nature (Hauser, Chomsky and Fitch 2002). Acknowledging that 'everything goes' as a defining principle of language contact is not admitting defeat; quite the contrary, it is a step forward in understanding that, if constraints exist, they must be sought outside grammar, in sociolinguistic patterns of language use. This is corroborated by at least three different fields of linguistic enquiry:

    i. linguistic diversity, or linguistic typology, which, with an increasing understanding of structural variation, is calling for a theory of language that aims at explaining diversity, rather than universality, as a defining cognitive capacity of humans (Evans and Levinson 2009);

ii. usage-based acquisition and language socialisation theory, which conclude that children acquire language largely through exposure, based on cognitive routines that are not language-specific, thus highlighting the role of society and, in particular, adults in understanding patterns of language use (Tomasello 2005; Kulick and Schiefflin 2007); and

iii. language evolution, which recognises that contact between different linguistic features is a fundamental underlying force in language evolution at large (Mufwene 2001; Ansaldo 2009a).

In this book, we approach the emergence of contact languages as a product of various forms of 'choices' that speakers in multilingual ecologies make. Our approach takes the view that contact languages including pidgins and creoles arise as solutions to specific contexts, as already noted in Baker (1995; see also Ansaldo, Matthews and Lim 2007).

1.1.2 Ecology and evolution

Language contact is as old as humanity, since it defines the earliest and most vital encounters between different human groups in contexts such as markets, intellectual exchanges, rituals and conflict. As such, it must account for one of the most important forces behind language change and speciation. In an evolutionary framework, it is reasonable to assume that there are two paths to the diversity that characterises human languages: (a) mutation – i.e. change that can occur in relatively isolated populations over time – and (b) adaptation – i.e. contact-induced change. Both are ultimately motivated by the same human need: identity construction, or alignment, as argued recently in Ansaldo (2009a). In other recent work, Dediu et al. (2013) similarly identify in-group-out-group oppositions as a force in the development of different languages. Whether through detachment from an original group or through admixture with a new population, humans manifest their social identity through the creation of new cultural traits that set them apart from neighbouring groups. Language is part of this cultural profile, and the emergence of diversity can thus be captured as the manifestation of new identities in human dispersal. The study of language contact is aimed at explaining (b). Considering that contacts between human populations have existed since the dawn of human society and permeate even the smallest and relatively isolated groups, it is fair to say that language contact must be a central part of any framework of linguistic theory.

In this book, we take seriously the notion of ecology as applied to the evolution of languages in contact, where ecology is used as a metaphor from population genetics and biology, a paradigm that has been developed most recently in linguistic contact by Salikoko Mufwene (2001 and other work). Language evolution, and the emergence of contact-induced varieties, can be regarded as speakers making selections from a pool of linguistic variants available to them in a contact setting. This feature pool consists of the sum total of the individual forms and variants that each of the speakers involved, with different language backgrounds and varying linguistic experiences, brings into the contact situation. Which variants from this feature pool are chosen as stable elements of the newly emerging variety depends on the complete ecology of the contact situation: the set of relevant conditions and circumstances, both extralinguistic and intralinguistic. All these parameters enter a complex 'contact equation', which allows for some degree of chance impact. The following components are involved: the numerical (demographic) and social relationships (including mutual attitudes and power distributions) between the participants in a contact situation; the amount and type of communicative events; and the nature of the linguistic input elements, in terms of cognitive and typological congruence between the systems involved. An evolutionary approach to contact language formation (Ansaldo 2009a) is elaborated on in Chapter 4, and an examination of the outcomes of language contact using the ecological approach is presented in Chapter 5. There the interplay of both external and internal factors in the selection of linguistic features from the feature pool, and the significance of the founder population, will emerge with clarity.

1.2 CONTACT PHENOMENA

When speakers of different languages come into contact, linguistic interference may occur. It is highly unlikely that speakers of different languages exist in each other's proximity without the other languages and cultures affecting the languages and cultures that define them. Even in the most resistant of cultures, as this book will show, transfer of linguistic features occurs. Language contact can be observed in even superficially multilingual contexts; it occurs frequently in bilingual and multilingual societies, in trading environments, through technological transfer as well as colonisation and globalisation.

A number of phenomena have been traditionally identified as linguistic outcomes of languages in contact, and in what follows we provide a preliminary sketch of these outcomes and other related concepts that define the field of contact linguistics. Note that here we use the terms conventionally used in the literature, so that the reader can, in this first chapter, make the necessary connections with what they may have encountered elsewhere.

1.2.1 Borrowing

The most common type of influence that a language exerts on another language is borrowing, which is the incorporation of foreign elements into the speaker's native language. Borrowing can include words, grammatical structures, phonology and the replication of linguistic patterns (Matras 2009). At its most common, in lexical borrowing – the borrowing of words – lexical items are borrowed and assimilated to the borrowing language. English is notorious for having a vast number of loanwords, estimated to comprise some three quarters of its vocabulary, with the majority from French and Latin, mostly after the Norman Conquest in 1066 and the subsequent contact between Norman French and English then. Lexical borrowing can involve a change in segmental phonology and the addition of lexical tone, as in English *cheese* becoming Cantonese[1] 芝士 *zi1si2*, and *taxi* becoming 的士 *dik1si2*. While lexical borrowing is used by monolingual as well as bilingual speakers, structural borrowing (Thomason and Kaufman 1988) entails intensive contact and widespread bilingualism. Nevertheless, it is recognised that any feature in any aspect of language structure can be borrowed, in the right circumstances. For example, with the majority of Uyghurs living in what is now the Autonomous Region of Xinjiang in western China, whose language belongs to the Turkic group of the Altaic language family of central Eurasia, Altaic case suffixes are found in Xinjiang Chinese. Structural borrowing can be so intense as to lead to deep grammatical change in a language (see Section 1.2.3).

1.2.2 Code mixing

Code mixing is the practice of mixing together features from different linguistic systems, in particular in describing more stable situations

---

[1] The romanisation system for Cantonese used is Jyutping (粵拼 *jyut6 ping3* [jy:t˩ pʰɪŋ˦]), which was developed by the Linguistic Society of Hong Kong in 1993; its formal name is *The Linguistic Society of Hong Kong Cantonese Romanization Scheme*. The name Jyutping is a contraction consisting of the first Chinese characters of the terms *Jyut6 jyu5* (粵語 'Yue language') and *ping3 jam1* (拼音 'phonetic alphabet'). In Jyutping, tone numbers are assigned to the nine tones in Cantonese. Tone 1 has a pitch contour of 55 or 53 where, in the Asianist system of tone level numbers, 5 represents a high pitch and 1 a low pitch; a pitch level of 55 would thus be a high level tone. Tone 2 has a pitch contour of 35.

where multiple languages are used, and emphasising a more hybrid form. This contrasts with code switching, which is usually used to indicate a speaker's movement from one grammatical system to another – that is, an alternation of languages within a conversation, usually at semantically or sociolinguistically meaningful junctures, which is associated with particular pragmatic effects, discourse functions or associations with group identity. Note, however, that the terms code switching and code mixing are sometimes used more or less interchangeably, and/or with code mixing used to encompass both practices. Research has focused on situational and contextual motivations for switching, as well as on the structural characteristics of code switching, aiming to identify general patterns. Code mixing, as a hybrid form that draws from distinct grammar, is very commonly observed in bi- or multilingual speakers and societies, which suggests that a rigid distinction of grammatical systems in the brain is not the natural state of bi/multilingual communities (Sridhar and Sridhar 1980; Muysken 2000). Such stabilised code mixed systems resemble lects (i.e. any distinguishable variety of a language) in their own right – they are also termed mixed languages (but see Section 1.3.4 below) or fused lects – and thus code mixing can be seen as one route to contact language formation (Auer 1999). Mixed codes will be discussed in greater detail in Chapter 2. And as we will see in the case of Sri Lanka Malay (SLM) in Chapter 4, code mixing is indeed the driving force behind the change that leads to the emergence of a new vernacular.

1.2.3 Contact languages

One of the most interesting research areas in the field of language contact concerns those contexts in which intense language contact between mutually unintelligible languages leads to substantial grammatical restructuring. Particular attention has been given to the phenomenon of language genesis – i.e. the 'birth' of a new language from a multilingual contact situation. The richest inventory of such cases known to us today comes from the centuries of Western colonial expansion. In this period Western nations settled and exploited various regions of the world, in particular the Caribbean, the Pacific and the Southeast Asian regions. In these contexts, trade languages referred to as pidgins (or jargons), as well as indigenous vernaculars known as creoles, emerged; these present a challenge from various points of view. Contact languages are usually studied along the following lines (e.g. in Holm 1988, 1989; Arends, Muysken and Smith 1994; Sebba 1997; Bakker and Matras 2013; Michaelis et al. 2013; Velupillai 2015).

1.2.3.1   *Pidgins*

Pidgins are contact vernaculars which emerge in situations where communities with mutually unintelligible languages are in close and repeated contact in specific situations and need a medium for mutual communication. At the time of their formation, pidgins are not the mother tongue of any speakers but a secondary language, typically used in certain limited contexts or as a lingua franca when communicating with speakers of other languages than their own. Pidgins are characterised by very simple and variable grammatical rules in which traits of the various input languages combine, by a limited vocabulary and by elimination of many grammatical devices such as number and gender (DeCamp 1971). Pidgins may exist for a long time, typically for as long as the contact situation exists; in the case of trade, they often fade with the dissolution of the trading community that created them.

Several typical situations are recognised in which pidgins arose, such as the category of trade and nautical pidgins. The earliest known recorded pidgin, Lingua Franca, was in fact a maritime or nautical pidgin, which was spoken from the time of the Crusades at the beginning of the second millennium and used in ports along the Mediterranean coast until the nineteenth century. Other well-known examples are Russenorsk (Lunden 1978), which developed in Russian–Norwegian fishing communities that met seasonally in coastal areas during the whaling season, and China Coast Pidgin – also known as Chinese Pidgin English. This emerged in Canton (present-day Guangzhou in southern China) in ports where trading with Europeans was permitted, to facilitate communication between Western and Chinese merchants, and survived for more than two centuries (Ansaldo, Matthews and Smith 2010, 2012). A trade pidgin which did not involve seafaring was Chinese Pidgin Russian (Shapiro 2010). The well-known China Coast Pidgin serial verb construction *look see* calqued on Cantonese *tái gin* 'look-see' = 'look' is shown in example 1.1 (Ansaldo, Matthews and Smith 2012: 82).

(1.1)

My wantchee look see counta
'I want to check the accounts'

Interactions between colonial people and locals led to another category of domestic workforce pidgins, such as Butler English in India, which emerged some 200 years ago in interactions between local domestic staff and their masters in colonial households. There are also multilingual workforce pidgins, the most well-known of these being plantation pidgins, which emerged as a consequence of mass importation of labour of workers from a variety of linguistic backgrounds to plantation sites. Examples of these are Tok Pisin (Smith 2002), initially primarily used on the plantations in the German territories of New Guinea, and Hawai'i Pidgin English (Sakoda and Siegel 2003), which arose in urban centres and in interaction with Anglophones and replaced Pidgin Hawai'ian as the main language used between plantation workers of different origins. A further category of mine and industry pidgins includes Fanakalo in South Africa, which originated about 200 years ago but is still used in workforce situations such as on farms, in mines and in domestic employment (Mesthrie and Surek-Clark 2013: 34).

A pidgin is typically distinguished from a jargon. A jargon can be regarded as an unstable/early/primitive/incipient/rudimentary pidgin or pre-pidgin. As a contact variety that is highly variable and lacks a stable set of norms, it represents essentially an individual solution and is subject to individual strategies. A pidgin can also be seen to develop into an extended or expanded pidgin when it becomes the main means of interethnic communication and is used in a wider variety of domains than at its origin. With such a transformation it develops a larger set of structural norms, becomes more stable and may even become a mother tongue for some of its speakers. A recent term that has been suggested is pidgincreole (Philip Baker in Bakker 2008: 131), indicating its affinity with both pidgins and creoles.

1.2.3.2 Creoles

Creoles are nativised contact languages that emerge from the restructuring of different – usually mutually unintelligible – varieties, a consequence of situations of intense language contact, when people of diverse ethnocultural and linguistic backgrounds were brought together and formed a distinct community. The term is primarily used for the languages that developed as products of European expansion and colonisation of the world between the sixteenth and eighteenth centuries, and which share the sociohistorical background of slavery, deportation and eventual emancipation that is found in the Caribbean and the Pacific and Indian Oceans. Creoles combine traits of the various input languages; they also display novel features not easily traceable to a specific source. Typically this involves a combination of features from the lexifier or superstrate, with features from one or several substrate languages. The superstrate or lexifier is the language usually associated with higher prestige as well as late arrival. The substrate usually represents the dominant language of the groups in subordinate position.

A fundamental divide between types of creoles has to do with whether the speakers were indigenous to the region (Chaudenson 1979). Exogenous creoles were formed in situations where none of the population groups in contact with each other were indigenous to the area. Instead, it was usually the mass importation of labour, typically of people from diverse backgrounds, that led to various languages in contact. The most typical example of this is a plantation creole; these arose in the contact of the colonial plantation economy, which required large-scale importation of labour – either slave labour, characteristically in the Atlantic, or indentured labour, in the Pacific – with European settlers numerically few but dominating the societies. Examples of plantation creoles are found in various regions. Those in the Caribbean include English-lexified Trinidad English Creole in Trinidad, French-lexified Haitian Creole in Haiti and Berbice Dutch in Guyana; in southern North America there is English-lexified Gullah; off the West African coast there are the Portuguese-lexified Cape Verdean Creoles in the Republic of Cape Verde; and in the Indian Ocean there is French-lexified Mauritian Creole in the Republic of Mauritius. Maroon creoles are languages of slaves who had escaped from plantations and formed settlements based on having a common ethnic origin or on having come from the same plantation. Well-known Maroon creoles include the English/Portuguese-lexified Saramaccan of Suriname and the Spanish-lexified Palenquero in northern Colombia.

Endogenous creoles (also called fort creoles), on the other hand, typically developed through contact between immigrant settlers, usually engaged in trade, and the indigenous population of the areas. This context was typically found along the West African and Indian coasts, when European merchants set up trading centres for their activities in the area. Examples include Guinea-Bissau Kriyol in Guinea Bissau and southern Senegal, Diu Indo-Portuguese on the island of Diu to the west of India, and Papia Kristang in Malacca in western Malaysia, all Portuguese-lexified. A most up-to-date and detailed discussion can be found in Velupillai (2015).

The social dynamics, as well as the structural typologies, change somewhat when we look at languages such as Melanesian Pidgin, Solomons Pidgin, Tok Pisin and Baba Malay. On the one hand, economic migration and/or political exile enter the picture as an alternative to slavery; on the other hand, we find contexts in which European colonial languages play a lesser role. We will explore such contexts in this book, for example in the case of Sri Lanka Malay in Chapters 4 and 6.

1.2.3.3   Mixed languages

Mixed languages have been identified as those relatively rare cases where 'two languages clearly make a significant contribution to the [new] language...frequently one provides the content words and another the grammar...[and] there is not necessarily any question of simplification' (Muysken and Smith 1994: 5). The specific idea behind these languages is that the variety spoken by the mother and the one spoken by the father intertwine: they combine aspects of each grammar – e.g. morphosyntax from the former and lexicon from the latter – which are still clearly identifiable in the new language (Bakker 1997). The main difference between pidgins and creoles on the one hand and mixed languages on the other is, therefore, that the former involve several input or source languages, while the latter are typically the result of contact between only two languages. Moreover, typically the source for both the lexicon and the structure of the language are identifiable, and most often both source languages are spoken in the same area, alongside the mixed language. In addition, there is general agreement that mixed languages emerge as in-group identity markers, rather than through the need for a communication bridge between population groups. Not every contact linguist accepts the mixed language as a bona fide class of its own, and it is indeed possible that new languages very often arise as identity markers (see Chapter 4). It is possible that pure mixed languages exist, but these would number very few. Classic examples are Michif in Canada, with French nouns and Cree verbs and morphology (Bakker 1994); and Media Lengua found in Ecuador, where Spanish vocabulary forms a mixed system with Quechua grammar (Muysken 1997).

The groupings above – namely those of pidgins, creoles and mixed languages – are the traditional categorisations in the literature. In this book, we tend to take a more integrated approach. Traditionally, creoles have been viewed as nativised pidgins (though see the discussion in Chapter 3). In this book we also discuss cases where creole languages emerge from multilingual contexts where pidgins are not necessarily present – such as SLM – or are present but as only one of the varieties in contact, and not necessarily a significant one – such as Singapore English (SgE), also referred to as Singlish. In addition, we prefer not to emphasise the traditional distinction between creoles and mixed languages: it has been argued that admixture and creole formation are essentially similar processes, which then blurs the distinction between these categories (see Chapter 4 and Ansaldo 2011). We point out that, structurally, the main difference between the prototypical creoles and other contact languages lies in the fact that the former show a substantial influence of their main substrate groups (West African) and/or lexifiers (Standard Average European[2]). Sociolinguistically they all share common traits: intermarriage in the early stages, endogamy in the later ones; displacement and new identity construction; multilingualism and complex variation. We will elaborate on these in Chapters 3 and 4.

1.2.4 New Englishes

One outcome of contact that is not normally encompassed in the field of contact linguistics is the category known as New Englishes. Creole studies and World Englishes developed as distinct subfields in linguistics, each with its own origins and history, and for the most part scholarship in each field has had its own concerns. Creole studies[3] became established as a separate subdiscipline as a result of the influential collection edited by Dell Hymes in 1971, with Valdman and Highfield (1980) laying out a number of theoretical issues. 1986 saw the volume edited by Muysken and Smith identifying the parameters of one of the core debates in the field – that of substrates versus universals – as well as the founding of the *Journal of Pidgin and Creole Languages*. The main subjects of creole studies have been prototypical creoles spoken in the Caribbean, which include plantation creoles and Maroon creoles, all of which emerged in the context of the African slave trade associated with European plantation agriculture in the period 1650–1750, and in areas with a large proportion of non-target language speakers in the overall population. In addition, there are other languages which differ in one or more of these features: plantation creole languages that emerged in West Africa, the Indian Ocean and the Pacific, rather than the Caribbean; or the involvement of speakers of different languages. Issues in creole studies have included, inter alia, what counts as a creole language, the genesis of creoles, the treatment of creoles as unique to their particular origin or as ordinary languages similar to any other languages, and so forth. The major debates in creole studies will be discussed in Chapters 3 and 4.

The idea of World Englishes was first raised in 1978 to examine concepts of regional Englishes globally, and the early 1980s marked the

---

[2] 'Standard Average European' is a term introduced by Whorf (1941/1956) to refer to Indo-European languages of western Europe on the basis of their sharing structural similarities. More recently, Haspelmath (2001) uses the term to refer to a number of traits characterising a Sprachbund, or linguistic area, defined by a core of twelve features that can be considered 'euroversals'.

[3] A snap review of creole studies is found in Muysken and Law (2001).

beginnings of the study of new varieties of English – or New Englishes – as a serious topic in linguistic research and a new subdiscipline of English linguistics. This led to the publication of some groundbreaking work – including Bailey and Görlach (1982); Pride (1982); Trudgill and Hannah (1982); Wells (1982); Platt, Weber and Ho (1984); Kachru (1986), (1992) – and the launching of scholarly journals devoted to the topic, *English World-Wide* and *World Englishes* in 1980 and 1982 respectively. The study of World/New Englishes concerns itself with emerging localised or indigenised varieties of English, especially varieties that have developed in territories influenced by the UK or the US. It consists of identifying varieties of English used in diverse sociolinguistic contexts globally and analysing how sociolinguistic histories, multicultural backgrounds and contexts of function influence the use of English in different regions of the world. Interest has tended to be in postcolonial English varieties whose origins lie in education – indeed, one of the defining features of New Englishes is that English is transmitted via education, typical examples being Indian English and SgE. These more acrolectal varieties – varieties that approximate most closely the standard prestige language – thus have much less in common sociolinguistically with creoles. It was with scholars who straddled – ideologically and/or institutionally – the two fields that cross-pollination of ideas emerged. With regard to Singapore, for instance, John Platt (1975) viewed SgE as comprising a post-creole continuum; and later scholars renewed scholarship of SgE from a contact perspective (e.g. Ansaldo 2004; Lim 2004, 2007, 2009a; Bao 2005; and others).

1.2.5 Linguistic areas

Language contact occurring over a prolonged period of time in a particular region results in the formation of what are identified as linguistic areas – regions in which a cluster of structural-typological features is shared amongst languages which are not directly genetically related. Linguistic areas that have been identified include Europe, the Balkans, Africa (especially West and Central Africa), Mesoamerica, the Pacific Northwest of North America, South Asia, Southeast Asia, Anatolia, Siberia and Arnhem Land in northeast Australia. In the Balkans, a region which very early on attracted the attention of historical and descriptive linguists, for example, the definite article is encoded by a suffix, as in Rumanian *lup-ul* 'wolf-the', Albanian *mik-u* 'friend-the' and Bulgarian *zena-ta* 'woman-the'. The Indo-Aryan, Dravidian and Munda language families of the South Asian region share contact features such as retroflex consonants, Subject-Object-Verb (SOV) word order, Dative

subject constructions, suffixing morphology and more. It is additionally interesting to see how the restructured variety of Malay in this
region, SLM, has evolved to acquire these very features (see Chapter 4). In
Southeast Asia, shared features include the absence of case marking and
gender, the presence of numeral class constructions, verb serialisation,
topic-prominence, sentence-final particles and the presence (in most
languages there) of lexical tone – the latter two features are explored in
Chapter 5. Southeast Asia also displays areal patterns of grammaticalisation, evident in the verb for 'acquire, get' grammaticalising to modal
'can', and/or 'get, become' grammaticalising to the passive 'be . . . -ed'.
As examples, Cantonese *dak (dou)* 'get' and Thai *dai* 'get' both result in
patterns like *sik dak* 'eat get = can eat' and *kin dai* 'eat get = can eat'
respectively.

1.2.6 Language shift

Another outcome when language communities come into contact is
somewhat distinct from the various consequences described above,
where, for the most part there is language creation of some nature –
borrowing, mixing, creating – that ensues. In contrast, in some situations, speakers of a language shift to another language, almost always
a language that is dominant in some respect, which affords the speakers
a greater amount of capital. One outcome can be that their original language is eventually no longer spoken. The phenomena of language shift
and endangerment, as outcomes of contact, are discussed in Chapter 6.
In the context of this book, we are particularly interested in the shifts
between languages that arise out of contact, as well as the types of
restructuring a language can undergo.

1.3 THE ASIAN PERSPECTIVE

Much of linguistic theory so far has been heavily influenced by lessons
learned in the study of English – think of wh-movement – and the history
and structure of (Indo-)European languages – think of the Stammbaum
model, a tree model of historical relationships amongst languages.
Given the history of modern linguistics, this has been a natural and
necessary point of departure; however, it is a problematic one when
these lessons are generalised to account for all languages. A parallel
situation is found in contact linguistics. Contact between communities, and thus languages, happens everywhere. Nevertheless, most work
in the field of creole studies has tended – until recently – to focus on
Caribbean creoles. In this book, we offer a less Eurocentric perspective

of languages in contact. This we do by largely drawing on research from Asian contexts, highlighting a number of case studies, and from contexts in which Indo-European languages and peoples do not feature as prominently. When we turn our observation to languages in contact of another kind, our generalisations often end up in need of serious revision. In particular, we find inspiration in what is considered Monsoon Asia: the region extending from the South China Sea to the eastern half of the Indian Ocean, including the Indonesian archipelago (Ansaldo 2009a). This is a region defined by the monsoon winds that, for most of the previous millennium (up to the nineteenth century), not only moved explorers, sailors and traders to different regions but also kept them in those regions for several months a year as they waited for the reverse monsoon to bring them home, affording periods of stability and contact amongst various communities. We also look further east to parts of Asia that, for twenty-first-century reasons, are the contemporary sites of contact. There are several other reasons why we find the Asian region significant and instructive for contact linguistics study.

Many of the excellent volumes on language contact draw on scholarship based on traditionally well-known creoles and pidgins. By definition, this has meant that, from a regional point of view, much illustration comes from the Atlantic and, to some extent, the Pacific, while Asia tends to be under-represented. This is changing, as can be seen in the *Atlas of Pidgin and Creole Language Structures* (*APiCS*) (Michaelis et al. 2013) whose seventy-six pidgin and creole languages comprise not only the most widely studied Atlantic and Indian Ocean creoles but also less well-known pidgins and creoles from Africa, Asia, Melanesia and Australia. These include fourteen varieties from both South Asia (Pidgin Hindustani, Korlai, Diu Indo-Portuguese, Sri Lanka Portuguese and SLM) and East and Southeast Asia (Chinese Pidgin English, Papia Kristang, Singlish, Singapore Bazaar Malay, Ambon Malay, Batavia Creole, Zamboanga, Ternate and Cavite Chabacano).

In Asia one finds types of contact that cover wide geographical areas and have significant historical depth. The Indian Ocean trading routes have connected the Arab world, South Asia and Southeast Asia since time immemorial. Contacts between China and East Africa, and everything in between, are attested since the tenth century. These numerous and diverse contacts pre-date Western colonisation and thus offer opportunities for the study of different linguistic and sociohistorical dynamics. Later, with the arrival of Portuguese, Dutch and British merchants, the contact world of Monsoon Asia becomes even richer and worth documenting. That it was the monsoons that directed the movements also meant that the flows of peoples and languages, and the contact that ensued, were not unidirectional.

Asia is particularly interesting for having been a very successful chapter in European colonisation, in particular that of the British, through the monopoly of the British East India Company and the corresponding spread of English in its non-settler colonies. The European colonial powers were also efficient at moving their peoples around. Soldiers and indentured labourers were shifted from one colony to another; this brought communities from different ecologies and with different repertoires in contact. One such example was peoples from various parts of the Malay and Indonesian archipelago brought as soldiers or indentured labourers by the Dutch and later the British to the island of Sri Lanka (known by its colonial name 'Ceylon' until it became a republic in 1972), eventually to become the Sri Lankan Malays. Members of the civil service (including teachers) also relocated, for example, from India and Ceylon to Singapore. In many cases, thus, the superstrate was not necessarily a single Standard Average European lexifier, such as a standard British English (and numerous other native English varieties, such as Irish English), but could well already have been a nativised variety, such as Indian English and Sri Lankan English.

Many countries in Asia are still vividly multilingual, having been spared the centuries of standardisation and national language policies that characterise the linguistic history of much of western Europe. The languages that abound come from diverse language families, which include Sinitic, Austronesian, Dravidian and Indo-European, to name the major ones. This makes for intriguing contact situations with widespread multilingualism, code mixing and shift, which can be observed in the present.

1.4 GLOBALISATION AND CONTACT

While many issues and topics in the study of languages in contact – whether in creole studies or New Englishes – are shaped by sociohistorical circumstances, ecologies are dynamic, and the nature of contact and the outcomes that arise are continuously subject to different and changing forces. The era of the kind of European expansion that brought into existence the majority of contact languages, for instance, is long over, but most of these communities still exist, generations on, in a qualitatively different place and time. In closing this first chapter, we briefly expound on the dimension of globalisation and its relevance in the study of language contact.

The notion of globalisation – the process by which regional economies, societies and cultures have become integrated through a global network of political ideas through communication, transportation and trade – really needs little overture these days. The term began to be widely used by economists and other social scientists in the 1960s, achieving widespread use in the mainstream press by the late 1980s, to the extent that in the new millennium many ask if 'globalisation' has become a global cliché (Lechner and Boli 2004). Nikolas Coupland, an early scholar in the field of language and globalisation, concedes that linguists actually have been 'late getting to the party' (Coupland 2003), but in the past decade this area of enquiry has grown rapidly. There are many good reasons why we believe it is something to be considered seriously in scholarship in general and, more specifically and pertinently to this book, in scholarship on contact.

First, even its harshest critics accept that the processes associated with globalisation, while not necessarily new in substance, are undeniably new in intensity, scope and scale (Coupland 2010a). Amongst the phenomena associated with the globalised era that we have experienced are the following (from Coupland 2010a: 2–3, excerpted, reordered and numbered here):

    i. the decline of the (British) Establishment
    ii. national boundaries becoming more permeable
    iii. massively increasing demographic mobility, often for economic reasons
    iv. developing ethnic pluralism, especially in urban settings
    v. the proliferation and speeding up of communication technologies
    vi. the growth of the middle class accompanied by the accentuation of the rich/poor divide
    vii. an upsurge in consumer culture and many new forms of commodification
    viii. greater subservience to global market economics, in the face of its demerits
    ix. a large shift to service-sector work, globally dispersed.

Each of the above has implications for bringing communities and their languages into contact with each other in new, contemporary contexts which, to echo Coupland, are distinct from those of the past in terms of intensity, scope and scale. Additionally, we feel strongly that the study of language contact in a globalisation perspective should turn its lens particularly to the Asian region because of two major factors in the region's ecology in what is largely acknowledged as the 'Asian Century'[4] – the belief that, if certain demographic and economic trends persist, the twenty-first century will be dominated by Asian politics and culture. The first factor comprises the great shift in the global economy's centre of gravity from West to East, which entails various phenomena of globalisation and economic growth in Asia, such as the pursuit of linguistic capital, mobility, trade, communication technology, etc. These all have significant implications for contact dynamics in terms of bringing together communities and their languages in new dynamics, providing new sites and potential for consequences of contact. The second factor is Asia's status as the site of the largest and most quickly growing number of English users – the only real global language for the predictable future, whatever one might feel about it. The total English-using population in Asia is some 600 million, far more than English speakers in the 'Inner Circle', defined as the set of Anglophone societies which are associated with ownership of English – i.e. the UK, North America and Australia/New Zealand (Kachru 1982). Taken together, it also means that Asian English speakers are interacting with other speakers of Asian Englishes, or speakers of other New Englishes such as African Englishes, more than with Inner Circle or 'native' English speakers. This, again, has consequences for a new kind of spread, contact and change. In what follows, we outline a number of phenomena which, in this era of globalisation, involve sites comprising new dynamics of contact – either 'superdiverse' contact (see below), or sites which by their very nature prompt more intense contact than would have occurred under more 'normal' circumstances.

The decline of the Establishment (Coupland's phenomenon i) has meant, amongst other things, that the ties that once bound communities to the exonormative standards of language – in particular English – of Britain and the US, are now loosened. This affords a freedom and flexibility for the restructuring that occurs in vernacular varieties and boosts confidence in recognising pluricentric standards, for example, of English. In tandem with such decline is the rise of other regions of the world – the BRIC states (Brazil, Russia, India and China), Asia more broadly and Africa – and the trade and communication that ensues amongst these communities, which promotes multilingual competences and 'non-native' varieties of English.

---

[4] The term 'Asian Century' is attributed to a 1988 meeting between the People's Republic of China leader Deng Xiaoping and Indian Prime Minister Rajiv Gandhi; this develops on the notions of the 'American Century', coined by *Time* publisher Henry Luce to describe the dominance of the US of much of the twentieth century, and the 'British Century', used for the nineteenth century.

The related phenomena (ii, iii and iv) of increased permeability of national boundaries, greater demographic mobility partly as a consequence of this and increased ethnic pluralism – also a consequence – are certainly recognised by globalisation scholars as contributing to language issues. Perhaps most notable in this regard is the influential article by anthropologist Steven Vertovec (2006), in which he coins the now familiar term 'superdiversity'. This he defines as a diversification of diversity, as diversity can no longer be understood in terms of multiculturalism alone, in the sense of the presence of multiple cultures in one society. Based on observations primarily on the demographic and socioeconomic changes in post-Cold War Britain, superdiversity is meant to encompass the vastly increased range of resources – linguistic, religious, ethnic and cultural in the widest sense – that characterise late modern societies. One of the sets of developments that can be observed most significantly in Europe, but also – it is claimed – world-wide, is the changing patterns and itineraries of migration from the outside into Europe and continued migration by the same people inside Europe, with 'more people now moving from more places, through more places, to more places' (Vertovec 2010: 86), bringing with them vastly more numerous and diverse resources and experiences. A number of (socio)linguists have drawn on this idea. Jan Blommaert (2010), perhaps most notably, talks of a sociolinguistics of globalisation – a new platform for thinking about language in society – since, he holds, 'old sociolinguistics' and its terminology can no longer address and do justice to new, unstable and unpredictable sociolinguistic realities resulting from superdiversity. It is obvious that this has great implications for the contact that ensues for communities and their languages, and we explore this further in Chapter 8.

Mobility for economic reasons has brought peoples to Asia who have not until recently been traditional migrants in the region. Since China's economic boom of the 1990s, thousands of traders and businessmen – with estimates of up to 200,000 – predominantly from West Africa and principally male, have migrated to the city of Guangzhou in southern China, for its proximity to factories and other manufacturing facilities making it the largest African community in Asia. An African diaspora is also found in Hong Kong, most prominently in a setting like Chung King Mansions in Kowloon. There, low-budget accommodation, shops and other services have made it a gathering place for some of the ethnic minorities in Hong Kong, including communities of South Asian, Middle Eastern and African origins, which has evolved into a globalised neighbourhood of the sort described in Europe by Blommaert (2010).

The twenty-first century has also seen internal migration as never witnessed before: most migration in the world today is in fact internal, with far more internal economic migrants than international ones – i.e. more internally displaced people than there are official refugees and asylum-seekers. In comparison to more than 200 million international migrants, there number some 740 million people who migrate internally around the world (United Nations Development Programme 2009; Abazov 2013). While this phenomenon is world-wide – for example, over the past two decades more than half the population in rural Tanzania migrated within the country – in Asia the two rapidly developing and urbanising countries of India and China have witnessed an explosion of rural-to-urban migration. The number of people living in cities in mainland China exceeded those in rural areas for the first time at the end of 2011, reaching 690.79 million and accounting for 51.27 per cent of the country's population (Bloomberg 2012). In India, internal migration accounts for 309 million – nearly 30 per cent of the total population (of which 70.7 per cent are women) – a noteworthy figure when compared with the estimates of a mere 11.4 million for Indian emigrants (UNESCO 2013). Such internal migration is in fact part of a larger global trend toward population concentrations in cities – half of the world's people (i.e. 3.3 billion) live in urban areas – which results in linguistic contact of immense diversity, intensity, and value.

The technological developments of this age have made new social media of communication accessible to the masses, with mobile phones and the internet (phenomenon v). These developments mean that the individual is likely to meet a much wider range of resources than just a few decades ago. The growth of mobile phone usage has been rapid: from just over 60 per cent of the world's population (4.1 billion) having access to a mobile phone in 2009 (United Nations 2009), the estimate now is that 6 billion out of the world's population of 7 billion have mobile phones. More significantly, nearly 5 billion of these are in developing countries (World Bank 2012).[5] While Sub-Saharan Africa has seen immense growth

---

[5] The growth of mobile phone usage in developing countries is especially strking when considered alongside another, more sobering, statistic – both revealed in conjunction with World Water Day on 22 March 2013 – that far fewer of the world's population – only 4.5 billion people – have access to working toilets (United Nations 2013a). In India, which alone is responsible for 60 per cent of the global population that lacks access to basic sanitation, in 2010 about half of its 1.2 billion residents were mobile phone subscribers, but only 366 million people – that is, one third of its population – had access to toilets (Wang 2013). We do, however, have to be cautious about the difference between mobile connections and individual mobile subscribers: while active mobile subscriptions were close to 6.8 billion at the end of 2012, many people own more than one SIM card, so the total number of unique mobile subscribers globally was approximately 3.2 billion. Thus, penetration in terms of individuals really stands at only 45 per cent.

in recent years, such that the number of mobile phone users in the region – 650 million subscribers – is more than that in Europe or the US, it is in Asia where mobile phone usage reigns. Some 2.43 billion people in Asia-Pacific are mobile phone users, which translates to 56.3 per cent of the world's population of mobile phone users (eMarketer 2013). The Asia-Pacific was the only region to show growth in mobile phone sales in the first quarter of 2013 (Gartner 2013), with the Southeast Asian market growing by 24 per cent in volume in 2011–2012 (GfK Asia 2012) and India now the fastest growing market in the Asia-Pacific, with quarter-on-quarter growth of 27 per cent in the third quarter of 2014 (International Data Corporation 2014). The other area of immense growth is the world-wide web. If we just take Facebook, the largest online social network in the world, as one example of the extent to which people are using social media, again the figures are impressive: as of May 2013 there were 1.11 billion users world-wide; notably, Asia comprised the second largest region of users, with 236 million.

What implications does such a widespread use of the internet and mobile phone technology have more specifically for language contact? Text messaging, developed and released in the early to mid-1990s, and other computer-mediated communication (CMC) comprise a rich and intriguing area for exploring contact dynamics, since they involve the interplay between what technology allows and what the communicator brings to technology. And nowhere is this more exciting for language contact and evolution, we feel, than in Asia, because of the way users employ such technology. Advances have certainly been made and continue to be made in developing keyboards for various orthographic traditions, such as Chinese characters or Devanagari script. While users of non-Latin alphabetic scripts (such as Arabic, Brahmic and Cyrillic scripts) have keyboards based on the QWERTY layout and can input Latin letters as well as the script of the language by a special key or through some combination of keys, input methods are more complex with East Asian languages Chinese, Japanese and Korean. Various methods have been invented to utilise a QWERTY keyboard to input the thousands of possible characters in these languages; however, there is no one-to-one mapping between keys and characters. Input may be, for example, by entering the desired character's pronunciation and selecting from possibilities, or by giving its component shapes, radicals and stroke count. Thus, even with such options, individuals often prefer to use a language like English when texting than a language like Chinese, because it is simply more convenient and more expedient to type in a Latin-based alphabet than to use character strokes. This means that there is more widespread use of English in CMC contexts than there would normally be for such a community, which results in the use of a mixed code, as well as phenomena such as relexification, direct translations and other linguistic outcomes of contact. Technology, in particular mobile phone technology, also means that communities who would have been non-literate now have access to languages. BBC Janala ('window' in Bangla), launched in 2009, is a service on multiple platforms including mobile phones, the web, television and print, providing access to English-language learning in Bangladesh. It is the largest multiplatform innovation to improve English language skills anywhere in the developing world, involving 95 million mobile phones and reaching two thirds of the population, including poorer communities. The spread of English and its contact with the other languages in the multilingual repertoire of these communities has immense implications for contact dynamics.

As is well recognised by scholars working in language and globalisation, the emergence of the globalised new economy has, amongst its consequences, new conditions for the production of language practices and forms, and new challenges to current ways of thinking about language. In the global economy, we find the movement of basic primary resource extraction and manufacturing production into hitherto peripheral zones of established industrialised countries (e.g. the Arctic) or out of them altogether (e.g. China, India); the development of new consumer markets (e.g. China, India); and an increase in the importance of symbolic capital in the development of niche and value-added products.

Monica Heller (2010: 349–52) outlines four consequences that global expansion has for language, summarised here.

i. There are many more social actors than before who are now involved in economic activities that have to deal with globalised forms of exchange; more markets involve wider networks. In other words, this experience is socially more widespread, such that it involves more people and deals more often with communication across social, cultural and linguistic differences.

ii. The management of these exchanges and networks involves a wider repertoire of forms of communication, and hence of language use. Today's technology affords a broader range of forms of mediation, which are used by a broader set of social actors, and arguably more often.

iii. A tension emerges between relatively anonymous, agentless and transferable forms of standardisation, and situated and identifiable forms of authenticity (for example, Taylorist industrial management practices, such as assembly-line production versus more specialised, local, authentic practices).

iv. Much work is computer-mediated, requiring literacy and numeracy skills versus controlled communication; language is not only part of the work process but also the work product. Language is made central: the call centre industry, for instance, sells mainly information, even if at the end it may be something concrete exchanged for money such as a car, airline booking, hotel reservation or replacement part. More generally, the global economy sees the emergence of 'language industries', where language is either the product or an important dimension of it, e.g. translation, speech recognition, language teaching.

The implications for the breadth and diversity of contact situations, in combinations not previously attested, are intriguing. In short, the new economy highlights language as a resource and a commodity. In classic Bourdieu (2001), the principal forms of capital comprise economic capital, which creates and maintains wealth and which is immediately convertible to money and property; cultural capital, which entails accumulated knowledge and skills that are potentially convertible to economic capital, such as educational qualifications; social capital, which is made up of group membership, social obligations or group connections, and also potentially convertible into economic capital; and symbolic capital, which comprises accumulated prestige and honour. While previously the pursuit of capital was directly linked to business and commerce, in today's new economy capital may be acquired more indirectly, usually through the prior possession of a premium language, which is then exchanged for economic capital. In other words, language itself may be regarded as linguistic capital, which possesses value and is a means by which people and nations may achieve varied goals, such as research, finance, manufacturing and public relations (Heller 2010).

The rise of the middle class and the increase in spending power and mobility (Coupland's phenomenon vii: see p. 17), together with the commodification of language (phenomenon viii), has resulted in the phenomenon of linguistic migration, where, when linguistic capital is not available in the aspirants' own country, families with the means send their children to other countries in its pursuit. Asia sees mainland Chinese 'study mothers/mamas' (Mandarin 陪读妈妈 *peidu mama*) and Korean 'wild goose mothers' (Korean 기러기엄마 *kirogi omma*) accompanying their children to English-speaking countries such as English-dominant Singapore for the sake of their education. These translocations bring various Asian languages, including various Asian Englishes, into more intense contact with each other than before.

The global economy has seen tremendous growth in business process outsourcing where multinationals and UK- and US-based companies outsource services, such as medical and legal transcription, to developing countries like India and the Philippines because of the factors of cheap labour, English fluency and literacy, and fast (usually overnight) turn-around time. One of the better-known business process outsourcing thrusts is the call centre industry – centralised offices used for the purpose of receiving and transmitting a large volume of requests by telephone, administering product support, fielding information enquiries from consumers, telemarketing, debt collection, etc. This is a recent but fast-growing industry in Asia, India and the Philippines being the call centre capitals of the world, contributing significantly to the countries' employment and GDP. With language playing such a central role in the industry, a number of sociolinguistic issues have also been identified and studied. A question arises as to whether, with greater and more intensive contact with Inner Circle English varieties once again, nativised varieties such as Indian English and Philippine English will see a shift towards or a reinforcing or focusing of features of more 'native speaker' or 'standard' varieties of English, particularly British English and General American English. Conversely, might it instead be the case that the currency of these nativised varieties will spread, with certain features becoming more widely known in other communities and potentially adopted there?

Finally, a prominent area in globalisation studies is popular culture – cultural forms that have wide public appeal – in particular popular music and the global, transcultural identifications that are made possible by global popular cultures and languages. Alastair Pennycook (2010) points out how the ease of cultural movement in this era is made possible by the transnational role of major languages (such as English, French, Chinese and Arabic) plus new digital media, which together allow popular culture to traverse the globe with speed and gregarity. Pennycook goes further to argue for the significance of the language of popular music as one of the central concerns of our times, in the construction, performance and confirmation of cultural identities. Focusing in particular on hip-hop music outside African American culture (Pennycook 2007, 2010) – since in rap, lyrics are more central than in other forms of popular culture – he explores what goes on with language use in 'global music' that is adopted in local contexts, in terms of both the mixing of codes and the indexing of identities that are possible. We explore in Chapter 7 these various contemporary situations for the implications they hold for language contact.

1.5 LANGUAGES IN CONTACT FOR TODAY'S SCHOLAR

In most (linguistic) books or courses on languages in contact, the usual topics addressed revolve around structural linguistic aspects, such as those outlined in Section 1.2, including code switching and lexical borrowing, theories of genesis of pidgins and creoles, substrate influence, synchronic structure, and so forth. In this book we are particularly interested in making connections between what goes on in the language and what is happening around it. To this end, what is found in this book focuses less on the structural and more on the social aspects, which are relevant in contexts in which languages come into contact with each other, and provokes thinking along the following lines.

i. What social factors are significant in language contact?
ii. Which varieties dominate in a given contact situation and why?
iii. How do the communities themselves respond in contact situations?
iv. What are the institutional responses to languages that have evolved from contact?
v. What are the ideological responses, and what should/could they be?

We therefore trust that this book will be of interest not only to scholars and students of language contact, pidgins and creole languages, and contact-induced change but also to a wider audience. The interdisciplinary threads that we pursue at various points will be of interest to scholars interested in the interaction between language and contemporary society, including migration, globalisation and cultural as well as linguistic diversity. This is what this book aims to bring to the study of languages in contact.

FURTHER READING

The classic reading for the field of language in contact is Weinreich (1953), while another seminal introduction is Appel and Muysken's (1987) textbook. Thomason and Kaufman (1988) lay the foundation of language contact from a historical and genetic perspective. For comprehensive accounts of pidgin and creole languages, see Holm (1988, 1989) and Arends, Muysken and Smith (1994); and for code switching, see Myers-Scotton (1993), Milroy and Muysken (1995) and Muysken (2000). Bakker and Matras's (2013) edited volume comprises state-of-the-art chapters by leading scholars on pidgins, creoles and mixed languages, as well as on more contemporary multi-ethnolects.

2 Contact and code choice

2.1 INTRODUCTION

One of the outcomes of languages and speakers coming into contact is increased multilingualism. It is worth identifying systematically the various scenarios that bring communities together and that put the pressure on adding language varieties to the repertoire. This chapter then proceeds to outline how, in such situations where more than one code is present, these codes may be (a) distributed in society and (b) exploited by the community. In the final section we examine some of the more recent, postmodern approaches which deconstruct the notion of multilingualism.

There was once a prevailing belief in some quarters that having more than one language in one's individual or collective repertoire could be considered a liability. Nineteenth-century nationalists promoted the 'one nation = one language' ideology, and even in contemporary times such an ideology persists. Theodore Roosevelt, as President of the United States of America, in 1906 declared: 'We have room for but one language in this country, and that is the English language, for we intend to see that the crucible turns our people out as Americans, of American nationality, and not as dwellers in a polyglot boarding house.' The motto of the Alliance for the Preservation of English in Canada is 'one language unites, two divide'. Such a monolingual perspective is a consequence of the possession of a powerful language of wider communication, accompanied by narrow cultural awareness and reinforced by state policies, which elevate one language to official status.

The stereotypical concept of multilinguals held by many in the US, Myers-Scotton (2006: 4) tells us, has been an exotic one. A multilingual is envisioned as a child either of European nobility (that is, from Transylvania, Monaco or another exotic locale) or of refugees (namely from Argentina, Chile or Russia), or, in more contemporary times, as a migrant worker (read: some Spanish speakers) or small businessman (read: Korean grocer or South Asian motel manager/owner). And for

Europeans from single-language-policy nations, being multilingual usually meant, until recently, being one of a prestigious few from a higher class with formal language education (thus speaking Latin, French and German). More unusual multilingual repertoires, as noted by Edwards (1994: 34–5), include the following impressive examples. The chief curator in the Vatican Library, Giuseppe Mezzofanti (1774–1849), reportedly spoke 60 languages fluently and could translate more than 150 languages and dialects. The Head of the Terminology Section of the United Nations (1965–1971), Georges Schmidt, was fluent in nineteen languages and less-than-fluent in a dozen more. The precocious editor of the *Oxford English Dictionary*, James Murray, in 1866 at age twenty-nine wrote in a letter applying for a post in the British Museum Library:

> I possess a general acquaintance with the languages and literature of the Aryan and Syro-Aryan classes... with several languages I have a more intimate acquaintance as with the Romance tongues, Italian, French, Catalan, Spanish, Latin, and in a less degree Portuguese, Vaudois, Provençal and various dialects. In the Teutonic branch I am tolerably familiar with Dutch... Flemish, German, Danish. In Anglo-Saxon and Moeso-Gothic my studies have been much closer... I know a little of the Celtic, and am at present engaged with the Slavonic, having obtained a useful knowledge of Russian. In the Persian, Acaemenian Cuneiform and Sanscrit branches, I know for the purposes of Comparative Philology. I have sufficient knowledge of Hebrew and Syriac to read at sight the O.T.... To a less degree I know Aramaic, Arabic, Coptic and Phenecian.

It is notable that all the above examples would seem to derive from the confluence of individual talents and professional development, resulting in some more formal and unusual acquisitions. But this does not have to be a necessary condition. In numerous individuals and communities around the world, multilingual repertoires do abound. Being multilingual is not an aberration, nor is it exotic or a privilege of the elite, but a normal and unremarkable necessity and existence for the majority in the world.

An everyday multilingual competence would include the oft-quoted situation of the Tukano people in northwest Amazon, at the border between Colombia and Brazil (Sorensen 1971), which is in fact the situation for most of Amazonia (Aikhenvald 2008). There, men must marry outside their language group, choosing from neighbouring tribes; the women move into men's households or longhouses, and thus in any village one finds the men's language, the numerous languages of the various women who have married into that community, plus the regional 'trade' language.

In urban contexts too, everyday multilingualism is unremarkable. Myers-Scotton (2006: 1) provides as one of her 'bilingual snapshots', here in example 2.1, a description of an individual in mainland China whose linguistic practices would sound absolutely familiar to most in this part of the world.

(2.1)

> Zhao Min speaks two dialects of Chinese as well as English. He's a commodity trader for a joint venture of the government of the People's Republic of China and an international conglomerate. He comes from Nanjing, China, but divides his time between Beijing and Hong Kong in China, with extended stays in Europe. He studied English as part of his secondary schooling and university education. Today his job demands a good deal of English; he writes emails and has long-distance phone conversations – always in English – with his customers, for whom English is usually a second language, too (e.g. Serbs in former Yugoslavia, now Serbia). When he visits his family in Nanjing, he speaks his home dialect, but when he deals with his Chinese colleagues, he speaks the standard dialect of the People's Republic of China (formerly called Mandarin, a name some still use, but called Putonghua in China). This is the variety he speaks with his wife, who was raised in Beijing. Zhao Min has little spare time from his job, but when he does, he often watches films and has a huge collection of English-language movies on DVD.

In the same vein, the range of languages and varieties in the repertoire of the individual from India in example 2.2 is again commonplace for most from the subcontinent (adapted from Edwards 1994: 4), as is that of the Singaporean in example 2.3 (Lisa Lim, field notes) and the Ghanaian in example 2.4 (Kofi Yakpo, personal communication 2012).

(2.2)

> The maternal tongue of a Bombay spice merchant is a Kathiawari dialect of Gujarati; he usually speaks Kacchi at work, however. In the market place he speaks Marathi and, at the railway station, Hindustani. English is the medium when he flies with Air India to New Delhi, and he sometimes watches English-language films at the cinema. He reads a Gujarati newspaper written in a dialect more standard than his own. He sometimes has dealings with a Bengali colleague who routinely speaks both 'high' and 'low' Bengali – a man whose 'primary' wife speaks a dialect strongly marked as a female variant, and whose 'secondary' wife normally speaks Urdu. His office manager speaks Dhaki and his servants variously use Bhojpuri, Awadhi, Maithili, Ahiri and Chatgaya. This Bengali businessman has a cousin in Orissa, an Oriya speaker married to a Tamil: they use English at home, but their children are more likely to speak Bengali; they employ a Hindustani nurse and a Nepali watchman.

(2.3)

> Dr Lim, now in his seventies, grew up in a time when Singapore was a British colony. While his home language was Hokkien, he eventually attended

English-medium mission schools, and English became just as important and dominant a language for him. He also studied Latin and French in school, as was the norm in such schools at the time. Amongst his siblings Hokkien is still the preferred language, though English is also used, and he still counts in Hokkien. He also speaks other languages widespread in Singapore during the colonial era, such as Bazaar Malay – the interethnic lingua franca in pre-independence days – and Teochew, Cantonese, and Hainanese, which he uses with Chinese from those ethnicities he encounters in markets, hawker centres or stores. He has a smattering of Tamil, one of the languages of south India common in Singapore, which he used to use with his gardener. In addition, he acquired Mandarin, which was made the official Chinese language at Singapore's independence. Dr Lim's wife is Peranakan, who, even with Baba Malay the language of the older generations of her family, grew up Anglophile and Anglophone, so they spoke English with their children. As a general practitioner in Singapore for half a century in an eastern suburb of the island, Dr Lim has had patients from all ethnicities and all walks of life. Thus he also has a basic repertoire (numbers, parts of the body, basic instructions, etc.) in languages such as Tagalog, Thai and Burmese.

(2.4)

I usually speak Siase with my father and Siase and Ewe with my mother. I learned Fanti from our next door neighbours' children when growing up. At school, we were supposed to speak English, which we did in class, but with my classmates I usually spoke Pidgin English in the breaks. School was in downtown Accra, so I learned Gã from the street traders, when buying lunch, for example. I did my national service in the North, that's where I learned Hausa. My French and Mina are also not bad because I went to school in Togo for two years. Now, most of the time, when I'm in town and with friends, we speak Twi. (Atta Gavu, 43 years, Accra, Ghana)

As can be gleaned from these snapshots, numerous factors responsible for the conditions which promote multilingualism may have been identified, many of which have to do with communities coming into contact with each other through close proximity. Research has documented many factors; a comprehensive collection may, for example, be found in Myers-Scotton (2006).

A number of social contexts induce close proximity amongst peoples of different linguistic backgrounds.

i. **Living in a linguistic archipelago.** This is when many (often unrelated) languages, each with few speakers, are spoken in the same ecosphere. This kind of ecology must have been common in the pre-colonial era – for example, in Aboriginal Australia – but is rare nowadays, though locales such as the Amazon Basin and Papua New Guinea are examples.

ii. **Living in a multilingual nation, especially as a minority group member.** This is a very common occurrence, as there are very few monolingual nations (perhaps Iceland and Korea). Even monolingual areas/enclaves are hard to identify in today's interconnected world, but in pre-Second World War Europe, for example, there were still isolated mountain villages with monolingual populations. This must still be the case in some remote areas of the world, such as among the ethnic minorities ('hill tribes') of mainland Southeast Asia living in relative isolation. Minority groups – i.e. groups who speak a mother tongue that is not the official language of the nation state, who typically lack political power and/or socioeconomic prestige – are compelled to become bilingual in the dominant national language for both instrumental and psychological reasons.

iii. **Living in border areas.** It is not uncommon for border areas to show bilingualism or even multilingualism. Think of the border between Romance and Germanic language families, through Switzerland (French, Italian, and Romansch in the south, Swiss German in the north) and Belgium (Dutch and German in the north, French in the south). Or the borders between Indo-European and Dravidian languages in India, characterised by rich linguistic diversity; the Mexican–American border and its English–Spanish bilingualism; the New England–Quebec border where American shopkeepers in Vermont develop French for Quebec shoppers, etc. At borders between ethnic groups too, neighbouring populations exhibit some bilingualism, although it is often not reciprocal: speakers of the less dominant language are more likely to learn the language of the dominant group. An example is in western Kenya at the border between the Luo ethnic group and the less politically powerful Bantu groups of the area, the Luyia to the north and the Kisii to the east.

iv. **Living in a multi-ethnic urban area: urban multilingualism.** Cities around the world today are generally very multilingual, such as Brussels, the capital of an autonomous region within Belgium. This has two official languages – French and Dutch – and several regional varieties, other European languages spoken by personnel of the European Union which is centred there, and languages of the various immigrant populations. Urban areas of a nation sometimes contrast with rural areas which are much less multilingual, as in the UK and the US. Harbour cities that have functioned as centres of trade since ancient times and later as centres of colonial administration have a long tradition of multilingualism. Lingua Franca arose in the Mediterranean from the interaction between the Christian and the Muslim worlds, with the

Genoese and Venetian trading colonies the first to use it. Lingua Franca was initially based mostly on Northern Italian languages and Occitano-Romance languages in the eastern Mediterranean, and later included more Spanish and Portuguese elements, borrowing also from Berber, Turkish, French, Greek and Arabic. In Asia, Bazaar Malay connected the trading routes of the Indonesian world and the Indian Ocean.

A number of fundamental social activities of human societies lead to language contact. The most important, in a historical perspective, are trade and exogamy.

v. **Engaging in trade.** Trade has brought people of different cultures together throughout history. Certain occupations involve many contacts outside one's own ethnic group and thus reasons to learn an additional language – such as market stallholders, as a classic example, found world-wide. Today globalisation and international finance are just the most recent incarnation of social patterns that are pervasive in our history.

vi. **Marrying outside one's ethnic group.** This was and still is very common practice in traditional societies, leading to the acquisition of family members with different linguistic backgrounds, and the creation of multilingual households in which children are brought up. In exogamy, children may learn the language of the mother or the father or both. The 'one parent – one language' environment which appears as a special case in modern times is commonplace in exogamous societies, as shown in language socialisation studies (e.g. Ochs 1988; Moore 1999).

Two conditions of displacement that run throughout the history of human societies are migration and war.

vii. **Migration.** Groups of people throughout history have moved, voluntarily or involuntarily. Motivations may comprise better jobs or education, or political or religious refuge. The outcome is always bilingualism in the mother tongue and the dominant language of the nation receiving immigrants. This occurs not always in the first generation but almost always in the second, with a shift to monolingualism in the dominant language in the third generation.

viii. **Conflict, subsequent colonialism and slavery.** These also need special mention: colonialism, sometimes preceded by war, often involves the imposition of the language of the conquerers on the local population; for example, the Roman legions who conquered part of Europe and spread Latin as language of governance; or the spread of French, Spanish, Portuguese, Dutch and English in Africa, Asia and South America during colonial times. This often involves deportation of slaves, which further accentuates language contact. War also leads to geopolitical changes, such as changes in national borders – another source of language contact. For example, the region of Alsace has passed between German and French control many times since the seventeenth century, with numerous German dialects spoken up until the nineteenth century, including the traditional vernacular Alsatian; today, French is the official language and the major language spoken, but heavy influence from German on the Alsatian dialect of French is evident.

It is actually quite instructive to plot the factors which have led to multilingualism across a number of generations in a community. This allows us to note patterns over time, which may be related to linguistic periodisation (see Chapter 5), thus bringing together sociohistorical information and macro-linguistic data. Table 2.1 charts the factors, based on those listed in Myers-Scotton (2006), which have led to diverse multilingual repertoires in three generations of a Peranakan Chinese family in Singapore.

2.2 ALLOCATING LANGUAGES IN SOCIETY

Until as recently as the middle of the last century, the notion that speakers use languages in their repertoire in a systematic way was in fact not explicitly recognised, surprising though that might sound to younger readers.[1] We owe the overt recognition in the modern perspective that speakers make allocations in language use to Charles Ferguson and Joshua Fishman (Spolsky 2011), who categorised such systematicity in terms of the phenomenon of diglossia and the pattern of domains respectively, and these concepts have been developed by numerous scholars after them. In spite of the criticism that such models may be too simplistic or reduce what often are grey zones to black and white, these approaches have great merit. In establishing and understanding how

---

[1] Hellenists wishing to describe the roles of dialects in Greek society had already introduced the idea of *diglossie*. French hellenist Psichari in the late 1920s saw as diglossic the contemporary use of both the ordinary spoken demotic Greek and the 'purer', more classic *katharévousa*. In 1930, French orientalist Marçais, examining *la diglossie arabe* of classicial and vernacular Arabic in North Africa, questioned whether diglossia could also be extended to different languages with separate social functions (Ferguson 1959: 326; Edwards 1994: 83–4).

Table 2.1 *Factors leading to multilingualism in a Peranakan Chinese family in Singapore (Lisa Lim, field notes)*

Interlocutor and dominant/home language

Factors for multilingualism	ego Eng	sibling Eng	father Hok	mother Eng, BM	maternal grandfather BM	maternal grandmother BM, Eng
1. multilingual nation, as minority						
2. border areas						
3. urban multilingualism	BZM, C	BZM	Eng, BZM, etc.		Eng, BZM	BZM, Hok, C
4. occupation	CM, SLM		C, Ch, T, Tag, Tam, etc.		Eng	BhM
5. exogamy	It		BM			
6. (grand)parent	BM	BM				
7. migration	D, C					
8. colonialism			Eng		Eng	Eng
9. change of borders						
10. national integration	Man	Man	Eng, Man			
11. socioeconomic mobility	D	Ge	J	J		
12. psychological attractiveness	Sp					
13. education	Man, Fr	Man	Eng, Lat, Fr	Lat, Fr	Eng	Eng, Lat

Abbreviations:

BM	Baba Malay	BZM	Bazaar Malay
C	Cantonese	Ch	Chinese
D	Dutch	Eng	English
Ge	German	Hok	Hokkien
J	Japanese	Lat	Latin
Sp	Spanish	SLM	Sri Lanka Malay
Tag	Tagalog	Tam	Tamil
BhM	Bahasa Melayu		
CM	Cocos Malay		
Fr	French		
It	Italian		
Man	Mandarin		
T	Teochew		

multilingual communities organise their multiple linguistic resources in more (or less) compartmentalised ways across society, we are provided with a snapshot of language use on a macro scale – that is, across a society or community. Examining the patterns across the different generations also provides an indication of how stable the bilingual situation is – that is, whether speakers are likely to maintain their first language (L1) or shift to another language that is more dominant in the community/society. This last point will be explored in Chapter 6.

2.2.1 Diglossia

In Ferguson's classic formulation of diglossia, functional differentiation exists between 'high' (H) and 'low' (L) varieties of a language exhibited in a society (1959: 336). This manifests itself in:

> a relatively stable language situation in which, in addition to the primary dialects of the language [L] ... there is a very divergent, highly codified (often grammatically more complex) superposed variety [H], the vehicle of a large and respected body of literature ... which is learned largely by formal education and is used for most written and formal spoken purposes but is not used by any sector of the community for ordinary conversation.

His formulation was based on his observations of four defining speech communities and their languages: classical Arabic (H) and various colloquial forms of Arabic (L) in the Middle East and North Africa; two varieties of modern Greek – katherevousa (H) and dhimotiki (L) – in Greece; standard German (H) and Swiss German (L) in German-speaking cantons of Switzerland; and French (H) and Haitian Creole (L) in Haiti. The defining features of diglossia identified by Ferguson are function, prestige, literary heritage, acquisition, standardisation, grammar, lexicon, phonology and stability.

Some societies show the functional specialisation identified by Ferguson, but with different languages rather than related forms of same language, or indeed with different styles and registers. H situations are not just those with more formality but those where status and prestige are salient – i.e. status-raising situations. The classic example of this, described by Fishman (1972) as extended diglossia, is Paraguay (Rubin 1968), where Guaraní is the mother tongue of 90 per cent of the population and the second language of much of the rest of the population, and Spanish is the official language of government and education but the vernacular of less than 10 per cent. In the capital, Asunción, the population is bilingual, while in the countryside, peoples are monolingual in Guaraní. The choice between Spanish and Guaraní depends on location, formality, sex, status, intimacy, seriousness and activity – i.e. situation. Notably, everyone speaks their own L1; but for some their L1 is also the H variety, while for others their L1 is the L variety – the consequence is that some have more access to participating in status-raising activities, by virtue of their background (compare the effect of schooling in classic diglossia).

This concept involving functional specialisation of linguistic varieties may be extended indefinitely. Triglossia, which describes the situation where there is a third language, dialect or style, may be found in East Africa, with the ethnic languages (L), English as lingua franca in status-raising activities (H) and Swahili as general lingua franca functioning as a 'middle' (M) variety, and in Tunisia, where there exist two H varieties – standard Arabic and French – and one L variety – Tunisian Arabic (Romaine 1989: 34). Tetraglossia may be seen in Morocco, with classical Arabic, vernacular Arabic, French and Berber (Edwards 1994: 86).

With communities and societies being as complex as they are, it is not surprising to note that a polyglossic spectrum (Mackey 1986) is in fact the norm in many parts of the world. The Arabic situation has been suggested to comprise a five-point continuum: Classical Arabic (H); Modern Standard Arabic, the current literary medium (only written); High Standard Colloquial, the usual spoken variety of educated people dealing with serious topics (part of Ferguson's L); Middle Standard Colloquial, the everyday language of the literate (part of Ferguson's L); and Low Colloquial, the everyday language of the illiterate (part of Ferguson's L) (Elgibali 1988). In Malaysia's Malay speech community one finds *bahasa di raja* – i.e. Royal Malay (H) – and Common Malay (L), which would approximate the H–L dichotomy. But the latter also encompasses *bahasa halus* (Refined Malay) and *bahasa terpelajar* (Educated Malay), and in addition to these there is a colloquial and coarse variety – *bahasa kasar* – and a variety which is colloquial without being coarse – *bahasa basahan* (Asmah 1986). It is in the multicultural, multi-ethnic speech community of Singapore that we see the vivid extent of polyglossia, as illustrated by Platt (1977, 1980). Gupta (1989), looking only at English, conceptualised Singapore as diglossic, where Standard Singapore English (SgE) (H) and Colloquial SgE (L) were seen to be in complementary distribution according to domains of use, with H taught in school and used in business and government, and L used amongst peers, in the army and generally in informal situations. Platt (1980: 64), much earlier, had suggested that it would be more appropriate to speak of polyglossia, as many Singaporeans possess a verbal repertoire containing more than two speech varieties, and as the speech community as a whole makes use of more than two codes in everyday interaction, each one having different functions. In fact, the different ethnic groups in Singapore – viz. the Chinese, Malays and Indians – would have diverse verbal repertoires. These would usually include one of the official 'mother tongues' Mandarin, Malay or Tamil, alongside their actual vernaculars, which could be any of the southern Chinese varieties such as Hokkien, Teochew, Cantonese, Hakka and so forth, or one of the Indian languages including Punjabi, Gujarati, Bengali and so forth, and of course English. Thus, Platt argues for a complex polyglossia, with not just one high prestige language and one low prestige language or dialect but a continuum, with possibly more than one high prestige speech variety, one or more medium varieties, and one or more low prestige varieties (Platt 1980: 69).

As has been noted by various scholars, one obvious implication of Ferguson's conception of diglossia and all its extensions is that members of a community would seem to be constrained in their language behaviour, merely reflecting a set of predetermined society-wide norms. The mixing of codes, for instance, as an outcome of contact between languages within and amongst speakers, would appear to be ruled out by this model. Adopting Ferguson's notion of diglossia thus means a focus on multilingualism at the macro-societal level – as can be seen in the various studies previously mentioned – on a dimension abstracted away from more concrete, interactional behaviour at the level of the individual speaker.

While one of the original defining features identified by Ferguson is that of diglossia being a stable situation, capable of persisting over several centuries, later scholars have extended the notion to account for communities showing changing patterns of language use over time – which is very much a reality for many communities. In Hong Kong, for instance, for most of the British colonial era English was the sole official (H) language, with Cantonese, the vernacular of the majority of the population, being the L language. In 1974 Chinese (meaning Modern Standard Chinese as the written form and Cantonese as the spoken form) was made a co-official language. Hong Kong thus displayed de jure diglossia pre-1974 and de facto diglossia after 1974 (Wright 2008: 267). Following the return of Hong Kong to Chinese sovereignty in 1997, the position of Putonghua – the official language of the People's Republic of China, based on the Beijing dialect – became much enhanced: it is Putonghua and standard written Chinese that are taught in schools. Nonetheless, Cantonese still remains the predominant spoken language of the majority of the population, and the written form of Cantonese is also still pervasive. The situation of Putonghua (H) and Cantonese (L) has been described as modern diglossia (Snow 2010: 157). Such a situation is found in societies that promote mass education and literacy to the extent that most or all of the inhabitants are proficient in both H (mainly as the written variety) and L (mainly as the spoken variety), with H and L being genetically or historically related varieties. H is a modernised standard language and not a classical language with prestige, is promoted as the national language in both spoken and written forms and has a large number of native speakers in the powerful nation that neighbours the smaller diglossic society. Thus, H is accepted because of its high utility value as well as its association with cultural traditions that are shared with the larger neighbour where H is the standard language. At the same time, members of the speech community strongly desire that L continue playing its role as a marker of social identity. The case of Hong Kong, as Snow (2010: 176) points out, is 'valuable for understanding what sustains [diglossic] patterns, especially during and after transition to modern society...examination of this subcategory of diglossia highlights the role that identity factors play in the sustaining of both traditional and modern diglossia – and the different kind of role identity plays in sustaining each'. If one takes into consideration all three languages of Hong Kong's biliteracy (written Chinese and English) and trilingualism (spoken Cantonese, English and Putonghua) language policy, a triglossic situation may be recognised.

2.2.2 Domains

Also concerned with establishing general patterns of language use in order to be able to characterise societies in terms of linguistic repertoire, but linking the analysis of societal norms and expectations with language use in face-to-face encounters, Fishman (1965, 1972) – writing at around the same time as Ferguson – developed the concept of domains of use. This is formulated as a sociocultural construct abstracted from topics of communication, relationship between communicators and locales of communication, in accordance with the institutions of a society and the spheres of activity of a speech community, in such a way that individual behaviour and social patterns can be distinguished from each other and yet are related to each other. In other words, speakers divide up when they use languages in terms of the 'major activity centres' in their lives, with the assumption that '"proper" usage dictates that only one of the theoretically co-available languages or varieties will be chosen by particular classes of interlocutors on particular kinds of occasions to discuss particular kinds of topics' (Fishman 1972: 15). Defined in terms of institutional contexts or socioecological co-occurrences, domains are intended to designate the major clusters of interaction situations that occur in particular multilingual settings. Domains enable us to understand that 'language choice and topic ... are ... related to widespread sociocultural norms and expectations' (Fishman 1972: 19). The majority of interactions in domain X are the same at some level – i.e. there is a usual, unmarked combination of elements in interactions in each domain; each domain has its own constellation of expected factors, such as location, topic and participants. In other words, congruence amongst domain components is key – in particular participant, topic and setting – as well as congruence of domain with specific language or language variety. It should be underlined that Fishman does not provide a taxonomy or set of principles for delimiting domains, and emphasises instead the need to establish relevant domains empirically, strongly rejecting the idea of an invariant set of domains applicable to all communities (Fishman 1972: 441). This makes absolute sense if one takes the reality of diversity seriously: different communities, even different groups in a community, with diverse cultural backgrounds, norms and values must surely have different conceptions of the domains in which they operate.

In one of the first studies to implement domain analysis, Greenfield (1972) gave members of the Puerto Rican community in New York City two congruent factors – for instance, talking with their parents (participants) about domestic affairs (topic) – and asked them to select a third factor comprising the most likely setting from amongst 'home', 'beach', 'church', 'school' or 'workplace' for such a communicative event to take place. In all but one instance the expected third factor was selected by no less than 81 per cent and up to 100 per cent of the informants, which would appear to confirm the theoretical validity of the domain concept. Greenfield also asked informants what the most likely language would be for the domains used in this study – namely family, friendship, religion, education and employment – and responses again were consistent, with Spanish regularly used in the more 'intimate' domains of family and friendship and English preferred in the other three domains, where a status difference between participants was involved.

However, the same domain may not be equally significant to different communities or even to all members of a single community, as Fishman also argues, and speakers' perceptions of what a domain entails will differ according to their backgrounds and social positions. The lack of criteria specified for domains means unconstrained lists of domains, which makes comparisons across communities difficult, if not impossible. A point of contrast is a study on language use in India, in which just three domains of family, friendship and institution are identified (Saghal 1991: 299). Thus, the lack of rigidity of the domain concept is at the same time its limitation. Another challenge is the congruence expected of domain components: it is not clear how Fishman's model can account for language choices in incongruent situations. In addition, other factors can override domains as predictors in language choice making, such as participants and their repertoire (e.g. in Lusaka, Zambia, higher socioeconomic status leads to a choice of English); topic (which interacts with participant); or addressee. And just as with the notion of diglossia, there can well be a change over time in the language for a particular domain.

While seemingly simplistic, and in spite of the criticism that in some communities a one-language-one-domain relationship does not hold, domains analysis is used widely in research precisely to identify certain broad regularities of language use – to establish societal or community patterns of language use, usually using large-scale surveys of speakers' reports of language use. There may, of course, be tension between languages: English in Kenya, for example, as noted by Myers-Scotton (2006), is an official language (with Swahili), and enjoys high social status, but constitutes a threat to local languages and cultures. And relationships between languages in bilingual communities may change. Social changes, such as migration, invasion, conquest and industrialisation, have been associated with the process of language shift, which can threaten viability of a language and even result in language death.

Furthermore, it is not simply a matter of allocation of language in different situations or domains but also a matter of allocation of power, where those who know the H variety have access to social and political power that is not available to those who do not. In order to participate in interactions where the H variety is used, one has to be able to use that variety or else not participate. In classic diglossic situations everyone's L1 is the L variety; the H variety is learned, so the opportunity for schooling is the gateway to potential power. In extended diglossic situations everyone speaks their own L1, acquiring it in the home; but for some their L1 is also the H variety, while for others their L1 is the L variety – the consequence is that some have more access to participating in status-raising activities by virtue of individual background in a particular society.

2.3 CODE SWITCHING

The research on code switching and mixing is vast, and here we can only mention some highlights. As outlined in Chapter 1, code switching refers to an alternation of languages within a conversation, usually at

semantically or sociolinguistically meaningful junctures, which is associated with particular pragmatic effects, discourse functions, or associations with group identity. Some scholars use 'code switching' for the
alternation of languages in between utterances or phrases, to contrast
with 'code mixing' for language mixing within the phrase or utterance.
Others use 'code mixing' to mean the practice of mixing together features from different linguistic systems, in particular in describing more
stable situations where multiple languages are used, and emphasising
a more hybrid form, as will be seen later in this chapter. Sometimes the
terms 'code switching' and 'code mixing' are used more or less interchangeably, and/or 'code mixing' is used to encompass both practices. A
distinction is also made between 'alternational code switching', involving alternating languages between utterances or sentences, as in the
well-known case from Poplack (1980) in example 2.5, and 'insertional
code switching', involving the insertion of a word or phrase into an
utterance or sentence in a particular base language, as in example 2.6
(Pfaff 1970, cited in Muysken 1997: 361) (English; *Spanish*).

(2.5)

Sometimes I'll start a sentence in English *y terminó en Español*.
'Sometimes I'll start a sentence in English and finish in Spanish.'

(2.6)

Yo anduve in a state of shock *pa dos días*.
'I walked in a state of shock for two days.'

Research has focused on situational and contextual motivations for
switching, as well as on the structural characteristics of code switching,
aiming to identify general patterns. It is significant that the study that
can be seen to mark the beginning of current interest in code switching
highlighted the communicative use of code switching to convey social
meanings. Jan-Petter Blom and John Gumperz's (1972) study on a bidi-
alectal community in Hemnesberget in northern Norway demonstrated
how Ranamål, a local dialect, symbolised local cultural identity and was
associated with home, family and friends, and locally based activities
and relationships. Meanwhile Bokmål, the standard variety, was associated with formal education and with official transactions, religion and
the mass media, and was also used by those occupying a high social
status in the community. Additionally, speakers would switch from
one variety to the other during the same social event depending on
the topic of conversation – for example, in clerk–resident exchanges,
greetings and enquiries about family affairs took place in Ranamål,
but when the conversation turned to the business transaction at hand,

this was done in Bokmål. Similar patterns of language choice to convey social meaning have since been documented in numerous other bilingual communities. Gumperz (1982), elaborating on Blom and Gumperz (1972), emphasises the role of code switching in helping the speaker redefine the conversational context.

A comprehensive account of social motivations for code switching comes from Carol Myers-Scotton's (1993) research in Africa, in particular her markedness model of conversational code switching. This suggests that speakers' language choices are predictable based on a set of indicators that are associated with each of the languages in their repertoire, on the assumption that in every multilingual community there are unmarked and marked language choices, where the language used is one that would be expected or unexpected, respectively, in that particular context. In Nairobi, the capital of Kenya, Swahili – one of the official languages of Kenya, along with English – is a widely used lingua franca between people who do not share the same L1 (and are not from the same ethnic group), especially in casual conversations. Various linguistic varieties from the ethnic groups in the country would be spoken as an L1 and used by in-migrants from that region to the city. Myers-Scotton identifies four main patterns: code switching (a) as a series of unmarked choices, (b) as an exploratory choice, (c) as a marked choice and (d) as an unmarked choice in itself.

Code switching may comprise a series of unmarked choices when aspects of the context, such as a change in topic or in the person addressed, make a different language variety more appropriate. A typical example in Myers-Scotton's (1993: 88) work in Nairobi takes the form of a visitor to a company and the security guard speaking initially in Swahili, the usual language for such interactions between strangers. But then the guard, followed by the visitor, switches to their joint ethnic language Luyia when it transpires that they come from the same ethnic group, the code choice indexing their common identity and marking their relationship as one between ethnic brethren rather than strangers.

When the unmarked choice is uncertain, as when little is known about the interlocutor's social identity or when there is a clash of norms, then code switching may be seen to have an exploratory function. When a local businessman meets up with a former classmate, now a university student who is home for a visit, he seems uncertain how to relate to his schoolfriend and tries English, a marked choice to be used in a local bar, as well as some Kikuyu and Swahili, either or both of which could be the unmarked choice. After such exploratory code switching, he ends up using English inappropriately and more frequently than his former classmate who, as a university student, would have more familiarity with the language (Myers-Scotton 1993: 143).

Code switching is considered marked when it does not conform to expected patterns. An example is seen in Myers-Scotton's (1988) unpublished corpus (given in Myers-Scotton 2006: 162), shown in example 2.7, which takes place in Nairobi between a Luyia man who is a passenger on a bus (L), and the bus conductor (C), who draws on *Luyia, Swahili* and English. Swahili would be the unmarked choice for any transaction with a bus conductor in Nairobi. The choice of the Luyia man's L1 in line 1 is thus clearly a marked choice, and can be interpreted as an attempt to establish solidarity through a shared group membership with the bus conductor, the aim probably to avoid being charged the full fare. Myers-Scotton (2006: 162) suggests that, because the Luyia man speaks loudly and in a joking voice, it is almost as if he recognises that he is making a marked choice.

(2.7)

1. L: [Holding out his hand with some money in it, speaking quite loudly and perhaps self-consciously]
   Mwana weru, vugula khasimoni khonyene.
   'Take only fifty cents, dear brother.'
   [Other passengers laugh]
2. C: [Also just laughs]
3. L: *Shuli mwana weru mbaa?*
   'Aren't you a brother?'
4. C: *Apana. Mimi si ndugu wako. Kama ungekuwa ndugu wangu ningekujua, ningekujua kwa jina. Lakini sasa sikujui wala sikufahamu.*
   'No, I'm not your brother. If you were my brother, I would know you. I would know you by name. But now I don't know you nor do I understand you.'
5. L: *Nisaidie, tu, Bwana. Maisha ya Nairobi imenishinda kwa sababu bei ya kila kitu imeongezwa. Mimi ninaketi Kariobang'i, pahali ninapolipa pesa nyingi sana kwa nauli ya basi.*
   'Just help me, mister. The life of Nairobi has defeated me because the price of everything has gone up. I live in Kariobang'i, a place to which I pay much money for the bus fare.'
6. C: [Taking some money out of the Luyia man's outstretched hand]
   Nimechukua peni nane pekee yake.
   'I have taken 80 cents alone.'
7. L: Thank you very much. *Nimeshkuru sana kwa huruma ya ngugu wangu.*
   'Thank you very much for the pity of this one, my brother.'

Finally there is the pattern where the act of code switching itself is an unmarked choice. In other words, no meaning is ascribed to any particular switch of language; rather it is the use of both languages together that is meaningful, as this draws on the associations that both languages afford and the dual identities they index. Myers-Scotton (1993: 118–19) sees this in the young people of Nairobi, who come from different ethnic groups and who probably do not know one another's ethnic languages. They use a mix of Swahili and English as lingua franca, as in example 2.8 of a conversation between several Nairobi teenagers including a Taita ethnic group member (T) and a Luyia speaker (L), using *Swahili* (with features from their own ethnic languages) and English (from Myers-Scotton's 1988 unpublished Nairobi corpus, in Myers-Scotton 2006: 167). What is notable is that they could well just be using Swahili – which has some prestige as an urban language while still being indigenous – but English adds the appeal of being the language of upward mobility, the international community and international mass media. To Myers-Scotton, switching between the two languages becomes their unmarked choice for making simultaneously two or more positively evaluated identities or memberships in both of the cultures that the languages index (1993: 122, 2006: 167).

(2.8)

T: *Ukisha ikanyaganganga hivi* pedals, *unasikia* air *umeshakishwa. Sasa unashangaa kama ni* bike *au ni ma*-ghosts.
   'When you step on the pedals you hear the air coming out. Now you wonder whether it's the bike or the ghosts [that do that].'
L: *Wewe pia una*-believe *habari ya ma*-ghosts *kumbe?*
   'You also believe about ghosts?'
T: *Ah*, ghost, *lazima una*-believe, *usiku unaona* something *kama* bones *na inatembea* on the road.
   'Ah, ghost, you have to believe [when] at night you see something like bones and it's walking on the road.'
L: *Kulikuwa na* table long *namna hii, mazee, imejaa tu chakula ya kila aina . . . Nilikwenda pale nikaangalia, nikapata chakula nyingine iko* grey, *nika-i-*taste *nikaona ina* taste lousy *sana.*
   'There was a long table like this, my friend, full of food of every kind . . . I went there and looked and I got another kind of food [that was] grey, and I tasted it and I thought it had a very lousy taste.'

2.4 MIXED CODE AS DEFAULT

It is this last pattern of unmarked code switching that is perhaps most significant in multilingual communities. This is when language alternation itself constitutes a default option that is meaningful as a signal of shared, multilingual identity. This is the observation made by Meeuwis and Blommaert (1998), who view the Lingala-French code used by Zaireans in Belgium as a single code in its own right, describing it as monolectal code switching. Auer (1999) proposes the notion of a fused lect to denote a combination of structures from different language sources, which no longer has any particular conversation-structuring function but instead is meaningful as a wholesale token of group identity and mode of conversation.

Many scholars, such as Canagarajah (2009), have pointed out that such plurilingual practices have been in existence and have been natural and embraced in regions such as South Asia since pre-colonial times. Canagarajah (2009: 6; based on research of scholars such as Silverstein 1996; Khubchandani 1997; Makoni 2002; Canagarajah 2007; Garcia 2009) summarises such plurilingual competence as follows.

   i. Proficiency in languages is not conceptualised individually, with separate competencies developed for each language. What is emphasised is the repertoire – the way the different languages constitute an integrated competence.
  ii. Equal or advanced proficiency is not expected in all the languages.
 iii. Using different languages for distinct purposes qualifies as competence. One does not have to use all the languages involved as all-purpose languages.
 iv. Language competence is not treated in isolation but as a form of social practice and intercultural competence.
  v. There is a recognition that speakers develop plurilingual competence by themselves (intuitively and through social practice) more than through schools or formal means.

Example 2.9 presents Canagarajah's (1995a) now classic illustration of plurilingual English, sometimes referred to as 'Englishised Tamil', as the unmarked everyday code in Jaffna, in northeast Sri Lanka (which was under the control of the LTTE – the Liberation Tigers of Tamil Eelam, a now defunct militant organisation that was based in northern Sri Lanka – until 2009). This is a situation that arose after independence in 1948 from British colonial rule, when there was strong social pressure amongst Tamils against excessive use of English but when the speaking of Tamil on its own could be considered excessively formal. Through this example, Canagarajah (2009: 15) provides an instructive account of how plurilingual practices are wielded to one's advantage. The senior professor (P), who is comfortable with prestige varieties of English (having done his graduate work in the UK), is interviewing a junior lecturer (L) for a faculty position in English, and begins the interview in the unmarked code. L, being locally trained and lacking advanced proficiency in English, draws from the plurilingual tradition to negotiate the conversation in his favour. He is able to understand P's questions because of his receptive multilingualism, and continues the interaction confidently. He strategically uses the English tokens at his disposal, mostly technical or scholarly vocabulary common in academia, to shift the conversation in his favour. Although L lacks the ability to form complete sentences in English, his mixing is effective – in fact, it is better than using Tamil only, as 'the mixed language, particularly its vocabulary, conceals the social and regional identity of the speaker and thus has a standardising (i.e. neutralising) function' (Annamalai 2001: 174). Canagarajah argues that, although initially P continues to speak English and maintains a certain amount of distance (perhaps deliberately, as English provides him with power and confirms his identity as a senior scholar), he is eventually forced to take L seriously because of his successful strategies. P finally converges to L's plurilingual English (in line 5), after which they speak as equals (English, *Tamil*).

(2.9)

1. P: So you have done a masters in sociology? What is your area of research?
2. L: *Naan* sociology of religion-*ilai taan* interested. *enTai* thesis topic *vantu*
   'The rise of local deities in the Jaffna peninsula'.
   'It is in the sociology of religion that I am interested. My thesis topic was "The rise of local deities in the Jaffna peninsula".'
3. P: Did this involve a field work?
4. L: *oom, oru* ethnographic study-*aai taan itay ceitanaan. kiTTattaTTa* four years-*aai* field work *ceitanaan.*
   'Yes, I did this as an ethnographic study. I did field work for roughly four years.'
5. P: *appa kooTa* qualitative research *taan ceiyiraniir?*
   'So you do mostly qualitative research?'

Such a mixed code is also found in second-generation bilinguals, such as younger-generation British-born Chinese in the north of England, originally from Ap Chau, a small island near Hong Kong, as documented by Li (1998). This is shown in example 2.10, which Li argues constitutes a distinctive linguistic mode (*Cantonese*, English).

(2.10)

A: *Yeo hou do   yeo* contact.
   Have very many have contact.
   'We have many contacts.'
G: We always have opportunities *heu xig   kei ta dei fong gaowui di   yen.*
   Ngodei xixi dou keep in contact.
                                   will know that other place church POSS. person.
   We   time always.
   'We always have opportunities to get to know people from other churches.
   We always keep in contact.'

In other multilingual contexts of Asia too, where English has become
part of the linguistic fabric, similar mixed codes involving English are
commonplace, viewed as single codes in their own right (Lim 2009b;
Lim and Ansaldo 2012). Examples 2.11, 2.12 and 2.13, all varieties of
SgE, illustrate the range that can be observed in such mixed codes. In
example 2.11 from Lim (2009b: 58–9) – from the Grammar of Spoken
SgE Corpus (Lim and Foley 2004), comprising data on naturally occurring spontaneous speech of young Singaporeans – linguistic features
from the local languages have evolved in the restructured New English.
These include zero copula, the *kena* passive, absence of inflection on
third-person singular and past tense verbs, *is it* question tag, use of *one*,
reduplication and Malay/Sinitic particles, all considered features of Colloquial SgE. Significantly, such a code is used by Singaporeans of all
ethnicities; here, A is ethnically Chinese, while B and C are ethnically
Indian. Example 2.12 from Tay (1993, cited in Kachru and Nelson 2006:
256) and example 2.13 from Lim (2009b: 60)[2] both exemplify the tight
and fluid mix involving English, *Mandarin* and **Hokkien** commonly used
by ethnically Chinese Singaporeans. In the latter example it is shown in
characters Mei and Seng, who are representative of the younger generation of Singaporeans, and in the older-generation father, Pa (Lim 2008,
2009c). (In all three examples: English, **Hokkien**, **Malay**, *Mandarin*, *Sinitic particles*.)

(2.11)

B: So just go down . . . ya just go down go straight down
C: Go straight down and turn into Zion Road *ah* [Bazaar Malay/Hokkien particle]
A: Careful! The *ah pek*! [Hokkien 'old man']
B, C: (laughter)
C: You remember that guy that was running across the other day? {Just run across like that. (laughter)
B: {****
A: Hey, you know that Razid in Pizza Hut, right?
B: Which one?
C: Razid *ah*, Razid . . . the other {**mat**. [Malay (slang) 'a Malay male']
A: {Razali . . . Razali's friend . . . you know what he was doing or not?
B: The one who always like to *kow peh* {is it? [Hokkien 'complain']
A, C: {Ya ya . . .

---

[2] Example 2.13 derives from the script of the award-winning Singapore film *Singapore Dreaming* (Woo, Goh and Wu 2006), whose dialogues are vouched for by Singapor-eans as being completely authentic.

C: The one who always making {noise . . .
B: {I don't like him, you know . . . he
       _ah_ . . . like **macam** [Malay 'like']
C: The **botak botak** {fella [Malay 'bald bald' = 'very bald']
B: {_Ah_ . . . the like ****
A: The fella centre **botak** three side hair {one [Malay 'bald']
       'The fellow is (has the quality of being) bald in the centre with hair on
       three sides'
C: {Eh, that guy got problem _ah_, that
       fella . . .

Note: Curly brackets represent overlapping speech; asterisks represent
unintelligible speech.

(2.12)

Oh I see, _guai bu de_ . . . _wo xie ing wen bi jiao kuai,_ **gua sia eng boon luan jut u**
luan ju sia, _jiaru_ move _de_ fast, **bo tek khak o**. _Dui bu qi._ I got to go.

'Oh, I see, no wonder . . . I write faster in English, when I write English, I simply
scribble and write, carelessly, if [I] move fast, [I'm] not sure. Sorry. I got to go.'

(2.13)

Mei: Seng _a21_, time to get a job _ho24_? Pa and Irene spend all their savings on
        you already _le21_. Are you waiting for Pa _to buy Toto [the lottery] and_
        get it all back me55?
Pa: You say other people for what? You are just a secretary.
Irene: _Aiya_, never mind, never mind. Anyway Seng already has a job interview
        on Monday.
Pa: _Wah_, real or not?
Seng: I arranged the meeting through email. Now American degrees _all in_
        demand.
CB: _Wah_, congratulations, man.
Seng: Thanks.
Ma: **What did they just say?**
Mei: _Seng said that on Monday_ . . .
Pa: Now you've come back, you can't play the fool anymore, okay? _What if_
        you end up selling insurance like this guy? **Don't make me lose face!**

Note: The data are represented as the idiomatic gloss in English here, with bold
and italics indicating the different language varieties used.

In the Philippines, code switching between English and the local languages is extensively used by urban Filipinos comfortable in both languages (Bautista and Gonzales 2009: 137). As in the case of Singapore's
plurilingual code, the mix of English and Tagalog – often referred to
as Taglish – is even said to be the usual code amongst Filipinos, with
'pure' Tagalog or English seldom heard, as in example 2.14 (McFarland
2009: 144). Most recently, such a mixed code has even been observed in
domains which usually do not exhibit this, including newspaper reports
such as an article for Yahoo! News Philippines on territorial disputes in

the South China Sea (Tordesillas 2013). This (example 2.15), while predominantly in English, mixes in a Tagalog item in the first sentence and a sentence in Tagalog to end the article (*Tagalog*, English).

(2.14)

Then they ask me, *ano pa daw* capabilities *ko* in singing . . . I did not told them . . . *gusto ko sila mag* find out.

'Then they ask me, what other capabilities I have in singing . . . I did not tell them . . . I wanted them to find out for themselves.'

(2.15)

Never have I felt so *kawawa* [Tagalog 'helpless'] reading the statements of Defense Secretary Voltaire Gazmin justifying his plan to allow American and Japanese military access to military facilities in the Philippines to deter China's aggressive moves in the South China Sea.
[Entire article in English]
Ano ba naman tayo?
'Oh, how helpless we are!'[3]

All the examples above demonstrate how the emergence of a mixed code is a very common and normal outcome of speakers of different languages being in contact with each other.

2.5 MIXING FOR MEANING

2.5.1 Mixing varieties for indexing meaning

In Hong Kong, an interesting consequence of mobility is the creation of a well-recognised community referred to as returnees: residents who emigrated from Hong Kong to another country – mostly Canada, Australia and the US – lived for an extended period of time in their adopted home, and subsequently moved back to Hong Kong.[4] Cantonese–English code switching has been observed in Hong Kong youth for some decades now, with English lexical items frequently mixed into (insertional) code switching patterns in an otherwise Cantonese conversation (Gibbons 1979, 1987), as in example 2.16 (Chen 2008: 61). Returnees, in contrast, maintain a unique in-group style distinctive from that of their local peers, involving insertion both ways, alternation between the two

---

[3] We thank Ariane Borlongan for regularly drawing our attention to such instances of mixed code in the Philippine context. *Ano ba tayo?* literally translates as 'What are we?'; the addition of the enclitic particle *naman*, used to express a critical or negative attitude, gives the gloss in this context (Ariane Borlongan, personal communication 2014).

[4] Most returnees left Hong Kong during the 1980s and 1990s, after the announcement of the handover of Hong Kong back to Chinese rule; nearly one sixth of the population is estimated to have emigrated between 1984 and 1997, and some 30 per cent of these are estimated to have returned to Hong Kong since.

languages and the use of discourse markers at the point of switching (Chen 2008: 61), seen in example 2.17. Such switching from one language to another occurs with high frequency within a single conversational turn (*Cantonese*, English).

(2.16)

M deoi jan ze o: zi gei personally *ze o jau hou siu tai pin le ze o m wui*
'and it is not personal. I myself personally I seldom get too biased. I will not'

(2.17)

It doesn't matter how you deal with them, it doesn't matter who you are
kei sat the way that you present yourself by *lei go* language
'actually the way that you present yourself by your language'
ji ging bei zo jat zung arrogant *ge gam gok bei keoi dei lei*
'already gives people an arrogant impression'

Yet another type of migration warrants observation: that of internal migration, which in this age far exceeds international migration. Over 700 million people migrate internally around the world (United Nations Development Programme 2013), and in Asia the two rapidly developing and urbanising countries of India and China have witnessed an explosion of rural-to-urban migration. The number of people living in cities in mainland China exceeded those in rural areas for the first time at the end of 2011, reaching 690.79 million (Bloomberg 2012), accounting for 51.27 per cent of the country's population, a consequence of the massive internal migration from rural areas – an estimated 200–250 million in the last three decades (Chan 2012) – to cities and special economic regions. In the multi-ethnic and multilingual context of China, such movements of peoples bring about a reordering of the sociolinguistic landscape of immigrant areas. As Blommaert and Dong (2010) explain, while certain accents mark a metropolitan, sophisticated identity, others mark rural origins, low levels of education and marginal socio-economic status. In these contexts people can also be expected to produce complex packages of accents, including various regional accents, social status accents, age accents and gender accents. Such accents can index identities and this indexical work is organised in a non-random way.

Blommaert and Dong (2010: 378–9) present an exchange on a Beijing street between a dumpling seller from the south of China (X) and a regular customer from Beijing (R) (example 2.18: transcript followed by translation). The entire conversation is in Mandarin Chinese, but different regional accents are used by X in a non-random way, with the shifts in accent part of a bigger series of shifts in the conversation. Blommaert and Dong highlight the microscopic shifts that occur, as a result of languages and speakers in contact, in accents that are often only perceivable and distinct to insiders. Nonetheless, their distribution and correlation with other discourse features – such as topic, style and identity – and the correlation with particular spatial orientations show that these shifts provide rich indexical meanings to these insiders, who pick up the shifts and project meanings onto them (2010: 380–1). The result of contact, whether of different languages or of regionally (and hence socially, culturally, politically) marked varieties, is a layered, multi-accented repertoire that can be mobilised by speakers to produce particular meanings, but can also be mobilised by their interlocutors, who ascribe particular meanings to them (Blommaert and Dong 2010: 381).

(2.18)

Transcript

{traffic noise, people talk unintelligibly}
1   X: ni yao *shen me [shrən^2 mə] de (baozi)*? {weak slow voice,
          noticeably trying to pronounce in local Beijing accent}
     R: ni zhe er dou you shen me de ya?
     X: you . . .
5   . . . {conversations about the kinds of steamed dumplings he offers}
     R: nimen zhe er de shengyi tinghao de, zheme duo ren dou mai nimen de
          baozi.
     X: {laughing voice} *jiushi* zaoshang hao, daole xiawu jiu mei ren chi
          baozi le {still making efforts to mimic Beijing accent}.
     R: zaoshang shengyi hao jiu xingle. Neige xia de ni fang jin (dai er li) qu
          le ma?
10   X: {nod with smile} nei tinghao de – women cong laojia dailai de.
     R: zhende?! Shi na er ya?
     X: {proud, smile} women de xia doushi changjiang li de xia . . . **tebie
          haochi** [t'ə^4 xo^{3}k'e^1] {his voice is noticeably higher and faster, and
          with clearer southern accent}
          . . . {conversations about how they brought the shrimps from that far
          away place}
15   R: ni Putonghua shuo de ting hao de, zai xuexiao li xuede?
     X: *hai xing ba*. You de (gu ke) ye buzhidao wo shuo shenme {end with
          laughing voice, indicating this is a humble response}
     R: wo juede ni de Putonghua zhen tinghao de, wo tingde ting qingchu de
          ya.
     X: en, zai xuexiao li xuede. Wo du dao **gao zhong** [kau^1 chrɔŋ^1] ne
          {switches from
20   noticeable southern accent to near-Putonghua}
          Ni jiu shi [ni^{3}chyiụ^4 shrị^4] Beijing ren? {smile, and switch to
          certain characteristics of Beijing accent}
     R: ai. Wo jiushi zhe er de.
     X: *jiushi zhe er de* [chyiụ^4 shrị^{4}chrer^4 de] {repeat in a low voice, still
          in an effort to produce a Beijing accent}

25 R: nimen zai xuexiao <u>quan</u> yong Putonghua?
    X: women xue (Putonghua in school), ye shuo nei zhong fangyan.
    R: na ni zenme lian de ya {smile}?
    X: wo... wo zai zhe er **dai guo** [tai¹ kuɔ]{switch to his Beijing accent with
        a higher, prolonged and jolly voice, indicating he was pleased by my
        comment on his Putonghua, and was proud that he was not a stranger to
30   the city of Beijing}
    R: na ni dou ting de dong zhe er ren shuo hua ma?
    X: ting de dong, jiu shi bie ren **shuo <u>fangyan</u>** [fɒŋ¹ ien²] wo ting bu dong
        {switches back to Putonghua}
    R: = nashi. Bie ren shuo fangyan wo ye ting bu dong.
35 X: = youde shuo <u>fangyan</u>. wo bantian buzhidao shenme ne {end with
        laughing voice, amused}
    R: jiu shi; erqie zhe di er ba, na er de ren dou you, suoyi na er de fangyan
        dou you...

Transcription conventions (as in original): (underline): stress, = : interruption or
next utterance following immediately, { }: transcriber's comment, **: segment
quieter than surrounding talk or weaker than the rest of the sentence, ( ): omitted
part in the utterance, bold: the shifts amongst accents.

Translation

1   X: *Which ones* (of the steamed dumplings) would you <u>like</u>? {weak slow
        voice, noticeably trying to pronounce in local Beijing accent}
    R: What kinds do you offer?
    X: Here we have...
5   ... {conversations about the kinds of steamed dumplings he offers}
    R: You are doing a good business: so many people get their breakfast from
        you.
    X: {laughing voice} *Only* good in the morning; <u>no one</u> comes in the
        afternoon {still making efforts to mimic Beijing accent}
    R: The morning business is good enough. Have you put the shrimp one in
        (the bag)?
10 X: {nod with smile} That's a good one – we brought the shrimps from our
        <u>hometown</u>.
    R: Seriously?! Where is it?
    X: {proud, smile} They are shrimps from the <u>Yangtze river</u>... **good
        shrimps** {his voice is noticeably higher and faster, and with clearer
        southern accent}... {conversations about how they brought the shrimps
        from that far away place}
15 R: You speak good Putonghua, did you learn that from school?
    X: *Just so-so*. Some (customers) couldn't figure out what I said {end
        with laughing voice, indicating this is a humble response}
    R: I found your Putonghua is really good, I have no problem understanding
        you.
    X: Well, we <u>learnt</u> Putonghua in school. I studied **up to** **high school**
        {switches from

20   noticeable southern accent to near-Putonghua}
      are you a Beijing person? {smile, and switch to certain characteristics
      of Beijing accent}
  R: Yeah, I am from here.
  X: *From here* {repeat in a low voice, still in an effort to produce a
      Beijing accent}
25 R: Did you all use Putonghua in school?
  X: We learnt (Putonghua in school) but also talk in our own dialect.
  R: Then how come your Putonghua is so good {smile}?
  X: I . . . I was here before {switch to his Beijing accent with a higher,
      prolonged and jolly voice, indicating he was pleased by my comment
      on his Putonghua, and
30   was proud that he was not a stranger to the city of Beijing}
  R: Do you (always) understand what people speak here in Beijing?
  X: Usually I can, when people talk in their dialects, I can't {switches
      back to Putonghua}
  R: = Sure. I can't if they use dialects.
35 X: = They use dialects when ordering steamed dumplings, for a few
      minutes I don't know what they are telling me {end with laughing
      voice, amused}
  R: That's right; also it is very mixed, you can find people from everywhere
      (of the country), and many dialects . . .

2.5.2 Hybrid competences for organising learning

If there is one domain that sees most resistance to the use of contact
language phenomena, whether restructured varieties or the mixing of
codes, it is education. Yet an increasing body of research is documenting
the presence of such practices in the classroom, revealing that they are
not only applied by students amongst themselves – whether in or out
of structured lesson time – but also by teachers in lessons. Further,
the research demonstrates that such practices are systematic and serve
pedagogical purposes. In what follows, examples are drawn from the
Asian context.

In the Singapore classroom, for instance, as shown in example 2.19
from Silver and Bokhorst-Heng (2013), language use during learning
tasks undertaken by multilingual Chinese–English Singaporean children shows a flow between Standard SgE, Singlish (the alternative
name for Colloquial SgE) and *Mandarin* (including **particles from other
Sinitic languages** found in both Singlish and Singapore Mandarin),
with a lack of neat, discrete boundaries. The authors argue that this
does not mean randomness; rather, the students are seen to be organising themselves around their learning tasks in ways appropriate in
the interactional moment. Going beyond categorising a restructured
variety such as Singlish in terms of hybridity, Silver and Bokhorst-Heng

(2013) consider the patterned mixing as hybrid competence enacted in a pedagogical space, and further query policy statements and pedagogical notions that only a standard variety of English is acceptable in school settings. Instead, they argue that hybrid competency can be seen as a 'principle for organising learning' (see Gutiérrez et al. 1999: 288), and rather than obstructing learning, hybrid practices can foster language development.

(2.19)

1. TJ: Number 3, A girl is sitting on a swing... *hao le ma?* ('are you done?')
2. JG: *hei, ni kan ni*... ('hey, look at what you did')
3. TJ: *hao le ma?* ('are you done?')
4. JG: *deng yi xia **lah**... wo... deng yi xia **lah**, ni chao si ren* ('wait a moment... I... wait a moment... you are too noisy')
5 TJ: *ni ye shi hen chao **leh**...* ('you are noisy too')
6. JG: *wo duo mei you chao ni, ni chao wo, hao **liao*** ('I didn't disturb you, you disturb me, it's done')
[...]
21. TJ: Number 8, a girl is skating
22. JG: A boy **lah** *ni* ('you')

Other classroom research focusing on teacher talk (Kwek 2005, discussed in Alsagoff 2010) shows the teacher using globalist – i.e. standard – features of English when she is organising the lesson, alongside localist features when she focuses on teaching content. The co-presence of standard and non-standard features is deliberate and purposeful. The shifts between a more formal globalist style – which signals her authority – in giving instructions about the organisation of the lesson and attending to classroom management, and a more colloquial localist and casual style clearly aligned to the pedagogical objectives and the role the teacher wishes to construct and present – which purposefully marks her not as distant and superior in status but as close and an equal – fulfil her authoritative and facilitative roles respectively in the classroom through her use of language. This is illustrated in example 2.21 (Alsagoff 2010: 122–3): when the teacher switches (back) to organisational discourse, much of her language is clearly in standard English, apart from the use of the particle *ya*, meaning 'yes' in Colloquial SgE. However, as she moves towards the end of her organisational talk in example 2.20 to a subject-specific content focus in example 2.21, the shift towards the localist orientation is quite apparent, with an increase in the occurrence of non-standard features. Thus, at the tail end of example 2.20, the teacher foregrounds her localist orientation through the use of several conditional clauses without subordinating conjunctions (e.g. [ ] *you want to film it, film it* 'if you want to film it, film it').

(2.20)

So you can do things like this . . . ok . . . [Long pause] *Ya*, I don't want to keep mentioning your name here. *Ya*, Go blush. Ok, structure. This is about the same structure as we did for action story. Recap, you are going to be given a template later. A template will be given; I am not going to reprint the template. This template is given to you as a model and this template you'll be using for all your work from now on from all the other passage I'll be giving, for all the writing that you are going to do, for even the production that you are coming. What is our end result of this production here, *ya*, Ian? That means our end result in two, three weeks' time, instead of coming up with a commercial you will be given a choice to come up with a production of your suspense story. *Ya*, but this time it need not be; *[] you want to act it out, [] you want to film it, film it, [] you want to make an audio tape out of it, make an audio tape out of it, []you want to write it, script it, go ahead.[] You want to make a comic script out of it, go ahead*, but we will lead on to it and we'll show you different types, ok.

As the teacher moves into a focus on content in example 2.21 (Alsagoff 2010: 123), a greater variety of non-standard features appear in her speech. These include the increased use of discourse markers (*ah, eh, then how*), expressions of clauses without overt subjects or objects (e.g. we *mark [ ]*; *[ ] Very hard ok to have [ ]*; *[ ] Cannot leave the, the reader hanging up there ah*; *Can [ ] remember [ ] or not?*), as well as the use of *don't have* in place of the existential construction *there isn't*.

(2.21)

Scaffold (. . .) always *ah*, in any writing. You it, eh, Band B, you need to know all this, you know, because when we *mark [] ah*, we'll check *ah*. Intro, that one, you all know *ah*, introduction, how you start. Very important, when I pick up a story, the first thing that does is the intro. *[] You go and buy a story book, the intro doesn't always start, 'long time ago, once upon a time, far, far away in a long lost land ter ra ra ra'. Don't have.* Theme? What theme? Although it's a suspense story, but what you doing, which theme are you going about? (Announcement on loudspeaker). *Eh*, 4G. Ok, the, whatever theme you set, the setting must match ok. If you want to do a theme of ok, maybe eh, where there are knights and castles or *whatever []* ok, Peter's favourite, then the setting must be there. You want to talk about the pirates and everything at that time, then the setting must be there. You want to talk about *eh* say the, what we did, we *watch* the roller coasters and it's about a fair and the modern times, then the setting must be there. So it must come down. Then comes your characters ok. *[] Very hard ok to have []* . . . you can have one character, but that means you must really write the person's inner feelings, the surroundings, the atmosphere and everything. Normally, average two to three, ok. Action. You need to add in a bit; that means you need to use *a lot of verb, adverb* because you need to *describe []*. Settings, character is adjective to describe the person. Conflict, complication, what happened, what led to it. *[]You always have little, little complication, then have ONE MAJOR complication that climaxed.* Always have *[] resolution*; how it's solved ok. Then you can conclude. *[] Cannot leave* the, the reader hanging up there *ah*. Climax, and then you put the all the dots there, dot, dot, dot, dot ok. Or some of you who wrote the 'chatasahib' the trap I finished, later I give it back to you and then you end up with 'hah' and then dot, dot, dot. *Then I go back, then how?* Ok, so, know this, anytime you do narrative you need this. *Can [] remember [] or not?*

Moreover, the teachers in the study are analysed by Kwek (2005) as skilled and deliberate in the mixing of codes, for example, by increasing the use of more vernacular Singlish features when there is small-group teaching, and moving towards a more standard form of English in whole-class lectures or discussions. Even while Singlish is officially stigmatised in the context of Singapore and the classroom, teachers are nonetheless observed to employ the linguistic resources that the mixing of codes affords in a complex play of identity construction and negotiation. Alsagoff (2010: 125) further comments that if we think of variation as fluid, and of users as selecting resources in the form of linguistic features as the 'need' arises, we are better able to see such variation in the context of use.

Plurilingual communicative practices are also found in educational contexts in South Asia, where, as noted in the examples from Singapore, teachers and students alike move in and out of diverse languages both to negotiate content and to facilitate language acquisition. Commenting on the interaction recorded in an English class in a secondary school in Jaffna, Sri Lanka, in example 2.22 (from Canagarajah 1995b; English, *Tamil*), Canagarajah (2009: 15) underlines the observation that, while students (S) do not respond to the general question posed in English, there is a torrent of response when the teacher (T) reframes the question more specifically in Tamil and relates it to their home. Note, though, that the Tamil statement (in the second half of turn 1 in the example) is not a direct translation of the preceding statement in English: students would have generally understood the statement in English, but what the use of Tamil provides is a local context and personal resonance for the students. Once the students become engaged, the teacher then proceeds to subtly introduce the English vocabulary items related to the lesson by translating the fruits mentioned by the students into Tamil. In this way, Canagarajah (2009: 15) explains, teachers and students often discuss culturally relevant anecdotes, explanations or illustrations to clarify the lesson content and, through this process, teachers relate the lesson content to knowledge gained outside the classroom, bridging the gap between school and home.

(2.22)

> 1. T: Today we are going to study about fruits. What fruits do you usually eat? ( ) *inraikku niinkal viiTTilai enna palankaL caappiTTa niinkaL? Cila peer kaalamai caappaaTTikku paLankaL caappiTiravai ello?*
>
>   'What fruits did you eat this morning at home? Don't some people eat fruits for breakfast?'
> 2. S1: *naan maampaLam caappiTTanaan*, Miss.
>   'I ate mangoes, Miss.'
> 3. T: Good, mangoes, eh? *Maampalam enRaal* mangoes.
>   '*Maampalam* means mangoes.'
> 4. S2: *vaaLappaLam caappitta naan*, Miss.
>   'I ate bananas, Miss.'
> 5. T: Okay, bananas.

Discussion of the significance of the presence of contact languages in educational and official settings is explored further in Chapter 8.

2.6 CONCLUDING REMARKS

Multilingualism is a very common and natural state of human societies, and is the result of practices that have always characterised the history of human populations: migration, war, intermarriage and trade. Language contact is thus to be taken as a pervasive phenomenon that has shaped languages over time. The fundamental practices we find in contact involve switching between codes and mixing of codes. We could even venture so far as to say that once a code-mixing system stabilises its basic rules it becomes a new (contact) language. We will turn to the topic of language genesis in the next chapter. Besides classical approaches to the study of contact, such as diglossia and domain analysis, we have today a whole array of new concepts to capture the increasing complexity of contact situations. Plurilingual societies are on the increase as a consequence of migration. Languaging and styling become significant practices in layered diasporic societies constructing new identities. Increased mobility and mega-cities offer us laboratories of superdiversity. The study of language contact today can no longer be restricted to neat, bilingual communities. In order to understand the needs of contemporary society, we must look at contact situations involving a wide range of varieties and registers, transient, varying competencies and multiple identities. The stakes have become much higher.

DISCUSSION POINTS

1. Document the generational change in language choice of your own family, from your grandparents' through your parents' generations. Note the dominant and less dominant lects in the repertoires and how these compare with current-day (i.e. your generation's) choices, exploring the factors for this.

2. Consider your linguistic practices and those of your community along the lines of some of the work outlined in this chapter. Is a mixed code the default code for your community? Do you observe plurilingual competence? Is there accent shifting to index different identities?

3. This chapter has exposed you to a number of views that call for a novel take on language use, which could have an impact on education. In particular, we have seen the possibility of allowing more fluid notions of codes in the classroom to the point of 'mixing' becoming an accepted strategy. Discuss this vis-à-vis the far more common and established normative views of language use we find in society and education.

FURTHER READING

A comprehensive account of the social motivations of code switching is Myers-Scotton (1993). For a conversational analysis approach to code switching, see the various articles in Auer (1998). A recent collection which addresses the role of social factors in determining the forms and outcomes of code switching, featuring new data from five continents and languages, is Stell and Yakpo (2015).

3   Contact and creole formation

3.1   *INTRODUCTION*

The question of why and how speakers in contact have, in specific contexts, created entire new languages with unique grammatical features occupies an important place in the field of language contact. The diversity of approaches this question has received, and the complexity of creole contexts itself, has led to a lively and at times controversial debate in creole studies. Some of the fundamental questions that creolists have grappled with include the following.

   i. Why do contact languages, and especially creoles, arise in the first place?
  ii. How are the new grammatical systems arrived at?
 iii. Which original languages of the contact situation influenced the new varieties most and why?

In attempting to answer these and other complex questions, a number of proposals have been put forward, including the following.

   i. Creole grammars reflect the expressions of innate constraints produced of sheer communicative necessity.
  ii. Creoles can be seen as continuations or dialects of their lexifier (superstrate) languages.
 iii. Creole grammars are based on their substrate languages.
 iv. Creoles are instances of second language (L2) transfer.

While some of these claims are compatible with each other, others are somewhat exclusive, a situation that has led to a number of controversies. This chapter is devoted to explaining and discussing these different positions. It is important to realise that what essentially distinguishes the different approaches is a matter of focus. In order to clarify this, the discussion in this chapter proceeds by focusing in the following sections on the role of Universal Grammar, the continuity of lexifier influences, the role of substrate grammars and language transfer in a plurilingual context. In the last section we discuss the more substantial arguments offered in favour of and against each stance. More recent theoretical developments in the field, including the notion of hybridity and evolutionary approaches to contact language formation (CLF), are discussed in Chapter 4.

3.2 FOCUS ON UNIVERSAL GRAMMAR

A number of theoretical approaches share the assumption that creole languages emerge out of pidgin languages through a process of nativisation. This position was explicitly taken by Hall (1966: xiv), who developed the notion of the pidgin–creole life cycle. In this model, a pidgin is regarded as having emerged as a vehicle of communication amongst people who lacked a common language. It becomes a creole through nativisation of the source pidgin, acquiring all the characteristics of a natural language in the process (Bickerton 1981). Creoles are seen as radically different from their pidgin variety due to communicative expansion and extensive regularisation. The process of morphosyntactic expansion that characterises the evolution of a pidgin into a creole is said to be brought about by nativisation – the process through which the speech variety gains native speakers and becomes the first language (L1) of children born in the community.

Hall's proposal was adapted and further refined by Mühlhäusler under the name of the 'development continuum'. Mühlhäusler (1986: ii) presents three such scenarios:

Type 1: jargon - - - - - - - - - - - - - - - - - -→ creole
         (Hawai'ian Creole English)
Type 2: jargon - - - - - - - -→ stabilised pidgin - - - - - - - -→ creole
         (Torres Straits Creole English)
Type 3: jargon - - - -→ stabilised pidgin - - - -→ expanded pidgin - - - -→ creole
         (New Guinea Tok Pisin)

The equation 'creolisation = nativisation' was tacitly adopted by the majority of creolists, becoming the cornerstone of Bickerton's Language Bioprogram Hypothesis (LBH), for which this assumption is crucial. This theory accounts for some typical pidgin traits, such as being a reduced code and the absence of functional categories such as gender, number, case, etc. It takes into consideration the fact that pidgins emerge in multilingual communities where the members need a lingua franca for communication. It also assumes that creoles emerge rapidly – in this case, in one generation.

Within this approach, the work of Derek Bickerton has been of primary significance for the development of the field of creole studies – in particular his LBH, conceived in his 1981 book *Roots of Language*. His hypothesis was the first theory of contact languages dealing entirely with creole genesis. Drawing possible parallels between creolisation and L1 acquisition, Bickerton argued that creoles were created by the children of adult slaves or contract labourers who grew up in the plantation societies in the Caribbean and the Pacific. Immersed in spoken pidgins that lack the structures of natural languages, they 'used their own innate linguistic capacities to transform the pidgin input from their parents into a full-fledged language' (Muysken and Smith 1994: 11), which developed into a vehicle for communication. Faced with the 'chaotic', variable and inadequate input of the adults' pidgin, the children learned the lexical items but acquired a new set of rules, guided by innate principles in the LBH.

Bickerton used Hawai'ian Creole (also known as Hawai'i Creole English, HCE) as the classic case of a creole, which is very different from the Hawai'i Pidgin English that preceded it. Hawai'i Pidgin English developed in the later part of the 1800s as the common language amongst the labourers on the sugarcane plantations in Hawai'i who came from origins as diverse as China, Portugal, Japan, Korea, Puerto Rico, Russia, Spain and the Philippines. The turn of the century saw the beginning of HCE, which had started to become the primary language of many of those who grew up in Hawai'i and the L1 acquired by children, and by the 1920s was the language of the majority of Hawai'i's population. Bickerton concluded that only some innate mechanism could have provided the set of regular rules to Hawai'ian-born children. Bickerton also claimed that the same set of rules could be found in other creoles which developed under similar circumstances. His definition of creole is very explicit: a language arisen out of a pidgin that had existed for not more than a generation and amongst a population consisting of dominant language speakers (at most 20 per cent) and linguistically diverse people (80 per cent). This would, however, exclude a number of varieties – including Tok Pisin and its relative Bislama, as well as West African Pidgin English – because of the prolonged pidgin stage they underwent.

Based on Chomsky's influential claim for an innate Universal Grammar possessed uniquely by humans, Bickerton defines the LBH as a set of unmarked parameter settings, adopting the concept from government and binding theory. According to the LBH, there are four main semantic distinctions that one can identify through the study of creole grammars, each of them leading to structural consequences:

    i. specific/non-specific
      consequence: the article system;
   ii. state/process
      consequence: differential marking of statives and non-statives in
      creoles, affecting the tense, mood and aspect (TMA) system;
  iii. punctual/non-punctual
      consequence: universal marking of non-punctual (viz. English
      'continuous') verbs in creoles, affecting the TMA system – e.g. *he*
      stay walk (Hawai'ian Creole) = 'he is/was walking';
   iv. causative/non-causative
      consequence: the existence of 'passive equivalents' (or pseudo-
      passive – i.e. they lack overt marking) – e.g. *di gon faiya* (Jamaican
      Creole) = 'the gun (was) fired'.

Bickerton also argued that, phonological influence aside, the substrate language can only have played a marginal role. According to his earlier versions (1981, 1984), substratal influence occurred only during pidginisation (through transfer or calques) or during later stages in the development of a creole (through borrowing). This pidgin-stage substrate influence, however, is in his view only temporary, since it will be obliterated by the LBH during nativisation. In Bickerton's theory, the similarity amongst creoles in the marking of TMA is of particular importance in upholding the LBH. While TMA markers are largely absent in pidgins, they typically occur in creoles as pre-verbal particles or free adverbial elements. Bickerton argues that TMA creole systems share functional similarities despite the fact that they appear in unrelated creole varieties; they therefore directly reflect universal aspects of the human innate language capacity. This will be discussed further in Section 3.6.2.

3.3 FOCUS ON LEXIFIERS

A rather different view of creole genesis argues that many creole varieties are in fact continuations of their superstrate or lexifier languages – the superstrate being the variety spoken by the colonial settlers, usually European, whose contribution to the new grammar is particularly visible in the lexicon – hence the term lexifier. In the work of Salikoko Mufwene and Robert Chaudenson in particular, we find a position which considers creoles as continuations of their lexifiers, following the normal processes of language evolution. By this logic, the genetic classification of creoles should, as argued by Mufwene (1990,

2001), be Germanic or Romance – that is, the same classification as their superstrate.

This framework highlights the importance of informal second language acquisition (SLA) in creole development. The initial stages of contact generated L2 varieties of the superstrate: in other words, the lexifier language underwent incremental changes and was gradually 'restructured' into the creole, which gradually and increasingly diverged from the superstrate through a process of 'basilectalisation' (Mufwene 1996a, 1996b) as a result of repeated SLA. The process is detailed in Chaudenson (1992, 2001, 2003) as follows. In the pre-plantation stage of some plantation colonies, with small farms or homesteads and often more indentured European workers than African slaves, the slaves had access to the European language (i.e. the lexifier) and learned close approximations of it – with only minor reductions in morphology and overgeneralisations – rather than developing a radically reduced pidgin. However, as the slave population increased and the economy changed from small-scale farming to large plantations, the version of the superstrate became further and further removed from the language of the masters. Newly arrived slaves had less access to the language of power, and thus learned only 'approximations' of the colonial language from other slaves; their approximations of this language therefore moved structurally further away from the European varieties. It is at this stage that strategies involved in informal SLA became important; these resulted in the reduced nature of early interlanguage, such as using temporal adverbs for tense and aspect instead of verbal inflection. Creolisation, as Chaudenson (2001:305) put it, 'is thus a consequence, or the ultimate result, of approximations of approximations of the lexifier'. Even more specifically, some superstratists hold that creoles do not derive from a superstrate in general but from specific superstrate dialects. This approach has been particularly popular amongst researchers who focus on French-based creoles and claim that many of their properties derive from the French dialects spoken by the first colonists – that they reflect a diachronic change (that is, a change over time) of French dialects which were spoken by the sailors involved in the slave trade (Chaudenson 2000).

In short, in this scenario it is thus not necessary to assume that everyone spoke or aimed at a stable superstrate-derived pidgin as the lingua franca for some period before its development into creole. As is also evident, the development of creole languages in a superstratist account must be gradual, without any significant gap in the acquisition process (also known as 'break in transmission') (see Section 3.6.4; cf. Chaudenson 1992, 2001, 2003; Mufwene 1996a, 2000, 2001, 2004a; and DeGraff

2001a, 2001b, 2003, 2005a, 2005b). Clearly, in this respect this view is not consistent with the fundamental idea behind Bickerton's approach, which requires a radical restructuring of a pidgin for creole formation. Superstratists also point out that all languages are mixed to some extent: in other words, the processes of change encountered in highly mixed languages such as creoles can be found in varying degrees in some cases of so-called 'normal transmission' (Thurston 1994; Mufwene 1998; DeGraff 2003).

3.4 FOCUS ON SUBSTRATES

A counterpoint to the focus on the superstrate is a focus on the substrate. This is an approach that has been favoured in particular by many researchers working on the creoles of the Caribbean region, which seem to display interesting resemblances to various West African languages. In this view, slave populations acquired the lexifier language through a gradual process during which they adapted it to the grammar of their own native languages. In substratist approaches, the focus is mainly on identifying particular syntactic, morphological or lexical features of a creole language that show similarities to African language structures. In addition, this approach needs to show that the (West African) language identified as a possible source was in fact present in the mix of languages used by the slave population at the time of the formation of the creole language.

It is worth noting that a majority of Bickerton's (1981) twelve features of 'true creoles' – word order, movement rules, articles, TMA systems, realised and unrealised complements of verbs, relativisation and subject-copying, negation, existential and possessive, copula, adjectives as verbs, questions, bimorphemic question words and passive equivalents (see Section 3.6.2) – can be readily identified in Kwa languages (Singler 1986; Sebba 1997). They are also areal features of West African languages. Other creole features most frequently noted as deriving from an African substrate include lexical calques (i.e. literal translations of idioms), predicate adjectives as verbs (also analysed as a type of stative verb and no copula used with the adjective), cleft and predicate cleft, serial verbs and phonological features.

A challenge often faced by the substratist approach pertains to the identification of precise sources of influence for creole structure. When the features under analysis are typologically unmarked – i.e. common amongst the world's languages – a debate opens up as to whether the features observed in the creole can really be ascribed to substrate influence or are a matter of universal traits. Thus, it is the presence of especially marked features in both the creole and the substrate(s) that can yield interesting terms of comparison. For example, in the area of serialisation, two features have attracted the attention of substratists: the use of the verb meaning 'say' as a complementiser, and the verb meaning 'give' to mean 'for'. These features are found in Sranan (also known as Sranan Tongo, Surinaams or Taki-Taki), an English-lexifier creole, also influenced by Dutch, Portuguese and some West African languages, spoken by most of the population as L1 or L2 or lingua franca in Suriname (formerly Dutch Guiana) in northeastern South America. As seen in examples 3.1 and 3.2 (from Holm 1988: 185 and Patrick 2004: 627), *tak* 'speak' is used as a complementiser and and *gi* 'give' means 'for' in Sranan.

(3.1)

m	sab	tak	a	tru
I	know	speak	be	true

'I know that is true'

(3.2)

A	tyari	a	nyan	gi	mi
he	carry	the	food	give	me

'S/he brought food to/for me'

Although not confined to the Caribbean and West Africa, these two types of serial verbs ('say' = 'that' and 'give' = 'for') are not very common typologically and are thus considered highly marked. They are therefore good candidates for constructions identifiable as being derived directly from West African sources. In the area of phonology, substrate influence is generally considered uncontroversial. The role of tone seems to be the most striking result of substrate influence on the Caribbean creoles: most African languages employ phonemic tone, and several Caribbean creoles – including Saramaccan and Papiamentu – make use of tone for lexical and/or syntactic purposes (see Chapter 5 for an account of tone in contact).

3.5 FOCUS ON TRANSFER IN SECOND LANGUAGE ACQUISITION

Similarities between creole formation and second language acquisition (SLA) were remarked upon as early as the nineteenth century (Hesseling 1897; Jespersen 1922). Most creolists today agree that creoles are the result of a special form of SLA (also see Section 3.3). Such an approach finds a robust beginning in the work of Andersen. Aiming to place pidgin and creole languages within the language acquisition framework, Andersen (1983) proposes the 'nativisation model'. According to this, both children and adults can construct a pidginised interlanguage at the initial stages of language acquisition. This means that creolisation, pidginisation and the formation of a unique interlanguage in both L1 and L2 acquisition in the initial stages are characterised by the same process of nativisation – the creation of an autonomous linguistic system. These individual interlanguages can be merged to create a new language, as in the case of creoles and stable pidgins. In the nativisation model, transfer is assumed to operate in conjunction with natural acquisitional processes (though the model does not deal with transfer in SLA explicitly) that cause a child or an adult to 'create a viable (although variable and dynamic) internal representation of a linguistic system' (1983: 13) under different circumstances. These include 'normal' L1 and L2 language acquisition, pidgins, semi-pidgins, creoles, etc. Individual acquisition as defined in L1 and L2 literature shows that in the initial stages of acquisition the learners infer structures very different from those of the input. Gradually, with increased exposure and over time, they begin to approximate to the L1 input. However, for pidgins and creole speakers, the input is not entirely adequate and the L1 structures are further removed from the original native source. In situations like this, individuals will start creating a unique form-meaning relationship so they can effectively communicate with conversational partners, who will probably accept the innovations and may propose similar innovations. According to Andersen, these unique form-meaning relationships will eventually generate the shared system of a pidgin or creole language based on cognitive or linguistic universals.

What is appealing in Andersen's account is that pidgins and creoles are placed in a continuum of acquisitional contexts, which includes also L1 acquisition, SLA, indigenised languages, diaspora languages, language attrition and language death. In all these contexts the same factors are at play, albeit in different degrees: linguistic, neuro-cognitive and social and affective factors. What distinguishes acquisition in pidgin and creole contexts according to Andersen can be summarised as follows.

i. In a creole context, the input is less adequate, or coherent, than in other L1 and L2 acquisition.

ii. This is because, aside from the target language, creole children need to acquire the languages of the parents as well as pidgin language(s).

iii. In creole communities, children and adults both contribute to the emerging language.

In addition to the factors above, one must bear in mind that social and psychological factors such as the distance between learners and native speakers can render pidgin and creole settings more complex.

A focus on L1 and L2 acquisition in an account of creole formation is also found in more recent work, notably developed by Jeff Siegel (1997, 2000, 2006, 2007a), where a number of 'availability' constraints are proposed. These include external constraints – such as the demographics of the groups in contact and the social context – and internal constraints – that is, linguistic ones, which determine the input of the earlier stages of creole development, i.e. the data at the learners' disposal that provide a target or model of acquisition. The internal factors constitute the constraints on learners' ability to process the L2 input, which leads to strategies of reduction and simplification of the input. (Note that such strategies are common for all initial efforts for communication across languages, including pidgin formation and early interlanguage.) It is essential to identify whether the available input is relatively full or simplified from the relevant L2. What learners take in from the superstrate is thus influenced by both the external and internal factors, and results in the actual L2 they learn and use in creating their interlanguage.

In addition to the overt retention of L1 forms, L1 influence in creole creation takes two general forms: abstract syntactic patterns are incorporated into superstrate phonetic shapes and superstrate forms are reanalysed as substrate morphosyntactic and lexico-semantic categories. Both these influences are explained via the concept of transfer (Siegel 1999, 2000). Examples of the second kind of influence are seen in seven core morphosyntactic characteristics of Melanesian pidgins – the set of English-based pidgins spoken in Melanesia, many of which have evolved to become expanded pidgins or creoles such as Tok Pisin in Papua New Guinea and Bislama in Vanuatu – derived directly from the relevant substrates, the Central–Eastern Oceanic languages. These include the organisation of the Melanesian Pidgin pronominal system, where contrasts such as exclusiveness and a four-way number opposition, as well as the morphemic composition of its pronominal forms, have direct parallels with those in Central–Eastern Oceanic languages. In Bislama, the use of a subject-referencing marker in the verb phrase and the use of property items as verbs show transfer from Tangoa, a language of Vanuatu, as illustrated in examples 3.3 and 3.4 (Siegel 1999: 14–15).

(3.3)

Haos   ya   i   big-fala   Bislama
house   DET   3SG   big-ADJ
'This house is big'

(3.4)

Tamioci   sei   mo   para mo   malokoloko   Tangoa
man   DET   3SG   fat   3SG   tired-tired
'This man is fat and tired'

Abbreviations: 3SG: Third-person singular, ADJ: Adjective, DET: Determiner.

A similar account is given for the emergence of various morphosyntactic features of HCE – for instance, the use of 'stay' as copula and progressive marker, interpreted as the result in part to L1 Portuguese learners who identified it with *estar*, the copula used in such functions in Portuguese.

Another important phenomenon in this approach is substrate reinforcement, where characteristics from different substrates reinforce the retention of reanalysed L2 forms. Several reinforcement principles (Siegel 1997) guide the selection process in transfer and determine which features will be retained and which discarded. A main principle appears to be that features shared across the individual interlanguages will be retained. In a situation of homogeneity of the population and typologically similar substrate languages being in the majority, similar strategies of L1 retention and similar kinds of L1 influence are likely to be found, which result in these characteristics occurring frequently. They may be seen to form some kind of common ground for learners in breaking the communicating language boundaries. On the other hand, where there are competing variants, it is the more transparent, frequent or salient features that survive. In general, features that are less marked because of similarity, frequency and transparency are most likely to be retained in the emerging community language.

We see how substrate reinforcement principles nicely account for patterns in emerging languages. Irish English is an example where one substrate language was involved in its emergence, whereas in the case of Singapore English (SgE; termed Singlish in the creole literature), the outcome was influenced by the dominance of numerous Chinese dialects. Chapter 5 explores aspects of SgE in greater detail from an ecological perspective; there, we look at competition and selection of features from a multilingual pool as the primary mechanisms for innovation. As preempted above, Melanesian Pidgin grammar retains a common core of features, features which are found across its Central–Eastern Oceanic substrates. And in the case of HCE's 'stay', Cantonese – another principal substrate – may well have reinforced its usage as copula and progressive, since it also uses the verb *haidouh* 'to be (t)here' as a progressive marker.

3.6 DISCUSSION

Until 1965, there was not much information about the distribution of pidgin and creole languages. Many of these speech varieties tended to be ignored and remained undiscovered, especially those based on non-European colonial languages. Little was known about the history of a language, which was essential for determining its creole or pidgin status, or the lack of it. It was not until the 1980s that creolists began to use historical documents that contained early linguistic material on creoles as sources of information about the genesis and historical development of these languages. Demographic evidence showed that the development of some slave societies such as Suriname and Jamaica was such that the nativisation of Sranan and Jamaican could only have been a very slow process (Arends and Bruyn 1994). The same evidence also brought about greater awareness of the diversity of ethnicities and languages involved in the slave communities. At the same time, a growing body of typological literature on non-Indo-European languages expanded the database within which creole studies could be situated. Together, these advances have led to a number of debates that continue today.

3.6.1 On the pidgin-to-creole cycle

The pidgin-to-creole view presumes, first of all, that these varieties – pidgins and creoles – can be distinguished. To a certain extent, this is possible. It is argued, for instance, that pidgins are very often based on the local language rather than on the colonial one, are strikingly different from creoles and may have considerably complex morphologies (Bakker 1994). On the last point, pidgins and creoles have in fact been argued to have very few structural traits in common:

i. all creoles have Subject-Verb-Object (SVO) word order, while pidgins can have any conceivable word order;
ii. TMA is expressed by adverbs (if at all) in pidgins, but mostly by preverbal elements in creoles;
iii. reduplication is a common, almost universal, process in creole languages, but not in pidgins (though common in extended pidgins).

The distinction between pidgins and creoles is, however, not always clear, whether in their life cycles or in their supposedly defining structural properties. Research has shown that not all jargons or pidgins are part of a pidgin–creole life cycle. Conversely, no evidence demonstrates that all creoles had a jargon or pidgin stage. For instance, there is no historical evidence of any Caribbean creole or Indian Ocean creole being preceded by a pidgin. In fact, the only language where there is documentation of both pidgin and creole stage may be Bickerton's (1981) HCE. Siegel goes as far as to suggest that 'no creole has evolved directly from a pre-pidgin, pidginised interlanguage or a stable restricted pidgin' (2007a: 176). Rather, in a language contact context, subsets of communicative features from pidginised L2 varieties of the lexifier, the lexifier itself, the substrate languages and other contact languages are employed in the creole formation.

A number of pidgins, such as Tok Pisin of Papua New Guinea, as argued by the gradualist theory, expanded and stabilised into fully fledged languages before being nativised. This has challenged the traditional distinction between pidgins and creoles, as well as the nativisation process, which does not seem to have played a significant role in the formation of languages created over a number of generations (Arends and Bruyn 1994). Furthermore, because these pidgin Englishes of the Pacific, especially New Guinea, may be L1 or L2 and spoken for generations, they are often not unambiguously examples of pidgins: they share both pidgin and creole language properties, with no structural difference between the varieties spoken as L1 by children or as L2 by adults.

3.6.2 On the Bioprogram

The LBH as formulated by Bickerton (1981) entailed ten characteristics for TMA markers. These are summarised and discussed in Bakker, Post and van der Voort (1994: 250–3) as follows.

    i. The zero form of verbs marks simple past for non-stative verbs and non-past for state verbs.

    ii. A marker of anterior tense indicates past for state verbs and past-before-past, or past, for non-stative verbs.

    iii. A marker of irrealis mood indicates 'unreal time' (= future, conditional, subjunctives, etc.) for all verbs.

    iv. A marker of non-punctual aspect indicates durative, habitual or iterative aspect and is indifferent to the non-past-past distinction.

    v. All markers are in preverbal position.

    vi. The markers can be combined, but in an invariant ordering, viz. anterior tense, irrealis mood, non-punctual aspect.

vii. The meaning of anterior + irrealis is 'an unrealised event in the past'.

viii. The meaning of anterior + irrealis + non-punctual is 'an un-realised event in the past, of a non-punctual nature': something like '[if only] X would have gone on doing Y'.

ix. The meaning of anterior + non-punctual is 'a durative action or a series of non-durative actions taking place either before some other event under discussion, or during a period of time regarded as definitely closed'.

x. The meaning of irrealis + non-punctual is future progressive.

Comparative work on TMA systems has shown that Bickerton's core TMA system is to a good degree shared by unrelated creoles: all creoles appear to have a grammaticalised TMA system that includes at least three markers – one for tense, one for mood and one for aspect. The core systems of the creoles such as Saramaccan – spoken in Suriname, with English and Portuguese lexifiers and West African substrates – and Fa d'Ambu – the Portuguese-based creole of Equatorial Guinea – seem to fit Bickerton's prototypical system, having the above ten characteristics.

However, it has also been noted that some creole TMA systems do diverge from Bickerton's core TMA. The core system of Negerhollands – a Dutch-based creole with Danish, English, Spanish, French and African elements, once spoken in the US Virgin Islands (known then as the Danish West Indies) – for instance, shows deviations from the markedness properties in Bickerton in a number of respects. This can be seen in the absence of distinction between non-stative and state verbs, the anterior marker *kā* being used for past tense in both cases. Absent in Negerhollands is also the clear distinction between tense, mood and aspect. The present tense marker *le*, for example, became later homophonous with irrealis *lo* (Bakker, Post and van der Voort 1994: 253).

In addition to the ten characteristics of the core system, Bakker, Post and van der Voort (1994) provide further examples from Saramaccan and Fa d'Ambu of mood-marking and aspect-marking morphemes, some with exact equivalents in other creole languages, some unique to Sara-maccan. For instance, the Saramaccan preverbal morphemes *fu* and *musú* mark 'obligation' (deontic mood). In addition to the core system marker *xa*, Fa d'Ambu has another preverbal aspect marking element: the auxiliary *sa*, which can be used in combination with *xa* to form sentences with a non-punctual or imperfect aspect. Bakker, Post and van der Voort conclude that both markers are essential in the Fa d'Ambu aspect marking system, with *xa* considered a grammaticalised prever-bal marker and part of the core system and *sa* being an auxiliary, but still fully integrated in the system. They also discuss serial completives, defined as an aspectual element marking completion of action. In Saramaccan, however, they are not pre-verbal but sentence-final, and can be analysed as either serial verbs or adverbs. Etymologically, they are often related to verbs meaning 'finish', such as Saramaccan *káá* from Portuguese *acabar* 'to finish', seen in example 3.5 (Bakker, Post and van der Voort 1994: 257).

(3.5)

A nján di fisí káá.
'He already ate the fish.'

Further evidence against the LBH comes from the work of John Singler (1990), who examined a set of seven languages and found that only two – Hawai'ian Creole and nineteenth-century Nigerian Pidgin – conformed to Bickerton's system for anterior tense marking.

The LBH has also faced challenges in terms of Bickerton's interpretation of the social and historical realities of creole formation. His theory presupposes the presence of a sufficient number of children during the formative period of the creole – that is, in the first twenty-five or fifty years of colonisation. However, demographic data on colonies such as Jamaica and Suriname provide counter-evidence to this (Arends 1995). For a long time, many plantation holders found it cheaper to simply work their slaves to death and then buy new ones, rather than create the slightly more stable living conditions that would permit the raising of children. Thus, because this type of society would have been childless for a considerable period of time, this means that nativisation of the pidgin to a creole would have taken a much longer time than Bickerton has assumed (Singler 1986), without the intervention of child language creators. These observations have led scholars to propose a gradualist view of creole development in which the new grammar undergoes a longer incubation time than assumed by Bickerton and proponents of the LBH (see Arends 1995; Selbach, Cardoso and van den Berg 2009).

In fact, more recent scholarship on the creation of HCE (Roberts 2000; Siegel 2000, 2007a) demonstrates how the development of this creole is in fact a more gradual, cumulative process. HCE involves the elaboration of an earlier English-lexicon pidgin that became a target for adult immigrants and their locally born children in the late nineteenth century. In addition, children of Portuguese and Chinese immigrants, who spoke both the ancestral languages and the pidgin, contributed much to the elaboration of HCE's grammar. This explains why many of its characteristics can be accounted for by substrate influence from Cantonese and Portuguese. For instance, several key features – including

TMA categories – previously attributed to the LBH have been shown to have arisen as the result of such substrate influence. In sum, the creation of HCE followed the typical three-generation process through language shift. Only after the restructuring of its grammar by previous generations did children start acquiring it as an L1, possibly also contributing to the regularisation of its grammar and introduction of further changes such as auxiliary combinations. Indeed, there are reasons to believe that children acquiring emerging creoles play a role in smoothing out the variation brought about by influences from different source languages.

Another objection deals with the assumption of broken transmission or communicative vacuum – that is, the idea that no concrete alternative language was available to creole-acquiring children, since not a single vernacular would have allowed access to all sections of the community. Critics have pointed out that it is likely that children were growing up bilingual, rather than monolingual, learning both the native language(s) of their carers and the pidgin/creoles (Sebba 1997). In a situation like this, the child would probably refer to the parental language, not the Bioprogram, for any guidance. This would also strengthen the effect of the substrate language on the emerging creole (see Section 3.6.3).[1]

3.6.3 On superstrate and substrate approaches

We evaluate the superstrate and substrate approaches together as they are more often than not rather compatible. It is generally accepted that both substrate and superstrate language contribute features to the emerging grammar, though they do so in different degrees. In examining SgE, for example, Bao (2005) proposes that substantial grammatical traits are indeed derived from the substrate, but that the lexifier exercises the role of filter to determine which features are exactly replicated and which are not (see also Bao 2015 for a framework that integrates substrate and superstrate reanalysis in creole formation).

Critics of the superstratist position have often pointed out that, apart from the obvious lexical influence of the superstrate, there is no direct evidence for this theory. There is no proof that specific superstrate

---

[1] Because of its relevance to general language acquisition theories, the LBH has also attracted criticism from linguists studying child language and linguistic diversity. Based on evidence from acquisition of languages such as English and Turkish, Bickerton claims that structures that conflict with the Bioprogram 'blueprint' are also more difficult to learn and are acquired at a later stage. Given that the Bioprogram prescribes the adequate minimum, Sebba (1997) finds it difficult to accept his claim that languages would develop structures that are unnecessarily difficult for children to learn. Mufwene (1986) also questions the assumption that all languages have started from the same Bioprogram, which would exclude linguistic diversity.

dialects were predominant at the time, nor is there a dialect which is able to explain all the phenomena the creole reveals. The lexical characteristics derived from their lexifiers have been noted to be frequently modified in various ways in the emerging grammar, with changes in semantics and function where the superstrate-derived lexical items do not match their counterparts in the European source language (Winford 2003: 334). With increasing understanding of the nature of substrate grammars, it has also become clear that creoles rely on both lexical and structural resources of the substrates. Furthermore, creole grammar is frequently the result of the interplay of both superstrate and substrate inputs. A good example for this interaction is the complementiser *se* 'that' in Jamaican Creole (JC), which shows similarities in lexis and phonetics to both English *say* and Twi *se* 'that', and is used after verba dicendi – words that express speech or introduce a quotation – and verbs of knowing (Winford 2003: 334).

A weakness of the substratist position, known as the 'cafeteria principle', is that it is simply too easy to look for substrate correspondences. It is generally acknowledged that finding superficial resemblances between a number of creoles and West African languages is not impossible due to the great diversity of the latter. For instance, most of the substrate languages have left lexical traces in terms of cultural practices and personal names. In addition, although many of them are lexically different, they share structures and grammars. However, tracing the influence of an exact African variety in a creole scenario is far more problematic. It is not sufficient to compare superficially similar structures and claim similarities, since all languages show some similarities and this could be simply a matter of coincidence. In this respect, the relexification approach has tried to move towards a deeper type of comparative analysis in which both syntactic and semantic features are carefully considered.

Clearly, lexifier and substrate approaches do not need to be mutually exclusive. In the framework of relexification, the assumption is that the grammatical features of creoles depend on the substrate while the lexicon depends on the superstate. This may be seen in Media Lengua, a mixed language spoken in Ecuador, which draws from Quechua – an indigenous language with agglutinative morphology – and Spanish – the other main language of Ecuador. While Media Lengua has a lexicon in which the phonological forms of lexical categories (i.e. nouns, verbs and adjectives) are almost entirely derived from Spanish, and the forms of the affixes and the functional category system are derived from Quechua, semantic content is derived from Quechua, as illustrated in examples 3.6 and 3.7 (Muysken 1981). In other words, Media

Lengua developed through a process of relexification, which involves the replacement of the phonological shape of a root of one language (Quechua) with a root with roughly the same meaning from another language (Spanish) (Muysken 1981; Bakker and Muysken 1994).

(3.6)

Si	llueve	demas,	no voy	a ir	Spanish
If	rain-3SG	too-much	not go-1SG	to go	

'If it rains too much, I will not go.'

(3.7)

Yalli-da	tamia-pi-ga,	mana	ri-sha-chu	Quechua
Dimas-*ta*	llubi-*pi-ga*,	no	i-*sha-chu*	Media Lengua
If too-much-ACC	rain-LOC-TOP	not	go-ASP-VAL	

'If it rains too much, I will not go.'

Abbreviations: 1SG: First-person singular, 3SG: Third-person singular, ACC: Accusative, ASP: Aspect, LOC: Locational, TOP: Topic, VAL: Valency.

Creolists in favour of relexification point out that the phonology of Atlantic creoles has many features which are also typical for many West African substrate languages (e.g. pre-nasalised and co-articulated stops). However, there have been some counterarguments based on the observation that the one-to-one relation between substrate and creole structure as assumed in the relexification approach is hard to come by. In addition, the choice of one specific variety of substrate as a term of comparison generates much debate, as scholars disagree on the nature of the variety and the exclusive reference to one – rather than several – substrate influence(s) in the process of creole formation.

In commenting on the differences between a relexification and a SLA approach, Winford (2003: 345) argues that the terms 'relexification' and 'transfer' really refer to the same 'objective psycholinguistic process of restructuring' and that the dichotomy between the two approaches is an illusion. The notion of transfer addresses the effects of L1 influence from the learner's perspective of the target language (or versions of it), focusing on the ways in which input is modified under that influence. In the context of relexification, the process is viewed more from the perspective of the L1 input, focusing on how L2 items are integrated into the learner system as labels for L1-derived semantic-functional categories. But in both approaches, creole creators as L2 learners retain certain abstract categories of L1, through which they reanalyse or reinterpret substrate- or L2-derived forms. According to Winford, whether learners 'project' L1 categories onto L2 forms or 'calque' the latter onto the former, the resulting reanalysis is the same. The process is regulated by the same principles and constraints on the reanalysis of L2-derived forms, whichever perspective we take. In addition, both appeal to the idea of congruence leading to interlingual identification between L1 and L2 forms.

3.6.4 The problem of transmission

As hinted at in several places above, an underlying debate relates to how we conceive of the process of transmission in a creole setting. Let us look at this issue in greater depth.

Historical linguists have argued that there is a difference between 'normal' and 'abnormal' or 'broken' transmission (Thomason and Kaufman 1988: 11). In the former, a language is passed on from generation to generation or parents to children with relatively small degrees of change over the short run. In this case, the entire language as a complex set of interrelated lexical, phonological, morphosyntactic and semantic structures is transmitted, and any changes over time are gradual and cumulative. If a particular language develops into another through the process of 'normal' transmission, the languages are considered genetically related, and the various components of the new language can be traced back to a single parent language, since the correspondences are regular and systematic. The label 'abnormal' or 'broken' transmission, on the other hand, is used when 'a whole population acquires a new language [i.e. an L2] within possibly as little as a single lifetime, therefore necessarily other than by parental or peer-group enculturation' (Thomason and Kaufman 1988: 10). This they describe as a process of 'abrupt creolisation', whereby a creole develops from a pidgin that has not yet stabilised, and becomes the primary language of a community and is acquired as an L1 by children born into this community. The result comprises mixed languages whose subsystems cannot be traced back to a single source language. Since not all aspects of the L2 have been transmitted and the L1 speakers are not integrated into the L2 population, the new language cannot be considered genetically related to the L2. Thomason and Kaufman claim that in this case it is impossible to trace either the grammar or the lexicon back to the L2 source. In short, because of the 'break in transmission' as a consequence of imperfect learning of L2 or the lexifier, an 'abrupt creole' does not have a genetic relationship with its lexifier; they are thus not a modified form of the lexifier language, but 'an entirely new language – without genetic affiliation' (Thomason and Kaufman 1988: 166).

It should be noted that in some contexts of creole formation the 'break in transmission' scenario is not relevant, because populations simply acquired a reduced, pidgin-like variety from the very beginning. In Hawai'i (and Fiji), for instance, there was no initial homestead phase during which European and non-European populations would have been integrated. This was because they were not typical plantation settlement colonies of the sort found in the Caribbean and Indian Ocean settlement colonies. Rather, colonised in the nineteenth century by the Americans rather than by the English, they were developed partly on the model of plantation exploitation colonies of the Pacific, with an abrupt transition from a whaling and trade colony into a plantation alternative. The Asian labourers – the Chinese and Japanese, and later the Koreans and Filipinos – arriving in Hawai'i in waves of immigration learnt a reduced English pidgin: Hawai'ian Creole. In Fiji, labourers learnt pidginised Fijian. Early Hawai'i Pidgin English spoken in Honolulu shows morphological simplicity: no inflections on nouns or verbs, adverbs used to indicate temporal relations (e.g. 'before' for past, 'by and by' for future, 'all time' for habitual), no copula, no existential marker, single preverbal marker and no complementiser (Roberts 2004; Siegel 2004, 2007b); it is similar to other 'restricted pidgins'. Similarly, in the Caribbean region, it was drastically reduced varieties that were spoken early in the homestead period of different colonies, such as Martinique (Siegel 2007b).

Scholars associated with a superstratist position such as Chaudenson and Mufwene, as well as DeGraff, hold the view that creoles, as versions of their lexifiers, developed via normal transmission according to the usual processes of language change (Mufwene 2000, 2001; DeGraff 2001a, 2003, 2005a). As mentioned in Section 3.3, the arrival of a large number of new slaves in the plantation stage increased the proportions of 'non-proficient speakers' and led to a process known as 'gradual basilectalisation' (Mufwene 2001), which involves maximum restructuring of the 'approximations' through cumulative divergent changes. Mufwene describes this process as 'more a by-product of imperfect acquisition of the target by second-language learners' (2001: 60). In this view it is typically pointed out that in language transmission there is always a certain degree of restructuring – i.e. intergenerational change – and that the difference between what is considered 'normal' and 'abnormal' transmission can be framed in terms of the grammatical changes that a language undergoes over time. In highly diverse contexts of restructuring, such as the creole ones, the structural differences between generations appear so much greater because of the great diversity of grammatical features in the contact situation. Another point worthy of note is that some diachronic processes are common to both creole and non-creole formation, as has been shown in grammaticalisation studies (Baker and Syea 1996). This can be taken as further evidence that the distinction between normal and abnormal transmission is not as clear-cut as it appears. The significant consequence here is to what extent we can determine whether two languages are genetically related or not. Recall that, within the superstratist approach, creoles are indeed considered variations of their lexifier languages.

Siegel notes that whether scholars argue for or against the idea of a break in transmission, both sides ultimately believe that SLA processes and exposure to L2 approximations or versions of the lexifier are relevant to creole formation (2007a: 176). The differences may therefore be more a matter of terminology:

> If there is a large degree of change (or restructuring) due to, for example, second language learning, the first side considers transmission to be interrupted, whereas the second side does not. In other words, if significant changes occur in the way a language is spoken due to adult second language acquisition, it is considered a break in transmission by one side but uninterrupted transmission by the other.

3.7 CONCLUDING REMARKS

This chapter has introduced the major theoretical frameworks that define the study of pidgin and creole languages. Each approach comes with a set of specific assumptions about the nature of speakers in contact and can be corroborated as well as criticised by different data sets. We have pointed out where different approaches can be reconciled, such as substrate and lexifier approaches, and we have discussed in depth the theoretical advantage of linking the study of contact-induced change with the field of language acquisition in general. We have chosen to keep the treatment of old and more recent creole controversies to the mere necessary, as it is our wish to place emphasis more on current and future directions in the field. In the next chapter we focus on two recent and contrasting approaches that have generated lively debate. We then summarise our position.

DISCUSSION POINTS

1. Consider the view of language implied in a Bickertonian approach to creole genesis: what does it reveal about the relationship between language and society?

2. According to a superstratist account, creoles can be categorised as varieties of the lexifier language. So, for example, Haitian Creole could be seen as a dialect of French. Discuss the implications of such a classification.

3. Think about non-creole contexts of SLA. Does the literature, or do your own experiences, shed light on the role of L1 transfer in SLA?

FURTHER READING

For comprehensive but more traditional accounts of pidgin and creole languages, the interested reader can turn to Holm (1988, 1989); Arends, Muysken and Smith (1994); Sebba (1997); Thomason (2001); Kouwenberg and Singler (2009); and Bakker and Matras (2013). A more recent, comprehensive compilation is Velupillai (2015). Work that looks specifically at mixed languages includes Bakker and Mous (1994); Bakker and Muysken (1994); Matras and Bakker (2003), and a state-of-the-art account is found in Meakins (2013). A recent project that presents comparable synchronic data on the grammatical and lexical structures of seventy-six contact languages, comprising four volumes and an electronic database, is *The Atlas of Pidgin and Creole Language Structures* (*APiCS*), edited by Michaelis et al. (2013).

4 Contact and language evolution

4.1 INTRODUCTION

When we move beyond creole genesis and look at the ways in which languages change over time, we realise we are actually contemplating a much bigger question. With our increasing understanding of linguistic diversity, one of the most challenging questions faced by modern linguistics is to explain how and why human societies have come to be characterised by such different linguistic systems over time. Does language contact play any role in the evolution of diversity? In this chapter we present two approaches that tackle this question.

4.2 THE CREOLE PROTOTYPE

Continuing on the discussion in Chapter 3, this chapter presents the most recent developments in the field of creole theory and contact language formation.

Probably the most debated approach to creole genesis since Bickerton, John McWhorter's (1998) 'Creole Prototype' (CP) develops a view of creole languages as a synchronically definable typological class, with a unique set of structural criteria. The data sample on which the CP is based includes eight languages which constitute examples of 'typical' creoles – that is, natively spoken languages that were allegedly created via rapid adoption as a lingua franca by slave populations five hundred years ago or less. These are Ndjuka English Creole, Tok Pisin English Creole, Saramaccan English Creole, Haitian French Creole, St Lucian French Creole, Mauritian French Creole, Fa D'Ambu and Negerhollands Dutch Creole. The three structural features shared uniquely by creoles postulated by McWhorter (1998, 2000, 2011) are the following.

    i. **Minimal use of inflectional affixation.** This is defined as the most salient feature of typical creole languages which, McWhorter claims, rarely have more than one or two inflectional affixes. For example, while Tok Pisin has two – the transitive marker *-im* and the marker *-pela* for adjectivehood (Mühlhäusler 1985) – Fa D'Ambu has one, which is marginally productive (Post 1994), and Negerhollands has one inflection – *sini* for plurality, which is optional. In addition, McWhorter claims that the inflectional affixes are always monomorphemic, and paradigms of allomorphs are not found in creoles. This he explains as the result of the stripping down of a system for its optimal learnability and processability.

ii. **Limited role of tone.** Tone is considered rare in creoles, and tends not to be used to mark lexical distinctions or to encode syntactic function. According to McWhorter, tone requires a subtlety of perception unlikely to develop in the rapid, utilitarian acquisition process of contact languages. Stress-language speakers tend to eliminate a lexifier's tone in transforming it into a pidgin or creole. In cases of tone language speakers transforming a tonal lexifier into a creole, the lexifier's tonal system has been reduced. Examples are Kituba, a creole variety of the Kimanianga dialect of Kikongo, and Sango, a reduction of the Ubangian language Ngbandi partly by West Africans and Kituba speakers. In some rare cases of tone contrasts in creoles, McWhorter claims that these resulted from subsequent internal developments, as in Saramaccan where the use of tone to encode morphosyntactic contrast is relatively recent and traceable to diachronic evolution.

iii. **Semantically regular derivational affixation.** Creole derivational systems display high regularity in comparison to non-creole languages such as Mon-Khmer languages. In creoles, derivation is generally semantically transparent. For example, the semantic contribution of the few derivational affixes in Tok Pisin is quite regular (Mühlhäusler 1985), as in *pasin,* from 'fashion', which renders a constituent abstract – e.g. *gut* 'good' > *gutpasin* 'virtue'; *isi* 'slow' > *isipasin* 'slowness'. Haitian Creole (HC) is similar, where the inversive prefix *de-*, to take one of various examples, with few exceptions transforms a word into its precise opposite – e.g. *pasyate* 'to be patient' > *de-pasyate* 'to be impatient', *respekte* 'to respect' > *de-respekte* 'to insult'.

McWhorter argues that since only languages with creole sociohistorical profile combine these three characteristics, a creole is a linguistic, typologically identifiable class, as well as a sociohistorical one. In his view, this class is the result of the pidginisation of the input languages (that is, the lexifier and substrates). What is crucial to the CP is that the three features shared by the eight creoles are not combined in an arbitrary manner. Instead, they have directly resulted from the interrupted transmission of a lexifier, which happened too recently to be undone by diachronic change (McWhorter 1998: 812). These features, McWhorter (2005) argues, are typical of young languages – languages in which the process of morphological development and accumulation of a certain amount of overt (at times redundant) marking has not yet occurred. This becomes a powerful argument for our understanding of morphological typology. In this view, early forms of language would arise without morphological elaboration, thus conforming to an analytic language type, and it is over time that morphological elaboration occurs (as a process of maturation, see Dahl 2004), leading to the development of synthetic languages.

McWhorter's CP has been criticised from several angles. First, the criteria for the general creole structural category reduce the set of prototypical creoles to a mere handful (Mufwene 2000), and, more importantly, each of these prototypical creoles in fact lacks one or another of the putative typological features. Also problematic is McWhorter's characterisation of creoles as simple (DeGraff 2001b; Lefebvre 2004), which, as DeGraff points out, harks back to earlier and similar claims by Seuren (1998) and Whinnom (1971). More pointedly, DeGraff (2003, 2004, 2005a) considers such an approach 'creole exceptionalism' – a colonial discourse which perpetuates the marginalisation of languages and their speakers by involving the 'postulation of exceptional and abnormal characteristics in the diachrony and/or synchrony of creole languages as a class' (DeGraff 2005a: 534).

With regard to the notion of simplicity itself, it has been argued by many (e.g. Siegel 2004) that morphological simplicity should be defined, and that it is not reasonable to compare whole grammars with each other, as McWhorter does, but that modular comparisons of individual systems such as tense, mood and aspect (TMA) marking yield more interesting results. Further, complexity can reside in places other than morphology and tone (Siegel 2004: 142–5). The issue of simplicity and complexity is taken up in the final chapter of this book.

Turning to McWhorter's criteria themselves, much empirical work has documented inflection, tone and opaque lexicalisations in a variety of creole languages. A survey of pidgin and creole languages on the whole does not find inflectional morphology lacking (Meakins 2011: 97–9), even if it is present in smaller quantities than in their lexifier languages. Obviously, a challenge in such an observation is not only that limited inflectional affixation is to be expected, since in the second language acquisition (SLA) of the European colonial languages inflection

is often lost during the initial stages of the process of creole formation (Muysken and Law 2001). More fundamentally, the contributing
superstrates (e.g. English, French, Dutch, Portuguese) and substrates
simply do not have a very rich inflection system either (Muysken and
Law 2001; Meakins 2011). In short, the lack of inflection may simply
be 'the accidental by-result of the limited typological spread in the
languages contributing to the proto-typical creoles' (Muysken and Law
2001: 49). Conversely, an examination of typologically different creoles
shows simplification and regularisation, but not loss, of inflection; for
instance, in creoles such as Berbice Dutch Creole, Papiamentu and Cape
Verdean, there is some inflection. In fact, if one examines those few
cases of creoles with highly inflected lexifiers, such as Kituba, with the
agglutinating Bantu language Kikongo as its lexifier (which has an elaborate noun class and bound pronoun system, subject-verb agreement
and verbal tense/aspect system), one finds that, although subject-verb
agreement has been lost, the noun class system and the grammatical
categories of bound pronouns and TMA suffixes have been preserved,
albeit with some changes (Meakins 2011: 99).

Where the criterion of tone is concerned, already in early work (not
cited in McWhorter's work) tonal contrasts have been shown to play a
central role in Saramaccan grammar (Voorhoeve 1961; Rountree 1972),
and it has been shown how Papiamentu lexicon and syntax depend
on tonal contrasts (Römer 1992). That tonal contrasts play a role in
Caribbean creoles should not be unexpected, as Muysken and Law (2011:
49) point out, since tone is so central in West African languages. They go
on to suggest that the only reason, it appears, that McWhorter puts so
much emphasis on this criterion is to maximise the difference between
the creoles and languages like Chinese, which shares many syntactic
features with the Caribbean creoles.

With regard to semantically derived derivational affixation, it has
been shown by other scholars – such as DeGraff (2000) – that HC, for
instance, manifests opaque lexicalisation as well as inflectional affixation, contra the predictions in McWhorter. Moreover, nearly all HC
affixes are etymologically related to French affixes; that is, virtually
none of these affixes result from grammaticalisation, thus casting further doubt on McWhorter's claims for diachronic change. DeGraff finds
no evidence of an earlier stage of (proto-)HC where all creoles were
consistently lacking all affixes. Given the fact that the HC lexicon is
etymologically French and that HC speakers were capable of dedu-
cing morphological (e.g. affixal) information from stored patterns in
their lexicon (similar to any other human speakers), he argues that 'an
affixless stage' is most unlikely. Since HC speakers would have created

this morphology at the beginning of contact, creole creators massively adopted, at the very least, French lexical forms, including opaque lexicalisations. DeGraff (2000) provides numerous examples of the HC affix *de-*, including near-synonymous pairs with subtle semantic and syntactic differences, and concludes that HC productive affixes are no more or less transparent than in other languages. Another derivational process in creole morphology – reduplication – includes examples of both semantic transparency and semantic opaqueness.

Despite these critical aspects, McWhorter's theory offers a powerful explanation for the diversity of morphological types. His ideas do indeed find corroboration when tested in quantitatively robust and empirically sound experiments. In a ground-breaking paper, Lupyan and Dale (2010) tested more than 2,000 languages with respect to social and structural traits. They divided languages into two classes: 'esoteric' languages – i.e. those spoken by small populations in confined areas with little or no exposure to neighbouring groups – and 'exoteric' languages, spoken by large populations over extended areas, with abundant contact with neighbouring groups. It may be noted that similar notions have appeared in the literature before, such as Trudgill's (2001) distinction between 'low' and 'high' contact varieties. Though such distinctions can only be upheld to a certain degree, we will for the purpose of this discussion retain Lupyan and Dale's terms. Their conclusions are very clear: morphological elaboration, and the resulting semantic opacity that goes with the process of inflection, occurs with far more frequency in esoteric languages. Exoteric languages, on the other hand, tend towards what typologists regard as analytic languages. This clearly lends support to the idea that in the widespread context of adult second language (L2) learning, morphology is unlikely to be retained or emerge in the first place. So is there something indeed complex, or perhaps just redundant, in morphology? The matter is not settled yet. Sections 4.3 and 4.4 will show concrete examples of how morphology can indeed arise in creole-like scenarios (or exoteric contexts), and we address the question of what triggers this.

4.3 THE EVOLUTIONARY APPROACH

Another recent development in the field of creole studies which impacts on the question of linguistic evolution is based on a theoretical alignment with the evolutionary notions of selection, competition and ecology (Croft 2000; Mufwene 2001, 2008; Ansaldo 2009a, 2009b). At the heart of this approach lies a uniformitarian view of language

transmission. In this view, the assumption is that all language transmission follows the same cognitive processes: whether in multilingual,
high-contact scenarios or more monolingual, homogeneous ones, speakers exist in contexts – often referred to as ecologies – in which they are
exposed to a variety of features. In many present-day, modern societies,
such as the western European context, these features vary marginally
amongst speakers; multilingualism, when present, is typologically
limited, and the educational system generally provides a uniform context for acquisition. But in a typical creole context, the linguistic ecology
would have exhibited a large degree of variation, characterised by the
presence of a lexifier, substrate languages and possible pidgins, all typologically unrelated; this is basically the difference between monolingual
and multilingual societies. This also reinforces the notion of plurilingual practices in such communities, as noted in Chapter 2. In learning
a language, speakers select from the features they receive as input from
adults, peers, instructors and so forth, and build their own grammar, or
idiolect. So in a monolingual society, the younger generation speaks a
variety very close, but not identical, to the older generation's language.
In a multilingual environment, there is the possibility of selecting
many more numerous and divergent features. Where transmission is
not controlled – that is, not constrained by schooling, standardisation
practices and normative pressures – this leaves speakers with a rather
wide freedom of choice. It is thus altogether possible that, over generations, speakers will find themselves using a very different variety from
the elders. This, of course, is of sociohistorical necessity: what better
reason to mark a new identity than being a disenfranchised, diasporic
community wishing to make a new start and declare its identity? This
view of identity is discussed further in Section 4.4.

Critical to this framework is a view of languages as all fundamentally hybrid (Ansaldo and Matthews 2001; Aboh 2006). When applied
to creole languages, the task is then to explain how the lexifier and
the substrate languages mix into a new system. The central idea here
is based on the early observations of Meillet (1921, 1929/1951), Hagège
(1993) and Mufwene (2001). In these works there is a shared assumption
that both first language (L1) and L2 acquisition are basically processes of
reconstruction. What this entails is that speakers select and recombine
from the variety of linguistic features they are exposed to in order to
construct their own idiolect. As argued in Croft (2000), variation exists
in language irrespective of the context. The distinction between high
and low contact scenarios is thus only a matter of degree.

What should be noted too is that the view of a linguistic ecology
in which features co-exist and are selected and replicated differently

by speakers is not incompatible with other frameworks such as the substratist approach (discussed in Section 3.4). The idea of substrate grammar influencing the choices available to speakers in a highly multilingual ecology, due to a general cognitive robustness as the L1, can be defended from an evolutionary perspective. This can be explained through notions such as cognitive salience, typological frequency and congruence, amongst others (see Ansaldo 2009a, 2009b and Section 4.4 below). Even the idea of a certain influence of the lexifier, perhaps as a filtering mechanism amongst the various variables, finds its place, which would explain why many creoles show lexifier-derived vocabulary but substrate-like grammars (see Siegel 2010).

When compared to the CP (Section 4.2), we can see that the fundamental theoretical divide is articulated along the following points.

i. The CP assumes that language is transmitted differently in different contexts. Where language contact is high and multilingualism is widespread, transmission occurs along different lines. In other words, the CP holds that there are non-contact languages that evolve along 'normal' lines of transmission and contact languages that evolve along special lines of transmission.

ii. The evolutionary approach assumes there is only one type of transmission. Whether languages evolve through heavy contact between diverse languages or not, they follow the same evolutionary path.

In order to understand better what causes these differential views, we look into the ideas that generate them.

4.3.1 Contact versus non-contact

First and fundamentally is the notion of creoles as an exceptional class. While creoles may in principle be classified as mixed languages, it does not follow – as argued by Mufwene (2000, 2001) – that they lack genetic parentage, a classification which has disfranchised creoles. As Mufwene has repeatedly pointed out – based on Hjelmslev's (1938) observation – all languages are mixed to some extent, and one should recognise a continuum of structural admixture which may be identified in any language, regardless of its evolution (Mufwene 1992, 2000). For example, the Romance languages started as mixed languages, and English itself has mixed language characteristics. Claims that creoles, but not other languages, are by-products of language contact should be disputed, since they strengthen the false distinction between creole and non-creole vernaculars. The structural distinction between 'normal, internally motivated language change' and 'externally motivated language change' has not provided much insight into language evolution. In contrast, in an evolutionary framework, while it is recognised that in contact language situations there may be more and diverse features available to speakers, the 'actual mechanisms of competition and selection remain the same, operating still at the level of interacting individuals before impacting the speech or language community' (Mufwene 2000: 72).

In this view, even during the plantation stage when non-Europeans became the majority, language transmission was still normal – 'from one group to another, from the creole or seasoned slaves to the bozal slaves [slaves introduced to the Americas or Spain directly from Africa], regardless of the structural variation in the target' (Mufwene 2000: 73). The difference in terms of contact and non-contact settings really lies in the number of systems competing with the lexifier and their structural dissimilarity from each other (Mufwene 1998). The contact setting also resulted in making language boundaries less rigid and the lexifier more 'osmotic', allowing mixing of systems and more substrate influence in the lexifier. Code mixing and code switching, phenomena associated with bi/multilingualism (see Chapter 2), present evidence for 'osmosis', showing that structures of languages can be mixed in different ways. Although it does not explain all creole formation, code mixing or imperfect replication as general principles of language acquisition are applicable to creole languages where substrate influences account for their development. In addition, grammaticalisation pathways go a long way to accounting for the emergence of novel creole structure. In this view, then, the words *creolise* and *creolisation* do not mean any specific type of structural diachronic process or special restructuring; they refer to the various linguistic evolutionary processes observable in any language but simply marked with special social values (Mufwene 1997).

4.3.2 The dynamics of the feature pool

The dynamic workings of the feature pool in the evolutionary approach is illustrated in Aboh and Ansaldo (2007), who discuss data from Suriname creoles and from Sri Lanka Malay (SLM), two contact languages that combine various features derived from different source languages in the contact situation. More specifically, they show how the features that form the feature pool are not equally competitive.

First, comparative analyses have been made of the general properties of the noun phrase, case markings and possessive constructions in English, Gbe and the Suriname creoles. Such research has shown that, in the phenotype – the surface form expressed in selected traits of syntax and semantics – of creoles or new languages that result from a process of recombination of the linguistic features from the competing languages that make up the feature pool through competition and selection, weak and semantically vacuous inflection is disfavoured. This also implies that functional categories – often associated with inflection – that are 'weak and semantically light, are less visible at the syntax-discourse interface and therefore are unlikely to be selected in the emerging language' (Aboh and Ansaldo 2007: 56).

Second, an examination of the case system and the structural features in Sinhala, Tamil and SLM shows that hybrid systems such as SLM emerged as a result of the acquisition of the substrate grammars together with reanalysis of lexifier elements. SLM retained Malay lexical items, but substantially modified its grammar along Lankan type – i.e. Sinhala and Sri Lankan Tamil. What has transpired is that typologically congruent features overwhelmingly dominate the feature pool because of semantic prominence and discourse frequency. A more detailed account of the SLM community and the evolution of SLM is found in Section 4.4. In contrast, when competing systems lack congruence, the result is a new grammar with ample space for patterns from the competing languages based on discourse salience and semantic transparency. A hybrid system, integrating competing features or their various aspects – thus forming novel constructions – may also emerge.

Third, a feature pool-based approach such as that used by Aboh and Ansaldo (2007) indicates that Suriname creoles should be described as more mixed than previously thought, and that SLM's abundance of morphological and grammatical features can be accounted for. The competition and selection in this approach are processes of admixture, where lexical, syntactic and semantic features of different grammars recombine into new grammatical – and typological – profiles, depending on the nature of a specific contact situation.

The units of selection from the feature pool may also involve smaller details which may potentially be disguised by the partial congruence between different languages. For example, as demonstrated in Aboh (2009), the morphosyntactic properties of Saramaccan display closer affinity with its English lexifier than with those of its substrate, Gungbe. A Saramaccan verb like *njan* 'eat' has the same argument structure, and therefore syntax, as the English verb *eat*; thus, the syntax of *njan* in Saramaccan maps onto that of English *eat*. At the same time, Saramaccan *njan* appears in sequences (e.g. to boast, to suffer, to have a headache) such as those shown in example 4.1 (cited in Aboh 2009: 333), which are found in Gbe, the substrate language.

(4.1)

a. Hédi tá   njan mí
   head PROG eat 1SG
   'I'm having a headache'

b. Nján búka
   Eat   mouth
   'To boast'

c. Kofi ta   njan suti   buka
   Kofi PROG eat sweet mouth
   'Kofi is boasting'

d. Njan pena
   Eat   pain
   'To suffer'

e. Njan yai
   Eat   year
   'To celebrate'

Abbreviations: 1SG: First-person singular, PROG: Progressive.

Thus Aboh (2009) suggests that the verb *njan* in Saramaccan combines semantic properties of both Gungbe *ɖú* and English *eat*, and maps them onto the syntax of English.

4.4 CONTACT LANGUAGE FORMATION IN EVOLUTIONARY TERMS

4.4.1 An evolutionary model of contact language formation ▬▬▬

Building on the evolutionary framework of language and the notion of the feature pool in language contact, Ansaldo (2009a, 2009b) presents a view of contact language formation (CLF) in which language creation in multilingual ecologies follows the same principles as language maintenance in monolingual ecologies – that is, the selection and replication of features available to speakers in a given environment. Three ideas underpin this CLF model.

i. Language is viewed as a set of cognitive patterns owned by all humans.
ii. Multilingual ecologies are normal environments, including CLF processes.
iii. Language change and contact-induced change are brought about by speakers; to understand grammatical outcomes, grammatical analysis must be integrated with sociolinguistic theory.

This model is also based on a functional-typological theory and usage-based view of language (Tomasello 2003). The stages of CLF, which should be treated not as separate phases but as occurring simultaneously and iteratively, involve:

 i. selection, which is a matter of social dynamics;
 ii. innovation, with frequency as a major factor in the creation of grammar, plus salience and congruence;
 iii. propagation, which occurs at the broader level of social organisation.

Crucial to Ansaldo's CLF model is the notion of a typological matrix, intended as the total set of linguistic variables available to a group of people related by shared patterns of communication, which is an especially relevant concept when considering in CLF the interaction between variables of different typological origins. In analysing typological matrices, the most salient factor is frequency, which comprises two types:

 i. token-frequency, which can be understood as discourse frequency, where linguistic items that are frequent in discourse may be those that are grammatically obligatory, semantically salient or pragmatically more relevant;
 ii. type-frequency, which includes linguistic items or constructions that are more common – or 'unmarked' – and the occurrence of the same type in two (or more) adstrates reinforces its presence in the matrix.

The use of the notion of frequency distinguishes the typological matrix from the notion of the feature pool, in which the significant factors that play a role in the selection process are markedness and discourse salience (e.g. perceptual salience and semantic transparency – see Mufwene 1991).

 The dynamics of CLF – specifically the stages of selection, propagation and innovation – and the contribution of the typological matrix are illustrated by Ansaldo (2009a, 2009b, 2010a, 2011) in a discussion of altered replication in SLM formation. The community of Malays came to be in Sri Lanka (then Ceylon) through one of the central practices of European colonialism – namely the displacement of subjects from one colonised region to another, during both Dutch rule (1656–1796) and British rule (1796–1948), a practice that brought diverse communities and languages into contact with each other. A large number of political exiles, soldiers, servants and prisoners were moved from diverse origins in the Malay and Indonesian world to Ceylon to help colonial powers in their struggle to settle and dominate the island.

The early Malays[1] (as they were later called by the British) in Ceylon spoke, besides a number of vernaculars of the Indonesian archipelago, the Malay lingua franca that had existed since the first millennium AD in the Monsoon Asia region. This is most often referred to as Bazaar Malay (Adelaar and Prentice 1996), and its varieties are referred to collectively as 'pidgin-derived Malay varieties'. This Malay variety entered into contact with two adstrates in Sri Lanka: Colloquial Sinhala, the dominant language of the population of Sri Lanka, and Lankan Tamil – Tamil in Sri Lanka has undergone considerable convergence and shows marked typological similarities with Sinhala – spoken by, amongst others, traders and plantation workers.

The typological matrix of SLM thus involved features from Malay/Indonesian varieties, Sinhala and Lankan Tamil for selection and replication to the early Malay immigrants in Sri Lanka. However, these features were not equally available for selection. In Sri Lanka, Sinhala was and is the language of the majority (approximately two thirds of the population), with political and economic prestige. Thus, we may assume that Sinhala features had very high token frequency in the ecology. At the same time, Tamil, even if less dominant numerically (one quarter of the population), has converged with Sinhala and they share many areal features. Tamil thus reinforces the type-frequency of Sinhala features. Word order is an example: Sinhala and Tamil both have Subject-Object-Verb (SOV) word order, while Malay is Subject-Verb-Object (SVO). A matrix with these typologies would imply the likelihood that the output be an SOV language, and in fact the basic word order of SLM is indeed SOV. Similarly, in terms of morphological processes, the typological matrix comprises inflectional (Sinhala) + inflectional (Tamil) + mildly agglutinative (Malay) morphology; the outcome is an inflecting language.

In short, innovation in SLM involved a thorough typological restructuring of Malay, on the basis of the typological matrix, with three notable developments: a case system where none was present in the ancestral language, inflectional morphology and a mixed tense/aspect system from a purely aspectual one. SLM is today a language of trilingual base, illustrated in example 4.2 (Ansaldo 2009a: 136), that preserves a predominantly Malay-derived lexicon, as in the verbs *pi, ambe, dudu, jato* – an indication of strong cultural vitality – but is broadly speaking

---

[1] In an earlier era, in fact, these peoples were known as *Ja Minissu* by the Sinhalese and *Java Manusar* by the Tamils: 'people from Java'. It was the British who, upon finding a community who spoke 'Malay', attached the corresponding ethnic label to the group, and it is this designation 'Malay' that has persisted.

Lankan in its grammar (Ansaldo 2005, 2008, 2009a, see also Aboh and Ansaldo 2007; Ansaldo and Nordhoff 2009).

(4.2)

Go market=nang   (e-)pi   ambe-ar-dudu si-jato
1SG market=towards (PST-)go take-PROG-sit PFV-fall
'While I was going to the market, I fell'

Abbreviations: 1SG: First-person singular, PFV: Perfective, PROG: Progressive, PST: Past.

The case system of SLM has received particular attention in the literature, as it offers a rare insight into morphological development as a product of language contact (Bakker 1994; Ansaldo 2008, 2009a, 2011).

The following examples (adapted from Nordhoff 2009: 483) illustrate the core cases: example 4.3 shows the use of Dative to mark experiential subjects, a typical Lankan (and South Asian) function; in example 4.4 we see the use of Accusative to indicate definite objects; and example 4.5 shows a typical Sinhala-like Instrumental/Ablative marking.

(4.3)

Go=dang karang bannyak thàràsìggar
1SG=DAT now   very   sick
'I am very sick now'

(4.4)

Titanic kappal=yang su-thìnggalam
Titanic ship=ACC   PST-sink
'The ship Titanic sank'

(4.5)

Police=dering su-dhaatang
Police=INSTR PST-come
'The police came'

Abbreviations: 1SG: First-person singular, ACC: Accusative, DAT: Dative, INSTR: Instrumental/Ablative, PST: Past.

The evolution of SLM is a good example of how what has until recently been seen to be anomalous development in CLF – such as morphological elaboration – is entirely possible when the typological feature pool allows it.

Two other concepts that are encompassed in Ansaldo's model of CLF – metatypy and identity alignment – deserve further discussion for their explanatory power. The concept known as metatypy not only captures what goes on in CLF; it holds implications for our understanding of why this happens in the history of language. Similarly, the notion of identity alignment provides an explanation for why a community of people is driven to create a new language.

4.4.2 Metatypy

The process of typological congruence that can be observed in prolonged and intense situations of contact due to widespread bi- or multilingualism may be conceptualised as metatypy. In this process, contact-induced transfer of syntactic and semantic categories leads to the formation of new grammatical systems that emerge as compromises between the actual grammars in contact. Simply put, metatypy means typological restructuring that occurs through language contact. This concept builds on the idea first coined by Ross (1996, 2001), who illustrates this in the 'papuanisation' of Takia, an Austronesian language that has undergone metatypy under the influence of the neighbouring Waskia language of Trans-New Guinea type, both spoken on Karkar Island, as seen in examples 4.6 and 4.7.

(4.6)

tamol an Nai i-fun-ag=da	Takia
Man DET me he-hit-me=IMP	
'the man is hitting me'	

(4.7)

kadi mu aga umo-so	Waskia
Man DET me hit-PRES.he	
'the man is hitting me'	
Abbreviations: DET: Determiner, IMP: Imperfective, PRES: Present.	

Other cases of metatypy have been found in Tariana, an Arawak language restructured on the model of East Tucanoan languages (Aikhenvald 2002), Semitic languages of Ethiopia remodelled on Cushitic grammar (Harris and Campbell 1995) and Arvanitic, the Albanian spoken in Greece, which has shifted towards a Greek type (Sasse 1985). They have also been found in more recent instances of CLF, such as Maluku Malay (Bowden 2005), Singlish and Mixe Basque (Ross 2007: 124).[2]

---

[2] In fact, metatypy can also help to account for the development of linguistic areas, introduced in Section 1.4.2, which arise through language contact occurring over

Table 4.1 *Case in Malay, SLM, Sinhala and Lankan Tamil*

Case	Malay	SLM	Sinhala	Tamil
			Functions	
Dative	∅	Exp, G, Ben, Poss	Exp G, Ben, Poss	Exp, G, Ben, Poss
Nominative	∅	Agent	Agent	Agent
Accusative	∅	Patient	Patient	Patient
Genitive	∅	Possession	Temp poss, Loc	Temp poss, Loc
Instrumental	∅	Instr source	Instr source	Source
Comitative	∅	Association	Association	Association

Abbreviations: Ben: Benefactive, Exp: Experiential, G: Goal, Instr: Instrumental, Loc: Locative, Poss: Possessive, Temp poss: Temporary possession.

In a bilingual or multilingual context, speakers may restructure (aspects of) one of the languages in their repertoire using another language of that repertoire as a model. While it is most often the case that the emblematic language in a multilingual context undergoes metatypy under the effect of a dominant language, the opposite can occur, as illustrated by the case of Singlish (Ross 2006: 97, 2007: 131). In this sense, differentiating between substratum transfer and metatypy simply helps in understanding the direction of forces, but does not entail ontologically different processes.

Metatypy is clearly illustrated in SLM in the nominal domain – in particular the case system. The emblematic Malay language has no morphological marking of case on the noun. In contrast, the dominant languages in the multilingual feature pool of SLM, Sinhala and Lankan Tamil both show typical case systems of the South Asian type, with a significant degree of functional overlap due to congruence between the latter two languages. SLM shows systematic restructuring of its noun phrase to map the case systems of Lankan type, as summarised in Table 4.1 (adapted from Ansaldo 2009a: 129–131, 2011).

But what exactly causes metatypy to take place? Metatypy can be seen as the result of a heavy psychological load that results from intense bilingualism requiring communication in distinct systems (Nadkarni 1975). The work of Sasse (1985, 1990) has explained a number of typical

a period of time in a specific geographical region in which neighbouring languages, usually unrelated to each other, share features. Typical examples mentioned include the Balkans, where the definite article is encoded by a suffix, and Southeast Asia, with areal patterns of grammaticalisation.

outcomes of contact as the result of bilinguals' needs to express the same thought in different languages. We are here not subscribing to a general claim that all multilingual situations are inherently unstable and must be resolved through some process of shift, be it convergence, simplification or metatypy. But, as clearly evidenced by the existence of well-documented linguistic areas, speakers of different languages in prolonged and intense situations of contact can affect each other to the point that their linguistic systems will become more similar to each other over time. This makes sense in light of the overwhelmingly accommodating nature of human communication, which results from a wider behavioural coordination characteristic of humans (Trudgill 2010).

As pointed out in Matras (2010: 66), bilingual individuals should be seen as possessing an enriched linguistic system (rather than two or more 'impoverished' ones), which they are capable of appropriately adapting to the context in which they function. In this sense, language contact phenomena can be seen as function-driven choices that speakers make, not necessarily consciously, in goal-oriented communicative interaction. Metatypy thus emerges as a process that 'offers speakers the opportunity to accommodate and generalise and yet still hold on to a mental demarcation between subsets of word forms within their repertoire' (Matras 2010: 76).

4.4.3 Identity alignment

At the outset of Chapter 3, we listed the following questions as being amongst some of the most significant for the field of language contact.

  i. Why do contact languages, and especially creoles, arise in the first place?
  ii. How are the new grammatical systems arrived at?
  iii. Which original languages of the contact situation influenced the new varieties most and why?

So far, we have focused more on the latter two questions rather than the first, which we now address.

One of the driving forces behind the formation of new varieties is the construction of a new identity, as demonstrated in the classic study by Robert Le Page and Andrée Tabouret-Keller (1985). Language creation is part of a process required in a new community to differentiate itself from the outside and strengthen endogenous forces. The motivation for the evolution of SLM, which – as seen in the previous section – involved the restructuring of the vernacular in which substantial features of Lankan grammar combine with a predominantly Malay-derived lexicon, has been explained as a process of interacting and of negotiating linguistic identities in a new environment. This is termed 'identity alignment' in work by Ansaldo and Lim (Lim and Ansaldo 2007; Ansaldo 2009a). The notion of identity alignment implies several things.

The overarching implication is that identity can be defined by being multilingual. This requires a loose view of 'community', in which identities can be adapted and renegotiated in an ever-changing ecology (Djité 2006). The idea of simultaneous identities – conceived by Woolard (1999) – in this context suggests that, instead of assigning one language a preferential status in a multilingual community, one's linguistic identity is shaped by the plurality of linguistic codes itself, regardless of the order in which they were acquired. In the case of the Sri Lankan Malay community this means that, even while SLM is their restructured vernacular – for which they are best known in the linguistics world – what should not be overlooked are the numerous other languages in their repertoire.

In the first place, what can be underscored is how the community of peoples from the Malay archipelago deported to Sri Lanka (then Ceylon) during Dutch rule – which included nobility, political exiles and soldiers, many with wives and families – swiftly settled in the new environment. As testament to their permanence there, when the British took over the island from the Dutch, the Malays as one refused to be repatriated because they had settled with their families and made Ceylon their home. A crucial part of such alignment was the acquisition of the main languages of the ecology in their repertoire, Sinhala and Lankan Tamil. As outlined earlier in this section, contact between their ancestral Malay languages and these two adstrates led to the evolution of SLM.

The significance of SLM in relation to the other languages in the Malays' ecology can still be seen today. In more peripheral and relatively isolated communities such as the fishing village of Kirinda, situated on the southern coast approximately 25 kilometres to the east of Hambantota, SLM is still the primary language for the Malays, especially in the home domain, but it is far from exclusive. With Sinhalese and Tamils also in the community and neighbouring areas, Malays in Kirinda frequently code mix with Sinhala and/or Tamil, and both these languages enter their lives from very early on, through play, school and the media. Sinhala and Tamil also occupy very significant functional roles in the community, as languages of education and economic opportunity. In other words, the Sri Lankan Malays can be seen as having a pluralistic identity, and are not conflating or changing identities; rather, this identity is simply multifaceted as is their linguistic repertoire.

The Malays' multilingualism not only included the indigenous languages. Many of the older Javanese exiles had a high proficiency in Dutch, which led them during Dutch rule to be appointed *Hoofd de Maha Badda* (Sinhala *maha badda* 'great trade', referring to the cinnamon industry first established by the Sinhala king in the 1500s for Portuguese trade) or *Hoofd de Cinnamon* – namely the 'captains' supervising the cinnamon gardens. Since the spice was one of the most precious commodities during Dutch rule, increased production of cinnamon meant that these superior officers would be rewarded with more power, promotions and privileges. Many others were enlisted in the military and were later retained under the British as members of the Malay Rifle Regiment, a prestigious division used to fight the local – i.e. Ceylonese – armies. Retired soldiers and officers of the regiment were later in a very good position to become police officers, supervisors and trusted guards in the British colonial structure. Many joined the tea estates and functioned as intermediaries between the English superintendents and the Indian labour force. In short, in both Dutch and British Ceylon, many Sri Lankan Malays were in privileged positions – intermediaries between colonisers and locals – not least because of their proficiency in the languages needed to interact with all parties concerned. Clearly, multilingualism was significant to the Malay community as it positioned its members in a powerful role between the colonial powers and the local Sinhalese and Tamil communities. The community in contemporary times is still clearly multilingual. In the most recent census of 2011 (Department of Census and Statistics Sri Lanka 2014), a significantly higher proportion of Malays report an ability to speak, and to read and write (49.7 per cent and 61.2 per cent) the three major languages Sinhala, Tamil and English. The other ethnic groups (Sinhala, Sri Lanka Tamil, Indian Tamil, Sri Lanka Moor and Burgher), in comparison, have proportions no higher than 12.8 and 10.8 per cent respectively, apart from the Burghers (20 per cent and 12.4 per cent) and the Sri Lanka Moors (26.7 per cent and 28 per cent), although these are still significantly lower than the Malays.

Overall, the Malays' multilingual repertoire put them in an ideal position as cultural brokers within Sri Lankan society, affording them the position to negotiate their social position within Lankan networks as well as between Lankan society and colonial structures. What is also evident is a multiple cultural and linguistic identity that is both Lankan *and* Malay, highlighted in the ease with which, until recently, these multilingual individuals mixed and shifted between codes, and in how they identify themselves as Sri Lankans *and* Muslim Malays (of Indonesian origin): there is neither conflict in this position nor separation of traits. The former identification is manifest in the absence of a wish to 'return' to Malaysia or Indonesia, while the latter is expressed in their interest in revitalising the Malay language in the community (more of this in Chapter 6).

Structurally, CLF can also be understood as a process of hybridisation, albeit grammatical, which is part of identity alignment. This alignment involves innovative construction of a new grammar based on multilingual resources, and is part of a more general process of new cultural identification that involves intragroup focusing and intergroup differentiation. On the other hand, differentiation does not mean total segregation, because the multilingual and multicultural resources of the group always allow contact to be maintained. Through this particular social positioning, the group often achieves an advantageous position in the political ecology. Identity alignment thus suggests that language creation is not the result of some exceptional situation in which speakers were denied the social, cultural or cognitive settings necessary for a 'normal' acquisition of a target; rather, it is a creative process in which speakers have agency in the transmission and transfer of linguistic features. Hybridisation is thus a perfectly 'normal' outcome of contact ecologies, as the combination of acts of maintenance and divergence that defines an emerging community in a new ecology.

Examples of identity alignment in CLF are many. In addition to the Sri Lankan Malays, the Peranakans of Malacca and Singapore and the Macanese of Macau, as other examples located in Asia, also share the following traits (albeit to different degrees; see Ansaldo 2009a, 2010b for an extensive discussion; also Ansaldo, Lim and Mufwene 2007; Lim 2010b, 2014a, 2016, forthcoming):

i. a relatively influential position as multilingual mediators in the ecology in which they functioned;
ii. a clear cultural and linguistic identity that set them apart as a discrete group from the rest;
iii. strong patterns of endogamy, despite various degrees of exogamy involved in the formative stages;
iv. multilingual repertoires, at both the individual and the societal level, as indicated by high degrees of variation, mixing and shifting through history;
v. cultural innovation which includes – but is not limited to – language creation, in which elements originally belonging to different systems are recombined in a new profile.

In a broader perspective, the notion of identity alignment relates to two important paradigms. First, identity alignment suggests that CLF is driven sociohistorically by the same forces that lead to speciation:

the evolutionary process by which new species – in biology, biological species; here, languages – arise. In other words, CLF is essentially the same as the speciation that leads, in the history of humanity, from allegedly one original language to a diversity of thousands of varieties. As humans migrated to new areas and settled in new environments, they detached themselves from the original group and over time formed a new community and a new culture. As part of that culture a new dialect of a language arose that, over time, diverged through natural variation to the point of becoming a different language. In CLF the same happens: a new community is formed in a new environment and evolves a new language. Second, the process of identity alignment is framed within an anthropological interpretation of language as socialisation. The views expressed within the socialisation paradigm build on notions of language transmission as acculturation, involving social participation in the construction and representation of identity throughout life (i.e. linguistic acts of children and adults), and assume a rich environment from which to select (linguistic) features (for a recent overview see Kulick and Schieffelin 2007).

4.5 CONCLUDING REMARKS

In this chapter we have discussed two recent theoretical developments in the field of contact-induced change: the CP and the evolutionary framework. An evaluation of these approaches points towards the latter as a promising model for future theoretical development in the field of contact linguistics. In particular, we have suggested the following.

   i. Contact language formation does not occur in a linguistic vacuum but rather in rich multilingual settings.
   ii. Contact language formation usually builds on previous experiences of trade languages, pidgins or lingue franche.
   iii. Contact language formation happens in concomitance with the evolution of a population of speakers that is negotiating a new position in the ecology in which it is situated. In other words, language creation is the product of identity alignment in a multilingual context.

In relation to these points, we propose that the processes of shifting and mixing codes – that is, the selection of features from different grammatical systems and their recombination in a new grammar – are the natural outcome of an identity alignment that typically occurs

in diasporic, ethnically heterogeneous contexts. Through these practices, the community achieves both integration within the new context and self-identification through cultural innovation. The multiple
linguistic resources on which the community draws in this process
of alignment constitute the de facto linguistic profile of the community, a profile that goes beyond notions of mother tongue and native
competence and includes multilingualism and mixing practices as the
defining points of linguistic and cultural identification.

Structurally, negotiation practices in multilingual ecologies translate
into processes of hybridisation through admixture, which may lead to
the formation of new linguistic repertoires; in Ansaldo (2009a), the process of linguistic hybridisation is treated as the outcome of a wider
process of cultural innovation. In our view, the way ahead is to test
these and other generalisations on an increasingly broad spectrum
of contact phenomena – in particular those that develop away from
the better-known Caribbean varieties, and especially where non-Indo-
European languages enter into contact. The most revealing test cases
will involve languages of radically different morphological type, as well
as diverse sociolinguistic dynamics. Is it really the case that more often
than not morphology erodes in exoteric contexts? If so, cases like SLM
must be treated as exceptions and occupy limited space in the theoretical debate. Alternatively, it is plausible to suggest that the typological
profile of a restricted language is directly related to the typology of the
languages in question (Givón 1979). If the contact involves languages
close to the analytic type, the outcome will be morphologically simple. On the other hand, where morphologically rich languages enter
into contact, we might see a morphologically rich outcome, as observed
in SLM.

DISCUSSION POINTS

1. The literature offers two claims about the nature of morphology:
   (a) morphology is stripped in L2 adult acquisition because it is too
   'complex'; (b) morphology may have developed in speech communities over time to make L1 child acquisition easier (i.e. to provide
   additional clues). Discuss how these two claims can be framed
   within one coherent theory of language.

2. Are there languages for which we have sound historical records
   that seem to have been morphologically analytic throughout their
   life-span? If so, how can this be explained?

3. Construct a possible database of some ten contact languages in which combinations of all different morphological types occur. Such a database should allow us to attempt to address the issues discussed in this chapter.

FURTHER READING

For an exploration of the CP, see McWhorter (1998) and DeGraff (2004, 2005a). For recent approaches to CLF that are based on ecology and evolution, see Mufwene (2001, 2008), Ansaldo (2009a) and Aboh (2015).

5   Contact and ecology

5.1   INTRODUCTION

At the outset of this book we underlined the significant role that ecology plays in the study of languages in contact. The ecology paradigm, a metaphor from population genetics and biology, has been developed most recently in linguistic study by Salikoko Mufwene (2001, 2008). The earliest instances of its invocation – Voegelin, Voegelin and Schutz (1967) and Haugen (1971), and later Mühlhäusler (1996) – use it in the sense of the social environment in which a language is spoken. Mufwene (2001: 153) is also influenced by its usage in macroecology as a cover term for diverse factors which are both external and internal to a species and bear on its evolution. These include population size, habitat requirements and genetic variation, as well as differences in initial conditions, stochastic (i.e. random) events, time lags, processes operating on different time scales and spatial subdivisions.

In this chapter we engage in a detailed examination of the role of ecology behind two linguistic features: particles and tone.[1] These features are germane to this book because they are extremely susceptible to contact. But, even more pertinently for this chapter, we highlight how a full appreciation of what happens with particles and tone requires us to look at the external factors which construe the ecology that creates the conditions for the dynamics of contact, and the close interplay between them. More specifically, we demonstrate how the identification of the substrates for certain features needs to call on an examination of demographic factors such as immigration patterns and population make-up at different points in time, as well as language policy. We also see how

---

[1] In the sections on particles and tone, where the information is available in the source data, tones are represented as pitch level numbers 1 to 5 where, in the Asianist tradition, the larger the number the higher the pitch; for example, 55 represents a high level tone, and 24 represents a rising tone.

the founder principle in the ecology paradigm helps to shed light on otherwise puzzling patterns in the restructured variety.

These linguistic features are extremely interesting to examine because they are features which can be seen to be quite distinctive for Asia. They are not exclusive to Asia, of course: particles are found in numerous languages of the world, and virtually all languages in Africa are tonal, with several clusters of languages with tones occurring in South, Central and North America. Nonetheless, these features are often closely associated with the Asian region. In the case of tone languages, which have marked regional distribution, it is languages with complex – as opposed to simple – tone systems that dominate in East and Southeast Asia: all varieties of Chinese, as well as Vietnamese and Thai, have tone systems that include contour tones. In fact, the region known as Mainland Southeast Asia, which provides a dramatic demonstration of the areal phenomenon in linguistics, has tone as one of its most well-known areal features. In contrast, although complex tone systems are in existence in Africa, in particular in West Africa (Maddieson 2013), most African languages have simple tone systems – essentially where there is only a two-way basic contrast, usually between high (H) and low (L) levels.

5.2 DISCOURSE PARTICLES

5.2.1 Particles in contact varieties of English

As a discourse-prominent feature, particles are very easily transferred in contact-induced change (Matras 2000). It is worthwhile examining this subset of grammar in the region of Asia, not least because most languages in Asia – such as Cantonese, Hokkien, Mandarin, Thai, Lao, (Bazaar/Baba) Malay, Tagalog and Hindi – have discourse particles, which are used widely in those languages to communicate pragmatic functions of various types. We see that, where a variety emerges as a consequence of contact in an ecology that includes particles, particles figure prominently and are considered a robust feature of the contact variety. We look first at particles emerging in the many contact varieties of English in Asia, as they have received increasing scholarly attention in recent years, perhaps because their appearance in a variety of English comes across as particularly marked. We will see later, though, that such contact-induced transfer is not exclusive to an emergent English.

In the stabilised, restructured variety of Indian English, for instance, one finds the particle *yaar* from Hindi. This occurs in with various clause types, such as declaratives, interrogatives, imperatives and exclamations, shown in example 5.1 (Lange 2009: 216). In the Indian component of the International Corpus of English, *yaar* occurs 127 times in the 'direct conversation' subsection, meaning a frequency of 0.58 per 1,000 words (Lange 2009: 211). This may suggest that it is much less frequent than, say, Singapore English's (SgE) *lah* as will be seen later. Nevertheless, it is significant to note that the particles *yaar* – originally from colloquial Hindi, which means 'mate' or 'guy' but has developed to serve to emphasise the speaker's intended meaning – and *na* – which indicates an expectation of agreement – shown in example 5.2 (Lange 2009: 213; idiomatic glosses ours) are used in Indian English by speakers regardless of mother tongue. Therefore, they are not constrained to Hindi mother-tongue speakers, and thus appear to be a robust feature of Indian English.

(5.1)

You'll <,> you must be really having good patience *yaar*
'You'll [pause and/or clause boundary] you must have a great deal of patience'
[emphasis]

(5.2)

Sunday will be more convenient *na*
'Sunday will be more convenient, won't it?' [expecting a 'yes' answer]

With Tagalog having some eighteen enclitic particles, it is not surprising that some of these also occur frequently in Philippine English, another stabilised, restructured variety of English. The Philippine component of the International Corpus of English testifies to their presence in Philippine English: there are seventy-five instances of *na*, which signals a relatively new or altered situation – seen in example 5.3 – and twenty-eight instances of *pa*, which denotes a relatively old or continuing situation. Meanwhile, the particle *ba*, a question marker obligatory in formulaic yes/no questions, is found in 11 utterances, illustrated in example 5.4 (Lim and Borlongan 2011: 62, 68).

(5.3)

We have an idea *na* of who we'll get yeah pero we're waiting *pa* for the approval.
'We already have an idea of who we'll get yeah but we're still waiting for the approval.'

(5.4)

You find this fulfilling *ba?*
'Do you find this fulfilling?'

Hong Kong English (HKE), a variety with Cantonese as its predominant substrate, displays numerous Cantonese particles (many of them similar to the Cantonese-origin particles in SgE, discussed in the next section). These are primarily documented in computer-mediated communication (CMC), such as the ICQ exchange seen in example 5.5 (James 2001; the idiomatic gloss is constructed from the explanatory notes in the article; also see other examples in Chapter 7). They are reported to be employed liberally in the Cantonese-English code-mixed text of users – such that 'almost every sentence they write ends with the little tag of a romanised particle' (Yang 2004:110) – as well as in natural conversation, as in example 5.6 (Multilingual Hong Kong Corpus, Katherine Chen, personal communication, April 2010[2]).

(5.5)

grace will not go to have lecture for huma *ar* ... can u help her to keep notes for her as i know u and she will have quiz on thu soon. Thanks very much. may be LG1 [Lower Ground 1st Floor] is much better *wor* ... noisy *ma* ... at G/F ... also u seem used to study there *ma*

'Grace will not go for her humanities lecture ... So, could you help take notes for her as I know you, and she will have a quiz on Thursday. Thanks very much. *Come to think of it,* maybe lower ground 1st floor is much better ... *Since, as we know,* the ground floor is noisy ... and *since, as I [and you] know,* you seem to study there [i.e. on LG1] usually.'

(5.6)

K: How are you *a33*?

The best known particle in SgE/Singlish is *lah*, exemplified in example 5.7 (Lim 2004: 46). Widely commodified, appearing on Tshirts detailing to users and viewers 'how to use lah', the particle has been included in the *Oxford English Dictionary* (OED) since 1997. The particle *lah* is also found in Malaysian English (MalE) – see example 5.8 (Baskaran 2008: 619) – and in fact Malaysians are up in arms about the OED ascribing *lah* to SgE. Another commonly found particle in both SgE and MalE is *ah*, as in examples 5.9 and 5.10 respectively (Lim 2004: 46; Baskaran 1994: 28). In the Singapore component of the International Corpus of English, the frequencies of *lah* and *ah* are well above 1,000 (Ler 2006).

---

[2] The Multilingual Hong Kong Corpus is in the process of being constructed, based on English–Cantonese bilingual data collected in Hong Kong in 2004–2005, and we are grateful to Katherine Chen for making the example available to us.

(5.7)

I don't know *lah*, I very blur *lah*.
'I don't know, I'm very confused.'

(5.8)

Please, *lah*, come home early.
'For heaven's sake, come home early.'

(5.9)

Then you got to do those papers again *ah*?
'Then you've got to do those papers again, do you?'

(5.10)

Where on earth you went *ah*?
'Where on earth did you go?'

But *lah* is only the tip of a complex and fascinating iceberg of particles
that have emerged in SgE (and MalE) as a result of Singapore's complex
contact situation over the years. What follows is a more detailed examination of the situation. This is instructive not only for what it shows us
about contact dynamics but also because it underlines the significance
of recognising ecology – or more specifically of recognising different eras
in an ecology – in order to be able to tease out the different influences
that different languages have had on an emergent variety at various
points in time.

5.2.2 Particles in SgE and the identification of substrates

Some eight to ten particles have been documented for SgE; in addition
to *lah* and *ah* mentioned in the previous section are the particles *what,
hor, leh, lor, ma* and *meh*, and a few others besides, illustrated in examples
5.11–5.14 (Lim 2007: 451).

(5.11)

My parents old fashion *a21*? Then your parents *le55*?
'Are you saying that my parents are old-fashioned? Then what about your
parents?'

(5.12)

The most I have fewer kids *lo33*.
'At the very worst, I'll have fewer children.' [resigned]

(5.13)

> He's quite innocent *la21 ho24*? Innocent.
> 'He's quite innocent, don't you agree? Innocent.'

(5.14)

> No *la21*! He's using Pirelli, you don't know *mɛ55*?
> 'No, he has Pirelli tyres; didn't you know that?' [incredulously]

The substrate sources for these are, however, different from those for *lah* and *ah*. The reasons for this are enlightening, but most work on SgE particles – until Lim (2007) – did not interest itself in comprehensively establishing their substrate origins. A handful of researchers attributed the sources of a few particles, explicitly or implicitly, to varying languages.[3] For example, *lah* has been ascribed to Hokkien (Richards and Tay 1977), to Cantonese (Besemeres and Wierzbicka 2003) or to Chinese in general (Mandarin, Hokkien and/or Cantonese) (Kwan-Terry 1978), to Colloquial Malay (Goddard 1994) or to Chinese or Malay (Pakir 1992). *Ah* has been ascribed to Tamil (Baskaran 1988), *hor* to Cantonese (Kwan-Terry 1992) and *what* to Chinese *ma* or *lo* (Kwan-Terry 1978; Pakir 1992), but the treatment was in most cases incidental. Richards and Tay (1977) do provide an account for SgE *lah* having originated in Hokkien rather than in Mandarin or Malay, basing their argument on the parallel in functions between Hokkien *la* and SgE *lah*. Similarly, Kwan-Terry (1978) presents her argument for *lah* and *what* being the result of transfer and calqueing respectively from Chinese, but treating Mandarin, Hokkien and Cantonese as equally possible sources.

In what follows, we draw largely from Lim's (2007, 2009c) investigation, in a triangulation of:

  i. the particles' forms and functions in the various potential substrate languages;
 ii. the dating of the appearance of the particles in the contact variety, SgE;
iii. the significant historical, social and/or political events in the ecology which would have elevated a particular community or language to a more dominant position, thus making that community, its language and hence its features a bigger player in the feature pool.

First we consider the languages involved. Several languages are widely acknowledged as being the main substrate languages in the formation

---

[3] In some cases, as suggested by Gupta (1992, 1994), this is to those languages that they are more familiar with.

of the contact variety SgE – namely Bazaar Malay, Hokkien, Teochew, Cantonese and, later, Mandarin. Comprehensive accounts are found in Lim (2007, 2010a), and the reader interested in the minute details is encouraged to turn to these works. Here, a distillation is necessary. We consider the particles that occur in these substrates, whose forms and functions are summarised in Table 5.1 for convenient comparison.

A few points regarding general features of the particles are also in order here.

i. Hokkien's sentence particles occur finally, typically with neutral tone, which is like the low tone but with very weak stress (Bodman 1987). While the number of particles in Amoy Hokkien is not systematically enumerated (Bodman 1987), Singapore Hokkien is said to have about ten particles (Tay 1968).

ii. Cantonese (Kwok 1984; Matthews and Yip 1994) can be said to be especially rich in particles, with some thirty basic forms (or more than 200 if all variants are counted), which vary in their pronunciation – including vowel quality, duration and intonation – to a greater extent than other Cantonese words. The vowel may be short or prolonged – the latter a characteristic of Cantonese which distinguishes it from other Chinese dialects. In Cantonese, sentence-final particles serve various communicative or pragmatic functions (which in English are often conveyed by intonation) – namely indicating (a) speech act types such as questions, assertions, requests; (b) evidentiality (showing source of knowledge); and (c) affective and emotional colouring. These particles sometimes correspond functionally to English question tags, but in Cantonese there is no pause between main sentence and particle.

iii. While in (Beijing) Mandarin (Li and Thompson 1981), sentence-final particles (*yu3qi4 ci2* 'mood words') number about six, Singapore Mandarin is said to have about ten (Lock 1988); they all have neutral tone and are unstressed. Their semantic and pragmatic functions are said to be elusive, and linguists have had considerable difficulty in arriving at a general characterisation of each of them (Li and Thompson 1981).

iv. Bazaar Malay is reported to have *la*, *ah* and *ka* as the most commonly used particles, with *ah* being said to be used extensively (Khin Khin Aye 2005); they carry no tone, as Malay is not a tone language. Note that Standard Malay does not have particles, save for the emphatic particle or clitic *lah*, used with imperatives to soften a command, and the question particle *kah*.

Table 5.1 *Particles in Colloquial SgE, Bazaar Malay, Hokkien, Cantonese and Mandarin (adapted from Lim 2007: 460–1)*

SgE	Bazaar Malay	Hokkien	Cantonese	Mandarin
lah draws attention to mood or attitude and appeals for accommodation; indicates solidarity, familiarity, informality [*la24*] is more persuasive [*la21*] is more matter-of-fact	*la* provides emphasis (like Malay *lah* emphatic marker); softens command; indicates solidarity, familiarity, informality	*la* indicates finality, completion, exclamatory or confirming meaning, emphasis, persuasiveness, dismissiveness, or listing	*la55* indicates definiteness or forcefulness; softens command *la33* like *la55* but less suppliant	*la* gives emphasis
ah [*a24*] signals continuation (in narratives or explanations) and keeps interlocutors in contact; softens command; marks a question expecting agreement [*a21*] marks a question requiring response	*a* indicates interrogative, exclamatory, and indicative moods; signifies continuation of utterance	*a* indicates completion, finality, slightly exclamatory; indicates interrogative, exclamatory, and indicative moods	*a55* indicates tentativeness in questions and requests *a33* softens force of statements or confirmations; accompanies A-not-A and copular questions *a23* checks addressee's meaning or intention *a21* checks validity of an assumption; turns declarative into question, tends to presuppose a positive answer, common in rhetorical questions; may suggest surprise, scepticism, disapproval	*a* reduces forcefulness in A-not-A and Qn-wd questions; gives emphasis

(cont.)

Table 5.1 (cont.)

SgE	Bazaar Malay	Hokkien	Cantonese	Mandarin
what [wat21] indicates that information is obvious, contradicting something previously asserted		**ma** indicates obviousness	**wo21** *indicates noteworthy discovery **ma33** (contracted from a55ma33): indicates obvious reason, excuse	**ma** provides emphasis (in listed items)
lor [lo33] indicates a sense of obviousness as well as resignation		**lo** indicates obviousness	**lo33** indicates obviousness, inevitability and irrevocability **lo55** points out what appears to be obvious	**luo** indicates obviousness
hor [ho24] marks a question asserting a proposition and trying to garner support for the proposition		**ho** marks a question with expectation of agreement	**ho35** expects confirmation of a statement or suggestion	
leh [le55] marks a question involving comparison		*ne ~ ni emphasises contrasts; indicates 'as for' le* marks informality and intimacy	**ne55 ~ le55** forms question; has comparative function; indicates 'what about?'	la* refers to currently relevant state *na* indicates response to claim, expectation or belief on the part of hearer

Table 5.1 (cont.)

SgE	Bazaar Malay	Hokkien	Cantonese	Mandarin
meh [me55] marks a question involving scepticism		**me** acts as a general question particle (in some Minnan varieties)	**me55** indicates a highly marked 'surprise' question, checks truth of unexpected state of affairs (common in rhetorical questions)	
ma [ma33] indicates obviousness		**ma** indicates obviousness	**ma33** (contracted from a55ma33): indicates an obvious reason or excuse	**ma** *acts as a general purpose question particle; **ma** provides emphasis in listed items; indicates emphasis, with enhanced note of disapproval or annoyance

* indicates that there is no match between the SgE particle and the particle in the substrate in form and/or in function.

~ indicates free variation between the two forms shown.

There are three aspects along which linguistic parallels between the particles can be drawn: (a) segmental form; (b) suprasegmental form (tone); and (c) function. We first consider the possible correspondences between particles present in the various languages for the eight SgE particles on the basis of two of these: segmental form and approximate function. Given the structural similarity of the Sinitic varieties, it is not surprising that a survey of Table 5.1 shows, at face value at least, reasonable comparability in the particles from Hokkien, Cantonese and Mandarin, with Cantonese in particular fielding possible candidates for all SgE particles and Mandarin with fewer contenders. Bazaar Malay sees similar particles in just two: *lah* and *ah*.

If one considers the tone of the particles in the substrates, however, because the Mandarin and Hokkien particles have neutral tone and weak stress, this would make explaining the emergence of prominent suprasegmental features of some of the SgE particles difficult to account for – in particular, the mid- and high-level pitch of SgE's *lor*, *leh* and *meh*. In other words, if one takes into account all three aspects of the make-up of the particles – namely segmental (phonemes) and suprasegmental (tone) form and function – what is most striking in Table 5.1 is that all the SgE particles, with the exception of *lah*, *what* and perhaps *ah*, can be seen to be the exact match of particles in Cantonese, including the maintenance of lexical tone (as noted in Lim 2007). For clarity, we take the reader through the analysis for SgE *lor*, as follows. In SgE, *lor* occurs only with a mid-level pitch, and indicates not only obviousness but a sense of resignation as well. While the corresponding particles in Hokkien and Mandarin are very close segmentally as *lo* and *luo* respectively, where suprasegmentals are concerned, both these have neutral tone and weak stress. Cantonese, however, does have particle *lo33* matching the mid-level tone in SgE *lor*. With respect to function, both the particles in Hokkien and Mandarin indicate obviousness, but Cantonese *lo33* also gives the sense of inevitability, irrevocability and resignation – again, a perfect match with SgE *lor*. The same parallels can be seen for *hor*, *leh*, *meh* and *ma*.

This wholesale import of the particles *lor*, *hor*, *leh*, *meh* and *ma* can in fact be seen to occur in two senses: (a) particles with their full phonetic form – i.e. both segmental and tonal features – and function as in Cantonese have been acquired into SgE; and (b) it is a substantial subset of these Cantonese particles that have been acquired. Lim (2007) analyses this along the lines of categorical fusion, a process first identified by Matras (2000: 577–8), by which is meant the wholesale import, over time, of an entire class of items in the contact language. In other words, the resources of one single language system (in this case, Cantonese) are drawn on for an entire functional category (in this case, particles), with no separation of form and function for that class of items (in this case, the phonetic form, tone and meaning of the Cantonese particles are taken as a package).

So far, with the particles *lor, hor, leh, meh* and *ma*, the picture looks quite neat. Things gets a little hazier, though, if one wishes to establish the origins of the remaining three particles – *lah, ah,* and *what* – and below we present the case of *lah*, following Lim's (2007: 463–4) reasoning. As is clear in Table 5.1, some form of *la* particle occurs in all the Chinese languages, and Bazaar Malay also has *la*, which indicates emphasis, solidarity, familiarity and informality, as with SgE's *lah*. But linguistic parallels are less clear cut, since SgE *lah* has numerous functions, and a number of pitch patterns can occur with the particle. Since the Cantonese counterparts are with mid (M)- and H-level tones, and SgE *lah* does not occur with either pitch pattern, Cantonese is perhaps a less likely source for *lah* than Hokkien or Malay. Kwan-Terry (1992: 67), however, maintains the possibility that particles may gradually lose their tonal feature over time as they become more fully assimilated into SgE, and it is suggested (Anthea F. Gupta, personal communication, cited in Kwan-Terry 1992: 67) that amongst the first particles, such as *lah* and *what*, this gradual loss of tonal feature is already underway. For this reason, one may keep Cantonese in consideration. Richards and Tay (1977) discount Mandarin *la*, as it serves a grammatical function and is used in both formal and informal situations. In short, on the basis of linguistic similarity, if one also allows for the potential bleaching of the tonal dimension of phonetic form over time, Malay and Hokkien, as well as Cantonese, are all likely sources for *lah* (since within the feature pool model, multiple etymology is a feasible option).

As the analysis above shows, establishing linguistic parallels between SgE particles and particles in the substrates, while convincing for a set of particles, is less clear with others. For further clarification, a look to the past is necessary in two respects – both significant and related to each other. First, the date of entry of the particles into SgE is not insignificant: given the changing linguistic ecology, establishing the period just preceding the appearance of a feature would point to the languages prominent in that period as being the most likely candidates for sources. In the absence of appropriate large-scale corpora of earlier decades, this is established deductively, based on the appearance of these particles in scholarship.[4] So: particle dating. Three particles – *lah,*

---

[4] The absence of documentation of features in scholarship, of course, does not conclusively show that those features were not present in the variety at the time; the locating of archival data from earlier decades (if any) and their analysis would be required to support such an assumption.

Table 5.2 *Some landmarks in the linguistic sociohistory of Singapore (adapted from Lim 2007: 452)*

Time period and historical circumstances	Language and education policies and practice		Linguistic ecology
pre-1800s Malay Sultanate			• contact varieties of Malay are main lingue franche
1819–1965 British colony			• Hokkien also serves as lingua franca
before 1900s to 1920s	• English-medium schools: majority of Eurasian teachers, smaller equal numbers of European and Indian teachers; majority of Eurasian and Straits-born Chinese students; extensive use of contact Malay varieties • Chinese-medium schools use other Chinese languages, not Mandarin		• numerous southern Chinese, Malay/Indonesian and South Asian languages spoken by respective communities • English spoken by communities such as Eurasians, Armenians, Ceylonese, Babas, British, Americans, Europeans
early 1900s		• sharp rise in Chinese students in English-medium schools • dramatic increase in Chinese teachers in English-medium schools (c.1927) • Mandarin replaces other languages in Chinese-medium schools (c.1912)	
1956–1965 leading to and at independence	• four official languages (1956) • English as compulsory school language (1965)		• English starts becoming widely used interethnic lingua franca, especially in the younger generation
after 1979	• Speak Mandarin Campaign (annually, from 1979)		• Mandarin becomes most frequently used home language for Chinese, and preferred intraethnic lingua franca for Chinese, especially in the younger generation
c.1980–2000 recent Cantonese immigration	• English is medium of instruction in all schools (1987) • Speak Good English Movement launched to counter spread of Singlish/SgE (2000)		• English is widely used lingua franca; Singlish/SgE also gains mainstream currency • Cantonese used more than Mandarin in Cantonese homes

ah and *what* – have been documented in the literature for SgE since the early days of SgE scholarship, and in fact are the first particles in SgE to have been documented. *Lah* and *ah* were noted as early as the early 1970s in Killingley (1972), the first description of English in Malaya; *what* first appeared a few years later in Kwan-Terry (1978). *Lah* is also the only particle to figure in the other pioneering work of Tongue (1974), as well as Kwan-Terry (1978) and Platt and Weber (1980), with *ah* next appearing in Platt, Weber and Ho (1983). All three particles are often mentioned in the same breath, and are also regarded as more common than the others (e.g. Gupta 1992). In short, these early particles already figure in SgE in the 1970s. These three particles were noted by Platt, Weber and Ho (1983: 21) to appear (only) in the 'even more colloquial style' of speakers at the basilectal end of the SgE speech continuum. In contemporary SgE, however, they figure not only in the colloquial SgE of proficient native speakers but also in what would be considered more formal or H domains, appearing in recent years, for example, in newspaper articles and election speeches.

The other SgE particles, in contrast, only start making an appearance in scholarship from the late 1980s (e.g. Platt 1987; Platt and Ho 1989; Gupta 1992; and other later work). Again, these were claimed by Platt (1987) to occur more in ethnically Chinese basilectal or informal mesolectal SgE and not further up the lectal or formality scale. However, a decade later their use is found in the colloquial SgE of proficient native SgE speakers of all ethnicities; Gupta (1992: 38; 2006) also disputes Platt's observation. We may surmise, then, that the later particles only become part of SgE from about the mid-1980s.

Following on from this, we must consider the likelihood of a language being the source of a particle within the appropriate era – that is, when it appeared in SgE – by appealing to the sociohistorical background of Singapore. This is summarised in Table 5.2.

In the case of *lah*, recognised as being part of SgE from at least the early 1970s, the sociohistorical facts would appear to support either or both Hokkien and Bazaar Malay as its source, since they were both the main and long-standing lingue franche in the previous decades. The existence of numerous functions of SgE *lah* makes for similarities to be seen in the corresponding particle in both substrates, since Bazaar Malay and Hokkien both have *la*. This may on one hand be interpreted as a case of typological convergence, when prolonged and intensive contact between different languages with similar features – in this case, Bazaar Malay and Hokkien – results in hybrid linguistic features in the contact language – here SgE. On the other hand, on the basis of the earlier history of the region, when the southern Chinese immigrants were the majority and were also the ones speaking Bazaar Malay, and where numerous bilateral lexical borrowings are attested, the view is that Bazaar Malay *la* has its origins in Hokkien itself (Richards and Tay 1977: 154; Khin Khin Aye 2005). In this view, then, the source of *lah* could be seen to be of Hokkien origin, regardless of whether it actually enters SgE via Hokkien or Bazaar Malay, and it would then simultaneously be reinforced by its usage in the other language, in the recognised phenomenon of substrate reinforcement (see Siegel 2000).

At the same time, one should be reminded of one more possibility to be entertained: that Bazaar Malay varieties may in fact pre-date the presence of Hokkien in Southeast Asia. In cases such as this, where there has been such long and intimate contact between the substrates and likely convergence of traits, as pointed out by Ansaldo and Matthews (2004), it is not always possible to unmistakably tease out the exact origin. We are, after all, ultimately getting into the reconstruction of contact situations, which is a notoriously difficult task (see Renfrew, McMahon and Trask 2000).

Cantonese, while the language of the third largest dialect group, would still not be as widespread – in the sense of being used for inter-group communication – as Hokkien and Bazaar Malay were. As for Mandarin, in those decades it was still an H variety in Singapore, used in education and official functions. It would certainly not have had wide currency in other domains, and the absence of functional and social overlap between that and the more colloquial – and therefore L – SgE would not have supported the acquisition of features such as *la* from Mandarin, in contrast with Hokkien or Bazaar Malay (Richards and Tay 1977: 149 on Hokkien). In fact, it is worth underscoring that the recourse to Mandarin as a major substrate in the restructuring of SgE that some scholars adopt is strongly contested, as Mandarin would not have been a dominant language in the ecology during the early evolution of SgE.

The later set of SgE particles, which on the basis of linguistic similarity have been ascribed to Cantonese, emerged in the mid-1980s, and their appearance can be seen to coincide with the burgeoning of Cantonese popular culture in the same period. Such an increase in presence and prestige of Cantonese in this more recent history would explain its con-tribution of a large number of particles to SgE due to greater and more successful pressure for items to be transferred. This, in fact, resonates with Matras's (2000: 577) model. There is clear direction in categorial fusion, where the orientation target – that is, the one from which items are acquired – is the pragmatically dominant variety, where dominance can be interpreted in a number of ways – for example, a language that is culturally prestigious or economically powerful, or one that is dominant for a particular domain of linguistic interaction. In both these respects, one can recognise the identification of Cantonese as a target. First, it is a language which was culturally dominant in that period. Next, it is one in which the range and variety of tonal categories – with level and contour tones used in three registers – is one of its rich and significant features, and whose particles offer a spectrum of form and nuanced meaning – in other words, dominant in terms of pragmatic resources. It is not difficult, then, to understand the import of the subset of Cantonese particles wholesale with their tone as in Cantonese, and SgE speakers' ready acceptance and use of them.

5.2.3 Particles in other contact varieties

We see how the acquisition of particles is truly a widespread feature of contact-induced change, their being such a discourse-prominent feature. In the Asian context, this is not limited to the contact varieties of English illustrated in the previous section but occurs more broadly across the various languages in the contact ecologies. Cantonese particles have also evolved in Kuala Lumpur Malay, Hokkien and Teochew (Sarah Lee, personal communication April 2013), and in Singapore Mandarin. Chinese Singaporean students, TJ and JG, discussing a task in class in Mandarin have *lor* to indicate obviousness and *hor* to indicate acknowledgement or agreement with the preceding statement in example 5.15 (Silver and Bokhorst-Heng 2013). In example 5.16 (Woo, Goh and Wu 2006), the Chinese man delivering fake miniature items to be burned during a funeral[5] has the Cantonese-origin particle *mɛ55* to express surprise that the character Seng does not realise that the funeral items comprise all the luxury items he lists, since the family had, after all, ordered the 'elite package'.[6] (In these examples the particles are highlighted in bold.)

---

[5] As part of traditional Chinese funeral rites, fake money and miniature items, mostly copies of luxury objects – in this example, a chauffeur-driven Mercedes Benz, a maid, a laptop, a VCR – made of cardboard and paper, which are symbolic gifts for the deceased, are burned so that they follow the deceased into the afterlife.

[6] In example 5.15, data are as in the source, where no tones are provided for the Mandarin dialogue or the Cantonese particles; note that the Cantonese particles are represented as in older literature on SgE. In example 5.16, the data are transcribed from the film dialogue, with the tones for Mandarin omitted for simplicity, as they are irrelevant here; the Cantonese particles are transcribed phonetically, including their tone; the English gloss comes from the film's subtitles.

(5.15)

TJ: *Kan shen me?*
    'What are you looking at?'
JG: *Kan wo ma ma lor . . .*
    'Looking at my mother PRT . . .'
TJ: A girl is skating.
JG: Oh, *dui hor.*
    'Oh, correct PRT.'

(5.16)

Seng: *Na ge shenme che?*
    'And what kind of car is this?'
Man: Merc *la! Limian yeyou siji.*
    'A Mercedes. There's even a chauffeur inside.'
Seng: *Siji?*
    'Chauffeur?'
Man: Aw . . . *Hai you* maid, security guard, laptop, VCR . . . *yi da dui dongxi a21!*
    'Yeah . . . There's also a maid, security guard, laptop, VCR . . . a whole bunch of stuff!'

    Nimen bushi order elite packet *mɛ33?*
    'You ordered the elite package, right?'

Abbreviation: PRT: particle.

Crucially, we see that it is not only into the contact variety of English that particles from the substrates enter. Particles from some of the Sinitic languages – notably Cantonese – also show contact-induced transfer into most other languages with which they have had contact. Two factors promote this, which are worth noting. First, Cantonese particles are perhaps more salient than other particles, occurring as they do with full tone – compared to weak or neutral tone in Hokkien and Mandarin – and thus may be seen to be more dominant in the feature pool in that respect (Lim 2007, 2009a, 2009c). Next, the other languages do have particles in their grammar, and are thus primed to take on particles from other languages they come into contact with.

5.3 TONE

5.3.1 Tone in contact

Tone is another linguistic feature that is interesting for the study of language contact. Suprasegmental features, including tone, are susceptible to being acquired in contact situations (Curnow 2001), and tone is often acquired in a non-tonal language by borrowing or imitation due to the presence of tone in the broader linguistic environment (Gussenhoven 2004). A classic example is the acquisition of tone in Middle Korean in the tenth to sixteenth centuries due to the prestigious status of Chinese in society then (Ramsay 2001) – worthy of note is how this is related to dominance in the external ecology. Another thoroughly documented account of tone spreading through language contact is that of the Chamic languages. While the language of the seafaring forerunners of modern Chamic speakers was essentially disyllabic, non-tonal and non-registral when they first arrived on mainland Southeast Asia some two millennia ago, under the influence of typologically different languages a variety of different phonological systems developed. These included the fully tonal system of Tsat, as a result of contact with the Southern Min language Hainanese, once the speakers arrived on Hainan and became bilingual in Hainanese (Thurgood 1999). Hybrid prosodic systems can also develop: the Austronesian language Ma'ya is documented as having developed both contrastive stress and tone, a result of contact with tonal Papuan languages (Remijsen 2001).

Tone is acknowledged as an areal feature, occurring in genetically unrelated languages spoken by geographically contiguous speech communities, as in Africa and Southeast Asia (Nettle 1998; Svantesson 2001). Indeed, in the context of Asia, tone is a feature that cannot be ignored, salient as it is in many Asian languages. In East and Southeast Asia it is languages with complex, as opposed to simple, tone systems which dominate – all varieties of Chinese, as well as Vietnamese and Thai, have tone systems that include contour tones. In the mainland Southeast Asia linguistic area (phonemic) tone is one of the most well-known features to have undergone diffusion (Enfield 2005).

Contact languages that have emerged in other settings have for some time now been recognised as having tone, acquired from their tone-language substrates, mostly in contact situations involving European accent languages and African tone languages. One such example in which this has been clearly demonstrated is Saramaccan, an Atlantic Maroon creole spoken mostly in Suriname, generally classified as an English-based creole, though its lexicon shows substantial Portuguese influence, with Gbe and Kikongo as substrates. There is evidence for a split lexicon in Saramaccan, where the majority of its words are marked for pitch accent, with an important minority marked for true tone (Good 2004a, 2004b, 2006). Similarly, Papiamentu spoken in the Netherlands Antilles – with superstrates of Spanish, Portuguese and Dutch, and West African Kwa and Gbe languages as substrates – shows use of both contrastive stress and contrastive tonal features which operate independently from stress (Kouwenberg 2004; Rivera-Castillo and Pickering 2004; Remijsen and van Heuven 2005). Another example is Pichi (also known as Fernando Po Creole English), an Atlantic English-lexicon creole spoken on the island of Bioko, Equatorial Guinea. It is an offshoot of Krio from Sierra Leone and shares many characteristics with its West African sister language Aku from Gambia, as well as Nigerian, Cameroonian and Ghanaian Pidgin, and has also been documented as having a mixed prosodic system which employs both pitch-accent and tone (Yakpo 2009). Nigerian English (NigE) too has a mixed prosodic system that stands 'between' an intonation/stress language and a tone language (Gut 2005): its pitch inventory is described as reduced compared to British English, and the domain of pitch appears to be the word, with high pitch triggered by stress, thus resembling a pitch accent language.

Relatively little research along these lines has been conducted in the Asian realm, which is curious considering how salient tone is. In the rest of this section we give an account of work that does examine tone in the Asian contact variety of SgE/Singlish, which draws from Lim (2009a, 2011a, 2011b). Tone in contact situations is already an intriguing topic of study for what it entails, as outlined so far. Compounding the interest is the fact that SgE's tonal prosodic patterns are, in fact, distinct from other contact varieties which have developed tone, whether the substrates are African tone languages – as in the examples above – or a similar Sinitic language substrate – as in the case of HKE, which we will also examine as a counterpoint. What emerges is a demonstration of the founder effect in the ecology paradigm.

5.3.2 Tone in SgE and the founder principle

As with a number of ecologies in Asia, Sinitic languages are dominant in Singapore. In its colonial and early independence eras, in addition to Bazaar Malay which was the local and regional interethnic lingua franca, Hokkien was the intraethnic lingua franca amongst the Chinese communities, as well as a widely understood and spoken language by ethnic groups (see Section 5.2). Soon after independence, Mandarin was made one of the four official languages of the nation, and very swiftly members of the Chinese population shifted from their own vernaculars to Mandarin as the main language in the home. In addition, Cantonese – always a significant Sinitic language throughout Singapore's history, as it was one of the prominent Chinese languages amongst the early immigrants – saw a resurgence in the late 1980s to 1990s with the golden years of Cantonese cinema and Cantopop, as well as significant immigration from Hong Kong (see details in Lim 2010a). Clearly, tone languages have been in the majority and dominant in the ecology, and tone has been a salient aspect of the feature pool. It is not surprising to find that SgE exhibits (Sinitic-type) tone not only in its particles – as seen in Section 5.2 – but also at the level of the word and phrase, where syllables are realised with L-, M- or H-level tones, as illustrated in examples 5.17 (Ng 2008; Wee 2008) and 5.18 (Lim 2004).[7] At phrase level, as observed in Lim (2004: 42), a characteristic pattern in the intonation contour may be analysed as comprising sequences of sustained level steps or level tones, which step up or down to each other rather than glide more gradually from one pitch level to another.

(5.17)

'manage, 'teacher	33–55 / MH
in'tend, a'round	11–55 / LH
'origin, bi'lingual	11–33–55 / LM
o'riginal, se'curity	11–33–33–55 / LMMH
o'riginally	11–33–33–33–55 / LMMMH

(5.18)

I think happier	LHLLM

An initial assumption would almost automatically be that the tone observed in SgE originates in the Sinitic substrates, as opposed to the other substrates – notably Malay – which are not tone languages. A slightly more complex and intriguing situation emerges, however, when we dig a little deeper. In this endeavour, we shall set aside the particles, which – at least in the case of the later Cantonese set – are clearly of Sinitic origin, and turn to the tone patterns at word and phrase level.

If we examine the prosody of other contact languages whose ecologies include tone languages, a curious picture emerges. In investigations of the Englishes of Hong Kong and China, for example, which have ecologies in which Sinitic varieties are dominant, the influence of tone on the emergent contact English variety is clearly noted and, at least superficially, is comparable to the presence of tone in SgE; the phonological patterning, however, is distinct. In HKE, H tones are located on stressed syllables and L tones on unstressed ones, as illustrated in example 5.19 (Chen and Au 2004; Wee 2008); this contrasts with the pattern for word-level tone in SgE seen above, where H tones are located on the final syllable. Similarly, at phrase level, HKE would have a pattern involving a sequence of tones as in example 5.20 (Luke 2000, 2008), which is based

---

[7] The tones on each syllable in examples 5.17–5.20 are represented in pitch level numbers as well as in the phonological tradition where L = low tone, M = mid tone, and H = high tone – the latter as in the original sources.

on a basic LHL! template and subsequent computation (Luke 2008). However, again, as noted previously, SgE tends to prefer prominence on the phrase-final syllable such that the pitch is perceived as relatively high. Other instrumental investigations have shown no significant decrease in fundamental frequency in the phrase-final syllable compared to the initial syllable of the phrase-final word (Low 2000). And even in utterances involving emphatic and contrastive stress, speakers do not place prominence on the contrastive element but systematically locate pitch prominence utterance-finally (Lim 2004; Lim and Tan 2001). This pattern of locating H tones on what would be stressed or accented syllables at word or phrase level observed in HKE is a general pattern that has been documented in other contact varieties in which tone has evolved, such as NigE and learner varieties of English such as those in China. What is going on with SgE would thus seem to be an anomaly.

(5.19)

in'tend	11–55 / LH
'origin, 'photograph	55–11–11 / HLL
o'riginal	11–55–11–11 / LHLL

(5.20)

I saw the manager this morning LHHHHHHHL!

One approach to accounting for this apparent disparity is to examine the ecology for other languages that may be influencing the prosody of SgE. Languages that are or have been in widespread use in the ecology are the obvious candidates, one of which is clearly (Bazaar) Malay, the main interethnic lingua franca in Singapore from the earliest era until as recently as the 1970s. In research on other Malay/Indonesian varieties (e.g. see various chapters in Gensler and Gil forthcoming), findings concerning word stress are diverse. Nevertheless, a number of studies (e.g. Goedemans and van Zanten forthcoming) do point to prominence on the penultimate and/or final syllable, and at phrase level there is a general consensus that prominence is located phrase-finally (with acceptability increasing closer to the right edge of the phrase-final word). Bazaar Malay as spoken in the earlier era of Singapore's ecology has not had its intonation described, but recent work by Ng (2012) suggests frequent word-final rises or H tone, as well as the use of level tones.

If we consider external factors of the ecology, at first glance it may seem curious that Malay should have exerted this influence on SgE, for three reasons. First, the Malays as an ethnic group have comprised a minority of the population (no more than 15 per cent) since the second decade of the populating of Singapore under British colonial rule which started in the early 1800s; thus, numerically, and consequently socially, they have not been as dominant in Singapore's ecology. This is, of course, not to downplay the significant presence of the early Malay royalty, as well as numerous influential and wealthy Malays and Arabs, such as the late-nineteenth-century community leaders. Second, even if Bazaar Malay was the interethnic lingua franca, it was dominant only until around the 1970s, when English started assuming this role, especially in the new generations of native English speakers. Malay is no longer widely spoken by Singaporeans outside the Malay community, although in that community the language is still very vital, being the most frequently spoken home language in 91.5 per cent of Malay homes in 2000. What this implies is that when varieties of Malay were widely spoken in Singapore's ecology, English was not: it would have been in the repertoire of a very small minority of the population (more of this in a moment), and would have been acquired in education again by a minority – those in English-medium schools. English started becoming more widespread in the ecology at about the time when Bazaar Malay lost currency. The timing, as it were, for contact and transfer would have been a bit off. And finally, even if we assume that Malay did influence SgE through the first and second points – that is, in the earlier era when Bazaar Malay was a dominant language in the ecology – why would it be that features of this earlier Malay influence appear to be maintained in spite of more recent Sinitic dominance?

Quite a compelling answer can be found if we consider the founder principle in the ecology paradigm (Mufwene 2001), which suggests that the founder population in an ecology exerts a strong influence on features – an influence which persists in the emergent variety. A feasible reconstruction, presented in Lim (2014a), is thus as follows. Another community of peoples in Singapore who were also Malay speakers are the Peranakans, also known as Peranakan Chinese, Babas or Straits(-born) Chinese (see Ansaldo, Lim and Mufwene 2007 and Lim 2010b for accounts of the Peranakan community and their languages Baba Malay and Peranakan English (PerE)). Descendants of southern Chinese traders who settled in Southeast Asia and who intermarried with local Malay/Indonesian women, they comprised one of the earliest and largest groups of the influential class of Chinese capitalists in the region. By the time of European exploitation colonisation in the nineteenth century, they had accumulated much wealth and become a prestigious subgroup. They are well known in the creole world for their vernacular, Baba Malay, a restructured variety of Malay with Sinitic – in particular Min – influences.[8] Crucially, the Peranakans were one of the earliest groups in Singapore to have held a high regard for English-medium education, and who had the position and the means to educate their children in English-medium schools, with several prominent Babas even pursuing higher education in Britain. Being one of the few and earliest communities in Singapore to have English in their repertoire further strengthened their prominent socioeconomic position vis-à-vis other local communities in relation to the British, and their knowledge of Malay and local ways allowed them to assume a significant role as intermediaries.

What of the linguistic features? Just as in most other Malay varieties, Baba Malay too has been documented as having phrase-final prominence, in the form of an utterance-final rise-fall, often manifested as step-up progressions across the final syllables of the utterance (Wee 2000). And while the Peranakans' distinctive variety of English, PerE – which the community would eventually shift to in the mid–late twentieth century – has been shown to comprise acrolectal features tending towards British English, it also comprises vernacular features reflecting contact with Baba Malay, including word- and utterance-final prominence in the form of pitch peak on the final syllable (Lim 2010b).

In short, in the Peranakans we find a plausible explanation for the prosodic patterns observed in SgE. In their Baba Malay vernacular lies the word-/phrase-final prominence that developed in PerE as a result of contact in their multilingual repertoire. While numerically more of the Singapore population might have been using Bazaar Malay, the Peranakans – though a small minority – can be considered dominant in the external ecology due to their political, economic and social status. As early English adopters, crucially during the British colonial period, theirs would have been the early features influencing the emerging variety of SgE, when the majority of the population would at that point hardly have been using English in any sustained, systematic way.

The examination of tone in the above contact situation is important on at least two counts. First, the presence of tone – or the evolution of a tone-language prosody – is perfectly possible in a contact variety, if the feature pool of its ecology allows for it; such mixed prosodic systems have been documented in a number of other creoles, though they have been far less acknowledged in varieties considered to be New Englishes.

---

[8] A detailed discussion of the distinction between Baba Malay and Bazaar Malay is beyond the scope of this chapter. For the purposes of this account, suffice it to say that Baba Malay can be considered a more focused variety than Bazaar Malay, as it is the linguistic variety of a particular cultural group (see Lim 1988 and Ansaldo 2009a for good discussions of this issue).

In other words, in an ecology where tone is an unmarked or dominant feature, then tonal features can indeed spread into a contact language. Second, even when the feature of tone may be ascribed to the tone language substrates, the actual realisation in terms of prosodic patterns – for instance, in the case of SgE, the location of the H tone at word or phrase level – can be influenced by the prosody of a non-tone language. In the case of SgE, this is (Baba) Malay, via PerE. What is also significant is that this is the language of a population – the Peranakans – recognised as having been an earlier or founder population in the ecology, which therefore exerts a significant influence on the structure of the emergent contact language.

5.4   REFLECTIONS ON THE SIGNIFICANCE OF ECOLOGY

In the study of languages in contact, we hope to have demonstrated in this chapter, the significance of ecology – both internal (e.g. the typology of substrates) and external (e.g. historical and social aspects) – needs more explicit attention for a more enlightened appreciation of the evolution of contact varieties. This is particularly the case for the identification of sources or substrate influence as a result of their contact dynamics. The ecology paradigm additionally affords a dynamic approach – as compared to classification, which is static – which can nonetheless be captured in a systematic manner through periodisation and the recognition of different eras. In a dynamic ecology, the language(s) which are dominant can vary in different eras as a result of changing population patterns, language policies and economic factors, to name just a few properties of the external ecology. Consequently, so do aspects of the internal ecology: the features in the feature pool can change in number and kind, depending on the typological make-up of the language(s) involved, as can their likelihood of selection, which also relates to external aspects such as the prestige of the speakers of a particular language.

To recognise the significance of ecology is then to recognise that anything is possible for the typology of the emergent contact variety, but this needs clarification on at least three counts. First, this is not a cavalier or anarchic free-for-all, but the recognition of an infinite potential within the possibilities that the typologies of the substrates afford. For instance, some scholars still baulk at the idea of English becoming a tone language, especially those less acquainted with Asian and African contexts and varieties. However, as demonstrated in this chapter, it is absolutely possible for contact varieties of English to evolve in this way, if tone is present in the feature pool and, better yet, a salient feature in their ecologies, as in the cases of NigE, SgE and HKE, and as with other creoles mentioned previously which have developed mixed prosodic systems. Second, this also does not mean resorting to the cafeteria principle (Bickerton 1981, after Dillard 1970), mentioned in Chapter 3, involving the ad hoc selection by a language of features from various sources like items chosen for lunch at a cafeteria. Scholars such as Roberts (2004) and Siegel (2008a), through careful and thorough linguistic and sociohistorical investigation, have shown how several aspects of the grammar of Hawai'i Creole have been modelled on features of different substrate languages. They have also shown, however, that this does not happen without certain principles and constraints: language transfer in second language use and substrate reinforcement of diffused features are two mechanisms that account for the features of one language ending up in another. Arends (1989), working on Sranan, also demonstrates the value of detailed sociohistorical investigation in the study of contact features. Third, ecology needs to be considered thoughtfully in ascribing influence to languages. Several scholars working on SgE, for example, have assumed Mandarin as a substrate, a practice that is largely refuted by others. While it cannot be denied that Mandarin is dominant in the ecology now, this would really be a much more recent source, relevant only from about the late 1970s or even 1980s, after post-independence language policies ascribed it the position of one of the four official languages and one of the mother tongues to be used in education, and aggressively promoted it via – inter alia – the Speak Mandarin Campaign. On the other hand, it is those languages that were present and dominant in an earlier period of SgE's evolution that have been shown to be more significant in many aspects: for example, SgE's reduplication and triplication patterns are convincingly shown to derive from Hokkien and Malay reduplication and Hokkien triplication (Ansaldo 2004).

A recognition of ecology also means a recognition that the similarity in typologies of substrates can account for otherwise unsupported observations of features that are found in varieties separated by categorisation (e.g. creoles versus New Englishes; 'Outer Circle' versus 'Expanding Circle' Englishes) or geography (e.g. Asian versus African Englishes). For example, serial verb constructions with directional function, derived from Cantonese, are found in both HKE and Hawai'i Creole English (HCE), and can be traced in the latter to Cantonese immigration to Hawai'i in the nineteenth century (Siegel 2000; Yip and Matthews 2007). Conversely, but for the same reason, one cannot expect across-the-board similarity within any one category. There may be common languages in the feature pool, but any difference can result in a different typological make-up of the emergent English. SgE and HKE, for instance, both have Cantonese and more recently Mandarin in common in their ecologies, but Singapore also has Hokkien as a dominant substrate, particularly in the earlier era when SgE was first evolving. While questions of the form 'X or not' are found in SgE grammar, they do not occur in HKE – this may be explained by the fact that 'X or not' questions are predominant in Southern Min varieties such as Hokkien and Teochew but are limited in Mandarin and Hong Kong Cantonese (Yip and Matthews 2007). Further, external ecology must be equally recognised. While consonant cluster simplification is noted in both SgE and NigE – a result of the substrate languages in their ecologies having simple codas – it is far more frequent in the former, most likely due to the attitudes of the communities towards a more endonormative – locally established – as opposed to a more exonormative standard in the latter (Gut 2007).

Time in the ecology paradigm is also critical. The population make-up in an ecology – and thus the composition and relative dominance of features in the feature pool – varies over different eras. By the founder principle (Mufwene 2001), however, features of the founder variety often had selective advantage as, amongst other things, it would be more cost-effective to speak the existing local vernacular rather than try to modify or replace it, which causes the founder population's features to become increasingly entrenched within the language community. Mufwene (2001) provides much compelling evidence for the founder principle in how many creoles' structural features are attested in the speech of the founder population. In this chapter we saw how the Peranakans may well be considered the founder population in the evolution of SgE.

Recognising the varying dominance of languages in an ecology is also particularly relevant in contexts where the linguistic ecology changes swiftly and/or frequently, as a result of factors such as political upheaval, migration patterns and language policies. Singapore is a case in point, with its fast-changing dynamics due to new immigration and language policies instituted in the twenty-first century (see e.g. Lim 2010a and Chapter 7); this could lead to a further restructuring of SgE as a result of new dominant languages in a global ecology.

DISCUSSION POINTS

1. Critics of an ecological approach may point out that ecology is just another term for 'social context' that adds little to our current understanding of contact phenomena. Based on the chapter, try

to point out where an ecological approach actually makes new theoretical and empirical contributions.

2. Conduct a brief research on the dimension of particles in language contact. What are the theories of language use that best explain phenomena such as the function of particles in contact described in this chapter?

3. Tone is given as one of the three complex features of language within McWhorter's Creole Prototype framework: according to this view, tone should not be found in young or new languages. Evaluate this claim in the light of the ecological perspective outlined in this chapter.

FURTHER READING

For a full account of the ecology paradigm, see Mufwene (2001, 2008). For a detailed account of the development of particles in SgE as a consequence of contact, see Lim (2007). For work on the evolution of tone in various contact languages, see Thurgood (1999), Remijsen (2001), Good (2004a, 2004b, 2006), Kouwenberg (2004), Rivera-Castillo and Pickering (2004), Gut (2005), Remijsen and van Heuven (2005), Lim (2009a) and Yakpo (2009).

6 Contact and shift

6.1 INTRODUCTION

There are good reasons to include the field of language shift and endangerment in a study of languages in contact. For one thing, language shift and language endangerment are themselves consequences of contact. Language shift, which is the replacement of one language by another as a primary means of communication and socialisation within a community, is a common response of communities in the face of competition from a regionally and socially more powerful language. In more extreme cases, language shift can lead to language endangerment and – eventually – obsolescence, when a language is no longer used by any community in the world. Second, in the course of shift and endangerment, outcomes of contact can still be observed, which are almost always illuminating for understanding the factors at play in such contact situations.

Scholars usually date the beginnings of formal identification and study of language maintenance and shift to Joshua Fishman's (1964) work. Since then, and especially in the last two decades, this field of scholarship – particularly for endangered languages – has seen immense growth. A few significant funding bodies have been supporting a large number of projects documenting endangered languages, resulting not only in the documentation of many hitherto unknown languages but also in phenomenal growth in the field in scholarship, methodology, technical expertise and equipment, as well as attention to issues of ethics.

In the first sections of this chapter, we provide an overview of the essential points and issues to be aware of when engaging with this topic; for full and comprehensive coverage readers are pointed to the volumes mentioned in the list of further reading. We then look in greater detail at the present situation of the Malays of Sri Lanka, an interesting case study for the various sociolinguistic factors that impacted on their choices, leading to situations of maintenance, shift and endangerment. We also return to the issue of identity alignment, addressed in Chapter 4, when a community is faced with choosing to keep or discard languages.

Numerous causes of language shift and endangerment have been identified in research in the past decades (e.g. see Crystal 2000; Nettle and Romaine 2000; Grenoble 2011; synthesised in Austin and Sallabank 2011a: 5–6, elaborated on below), and these factors often overlap or occur together. What is particularly worth noting is that – apart from the factor comprising natural catastrophes, famine and disease – for the most part the causes have to do with communities, and thus their languages, coming into contact with each other, in relationships of unequal power. The first factor involves natural catastrophes, famine and disease. The Indian Ocean tsunami, created by a massive earthquake on Boxing Day 2004, for example, caused devastation in fourteen coastal nations and killed almost 300,000 people around the Indian Ocean region. The Nicobar and Andaman Islands, which lie north of Sumatra and closest to the epicentre of the earthquake, were struck by tsunami waves within thirty minutes of the earthquake. The Nicobarese – the most numerous of the populations, numbering some 20,000, who live on all twelve inhabited islands of the archipelago – was the only indigenous group to have suffered extensive deaths with all twelve villages on the island of Car Nicobar destroyed. One fifth of the population of the Nicobar Islands were estimated to be dead or missing; losses in such small populations hold implications for their languages, and the Nicobarese languages are already considered endangered.

The second factor includes war, conflict and genocide. An oft-cited example of genocide is that committed by colonists in Tasmania (then Van Diemen's Land) over the course of five decades beginning in 1803, when it was claimed as a penal colony for criminal offenders from Great Britain and Australia. Disputes between the settler convicts and the indigenous nomadic hunter-gatherer Tasmanians over foodstuff (kangaroo), land rights (Tasmanians crossed into territory that settlers claimed ad hoc) and women (Tasmanian women were kidnapped for partners) led to an escalation of conflict resulting in the Black War in 1828. This extermination was so extreme that the original estimated population of 4,000 to 10,000 Tasmanians was reduced to just a few hundred. In 1835 some two hundred Tasmanians were resettled on Flinder's Island – effectively a prison camp with such poor conditions that three quarters died before repatriation – and the last full-blooded Tasmanian died in 1876. The consequence of all this is that little remains of the Tasmanian language in Australia other than place names and word lists.

The third factor comprises overt repression, often in the name of national unity or assimilation, which includes forced resettlement. This has taken place in many countries around the world, and has affected languages such as Welsh, Kurdish and Native American languages. For example, in 1932 following an uprising against the government over perceived political abuses and broad social inequality between landowners and peasants, the El Salvador military murdered between 10,000 to 40,000 peasants and other civilians (this became known as 'La Matanza', 'the massacre'). Many were indigenous people, who for the most part were descendants of the Pipils, a migrant Nahua-speaking group from central Mexico, and the Lenca. While in the late nineteenth century there was already abandonment of indigenous language, culture and other ethnic markers, the fear in the aftermath of La Matanza, combined with state policies marginalising indigenous peoples, deterred many from wearing traditional clothing or practising their customs and culture, and led to their adoption of the mainstream Spanish language and Catholic religion.

The final factor relates to cultural, political and economic dominance. Dominance along these various dimensions within a nation often disenfranchises languages like Ainu in Japan, and is found with many other languages in other territories. This category, which is the most common, comprises five factors (see also Grenoble 2011; Harbert 2011).

  i. Economic: Rural poverty leading to migration to urban centres and abroad, as well as rapid urbanisation of cities, position rural varieties alongside urban and global ones. If the local economy improves, tourism often brings speakers of majority languages.

 ii. Cultural: The majority community tends to dominate culturally, most commonly when education and literature are transmitted through the majority or state language only, and the indigenous language and culture tends to become downgraded into folklore and folk culture. This leads to social and cultural dislocation for the minority community.

iii. Political: Education policies very often ignore or exclude local languages, and these languages lack recognition or political representation. In more extreme scenarios, there may even be bans on their use in public life.

 iv. Historical: Colonisation and boundary disputes often result in the rise of one group and their language variety to political and cultural dominance.

  v. Attitudinal: Minority languages usually become associated with poverty, illiteracy and hardship, while the dominant language is associated with progress, success and escape.

6.2 LANGUAGE SHIFT

6.2.1 Pioneering language shift ▬▬▬▬▬▬▬▬▬▬▬▬▬▬

In approaching the topic of language shift, the now classic study conducted by Susan Gal (1979) in Oberwart, a town in eastern Austria near the border with Hungary, needs first mention for both its findings and its methodology. Gal documents the process of language shift from Hungarian to German as the town transformed from a peasant agricultural village, in which the majority of inhabitants were Hungarian speakers who were also bilingual in German, to a more ethnically diverse town where educated upper-class monolingual Germans had become the majority. Gal's study is significant, not just for being one of the earliest major works on shift, but for its in-depth focus on the detailed processes by which shift occurs: the changes in the linguistic habits of individuals and groups of speakers, and the motivations for these. As Gal argues compellingly at the outset of her book (1979: 3):

> What is of interest to know is not whether industrialisation, for
> instance, is correlated with language shift, but rather: By what
> intervening processes does industrialisation, or any other social
> change, effect changes in the uses to which speakers put their
> languages in everyday interactions? How does the social change affect
> the communicative economy of the group? How does it change the
> evaluations of languages and the social statuses and meanings
> associated with them? How does it affect the communicative strategies
> of speakers so that individuals are motivated to change their choice of
> language in different contexts of social interaction – to reallocate their
> linguistic resources radically so that eventually they abandon one of
> their languages altogether?

As is now well known and also often the pattern in many communities undergoing shift, the choice between Hungarian and German in the community, as Gal found, was first and foremost associated with a speaker's age: older speakers used Hungarian across a wider range of contexts than younger speakers. Then, for any speaker, the most important factor influencing their choice of language was their interlocutor.

Especially striking about Gal's study is that her results are represented in an implication scale, as in Table 6.1, where the further right of the table one goes, the more frequently German is used. Gal argues that the ordering of the interlocutors corresponds to an underlying dimension which she refers to as 'peasant' ←→ 'urban'/'Austrian'; in other words, the interlocutors towards the right of the table are perceived as more 'urban' or 'Austrian' than those to the left. Because the left-to-right order

Table 6.1 *The choice of Hungarian (H) or German (G) by women speakers in Oberwart (adapted from Gal 1979: 102, here shading added)*

Number of speaker	Age of speaker	Interlocutors												
		1	2	3	4	5	6	7	8	9	10	11	12	13
1	14	H	G		G	G	G	G	G				–	
2	14	H	GH		G	G	G	G	G				–	
3	25	H	GH	GH	G		G	G	G	G	G	G	–	
4	15	H	GH		GH	GH	G	G	G				–	
5	13	H	GH		GH	–	G	GH					–	
6	13	H	H		GH	–	G	G	G				–	
7	27	–	H		GH	–	G	G	–			G	–	
8	3	–	H		GH	–	GH		–				–	
9	4	–	H		GH	–	GH	GH	–				–	
10	17	H	H		GH	–	–	GH	–	–			–	
11	39		H		GH	–	–	GH	G	G	G	–	–	
12	52	H	H	–	GH	–	GH	–	–	GH	G	G	–	G
13	23	–	H	GH	GH	–	–	GH	G		GH	G	–	
14	22	H	H		H	GH	GH	GH	–			G	–	
15	33	H	H	H	H	–	GH	–	–	H	GH	G	G	
16	35	H			H	–	GH	GH	–	GH	GH	G	–	
17	40	H			H	–	GH		–	GH	GH	G	–	
18	42	H			H	–	GH	GH	–	GH	GH	G	–	
19	43	H			H	–		–	–	GH	GH	G	–	
20	35	H	H		H	–	H	GH	H	H	GH	–	–	
21	40	H		H	GH	–	H	GH	H	H	G	–	–	
22	40	H		–	H	–	H	–	H	H	GH	–	G	
23	50	H			H	–	H	H	GH		G	–	–	G
24	61	–	H		–		H	GH	–	GH	GH	–	–	G
25	54	H	H	H	H	H	H	–	H	GH	GH	–	–	
26	55	H			H	–	H	H	–	H	GH	–	–	GH
27	61	H			–		H	H	–	H	GH	–	–	
28	59	H	H	H	H	H	H	H	H	GH	H	–		GH
29	50	H			H	H	H	H	–	–	H	GH	–	
30	50	H		H	H	–	H	H	–	H	H	GH	–	–
31	60	H		H	H	–	H	H	–	H	H	GH	GH	–
32	60	H			–		H	H	–	H	H	GH	–	GH
33	63	H			–		H	H	H	H	H	H	–	GH
34	64	H			–		H	–	–	H	H	H	–	GH
35	66	H			–		H	H	–		H	–		GH
36	68	H				H	–	–	H	H	H	H	–	H
37	71	H			–		H		H		H	H	–	

Interlocutors: 1 God; 2 grandparents and their generation; 3 black-market clients; 4 parents and their generation; 5 Calvinist minister; 6 age-mate pals, neighbours; 7 brothers and sisters; 8 salespeople; 9 spouse; 10 children and their generation; 11 non-relatives aged under twenty; 12 government officials; 13 grandchildren and their generation.
Empty cells = no data, not applicable; dash = not enough data

of the interlocutors in the top row of Table 6.1 was determined by an attempt to make the scale as perfect as possible, it is indeed interesting to observe just what order transpires. First, an unsurprising finding, as mentioned above, is that older-generation family, relatives and friends are more likely to be addressed in Hungarian and younger ones in German. What is striking – as pointed out by Fasold (1984: 199), who also provides an instructive account of Gal's methods and analysis – is that 'black-market clients' are the most likely people to be addressed in Hungarian, weighing in only after God and the grandparents' generation, and before parents. This 'black-market' activity actually simply refers to the community's traditional practice of mutual exchange of services – a Hungarian-speaking carpenter doing some work for a neighbour that legally can only be done by a licensed skilled contractor, for instance – in the face of the strict Austrian regulations for the licensing of skilled labour. Because this activity represents the maintenance of traditional peasant values, requires a high degree of mutual trust and is in defiance of 'Austrian' law, it is understandable that the community language is what is used most.

In short, the two languages have assumed different symbolic values, with Hungarian associated with 'the old ways of life, the old forms of prestige of the peasant community' and German symbolising the higher status of the worker and the 'prestige and money that can be acquired by wage work', and thus modernity and economic success (Gal 1979: 106).

6.2.2 Ethnolinguistic vitality

Before we look at several other instances of language shift, an examination of ethnolinguistic vitality is in order – a construct widely turned to as an explanatory model when examining the factors for shift in a community. A concept arising from work on the social psychology of language, notably by Howard Giles and colleagues (1977), ethnolinguistic vitality is defined as 'that which makes a group likely to behave as a distinctive and active collective entity in intergroup situations' (Giles, Bourhis and Taylor 1977: 306). It proposes that groups' strengths and weaknesses may be assessed 'objectively' as well as 'subjectively' (Bourhis, Giles and Rosenthal 1981), on a number of political, social and demographic – as well as attitudinal – dimensions to provide a rough overall classification of ethnolinguistic groups as having low, medium or high vitality (see Figure 6.1).

Objective ethnolinguistic vitality is evaluated along three clusters of factors: the status either of a variety or of the speakers of that variety in different contexts; the demographics of the group identified and

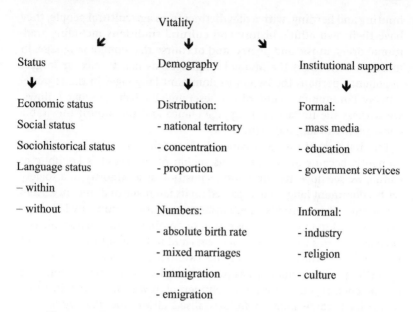

Figure 6.1 Factors contributing to ethnolinguistic vitality (Giles, Bourhis and Taylor 1977)

identifying with that variety; and institutional measures supporting or recognising a variety, both formal and informal. It was argued that the more vitality an ethnolinguistic group has the more likely it would be to survive as a distinctive linguistic collectivity in intergroup settings. A high vitality is then a good indicator of whether or not that particular language will continue to be spoken in successive generations, or whether speakers are likely to shift to another language. Conversely, groups that have little or no group vitality were expected to assimilate linguistically or to cease to exist as distinctive groups.

6.2.3 Shift in Asian contexts

To pick up from Gal's Oberwart community, a similar pattern is observed with the Mongols of Inner Mongolia in recent times, whose situation exemplifies many of the textbook factors that lead to shift (Wu 2008). The Mongols, who trace their origins to Mongol tribes in the twelfth century and the Great Mongol Empire of the thirteenth century, were expelled to the north or south of the Great Desert in the time of the Ming Dynasty after the fourteenth century, the latter forming Inner Mongolia. Known as the 'horse-back tribe', the Mongols of Inner Mongolia clearly have a distinct culture: living a nomadic pastoral life involving hunting and herding, with a diet distinct from agricultural people, they have their own ethnic history and cultural traditions including traditional dress, music and poetry, and of course the Mongol language. In more modern times the Mongol language has had to face its largest opponents, perhaps the two most dominant languages in the region – namely Putonghua (standard Chinese) and English. In what follows, we witness the impact on language choice and the almost inevitable consequence of language shift.

The first part of the story concerns Putonghua: in 1947, when Inner Mongolia became an autonomous region of the People's Republic of China, we see how the population's position as a minority in a society with a dominant language impacted on its language maintenance. As in numerous other contexts where industrialisation in minority-language areas has led to massive in-migration of dominant-language speakers – such as in Wales with English speakers and in the Basque Autonomous Region in the third quarter of the twentieth century with Castilian Spanish speakers, making Basque a minority in its own region – so it happened in Inner Mongolia. Numerous towns and cities in Inner Mongolia became modern industrialised cities, and the region saw substantial Han Chinese immigration from other parts of China, for industry and settlement in this newly developing area. Not only did the Mongols exchange their traditional nomadic pastoral economy for Chinese farming culture; more significantly, many started migrating to urban regions in search of occupational and economic opportunities in industrialising China. With in-migration of Han Chinese into Inner Mongolia and internal migration of Mongols to urban centres, demographic factors changed significantly. Younger-generation Mongols have grown up in a society dominated by Han Chinese and their language, Putonghua. Increased contact between Mongols and Han Chinese has also led to substantially greater numbers of mixed marriages: 38 per cent of Mongols are married to Han Chinese. In terms of institutional support, Putonghua clearly dominates. In education, before the Cultural Revolution in 1965, the Mongols had their own Mongol education system. At present, while there is support for minority languages, there is clear encouragement of Putonghua and dominant Han Chinese culture, with Putonghua (and English, which entered the picture in particular with globalisation and education reform in China in 1949) compulsory from primary school and necessary for the college entrance exam. In addition, textbooks have little by way of information on Mongol history, culture and language. In the media, there is only one radio channel and one television channel in Mongolian at the provincial level. While young Mongols still feel strongly about speaking and learning their mother tongue in the home and school domains, they nonetheless hold more positive attitudes towards the two dominant languages, as well as Mongolian–Putonghua bilingualism for instrumental and integrative motivations, such as job opportunities and cultural integration (Wu 2008).

The effect of the appearance of these two major languages in the ecology of Inner Mongolia on the language choices of the Mongols is clear, based on a survey of language use by university undergraduates at the Inner Mongolia Normal University (Wu 2008; Lim, Karregat and Wu 2009). There is a significant language shift from Mongol to Putonghua. The use of Putonghua by young Mongols with their parents in the home domain is as much as 25 per cent, compared to 10 per cent in their parents' generation, while in the media domain usage by young Mongols is 75 per cent, compared to 25 per cent in the parents' generation. There is also a significant increase in English: usage is 100 per cent in school and 25 per cent in the media, compared to not at all in their parents' generation. Notably, a bilingual mixed code of Mongolian–Putonghua is the increasingly frequent code amongst the younger generation. The various demographic, institutional, status and attitudinal factors outlined above clearly impact on language choice and consequently language shift within the Mongol community of Inner Mongolia.

But we do not need to venture far to look at rural communities or communities which have seen dramatic border changes to find shift happening. This is a story that repeats itself in numerous minority communities around the world. It is a phenomenon on the rise, in both rural and urban contexts, due to the spread and penetration of global languages. In Asia, for instance, small communities in urban areas in nation states such as Singapore and Malaysia with non-inclusive language policies see shift occurring before their very eyes, in a matter of a generation or two.

Malaysia's population comprises some 61 per cent Malays and Malay is enforced as the national language, with English as the second most important language. Here, minority groups such as the Sindhi and Punjabi Sikh communities show clear shift away from their ethnic languages – Sindhi and Punjabi respectively – both in the home and outside, to either English or a mixed code consisting of three languages, English, Malay and the ancestral language (David 2001; David, Naji and Kaur 2003). This pattern is particularly strong in the younger generation, who admit to having low proficiency in the ethnic language. Factors such as the minority community's members' awareness of their minority status in a multilingual setting and level of education are found to be factors affecting choice and shift. As noted by the researchers, 'education

Table 6.2 *Patterns of language choice within and across generations (adapted from Li, Saravanan and Ng 1997: 374, here shading added)*

	Grandparents		Interlocutor Parents		Children	
Speaker	Languages spoken	% of users	Languages spoken	% of users	Languages spoken	% of users
Grandparents (2 speakers)	T	100	T	100	T	100
Parents (26 speakers)	T	100	T	46	TM	31
			TM	26	T	26
			TME	8	M	19
			H	8	TME	8
			E	8	ME	8
			M	4	E	8
Children (44 speakers)	T	85	TM	27	TME	26
			T	23	ME	23
			M	16	E	21
			ME	11	T	9
			H	7	TE	7
	H	6	HM	7	HM	7
	ME	6	E	7	HME	5
	TM	3	TME	2	HM	2

E: English; H: Hokkien; M: Mandarin; T: Teochew

for this rapidly upwardly mobile community appears to have come with a price, the loss of their ethnic language' (David, Naji and Kaur 2003: 23).

In Singapore, the Teochew Chinese community – the second largest Chinese group in Singapore – has, since the late 1970s, seen significant language shift to the officially recognised national languages. As documented by Li, Saravanan and Ng (1997), in the Teochew community as a whole there is still a certain amount of maintenance of the vernacular, with some 40 per cent reporting their preferred language(s) at home being Teochew or Teochew and Mandarin. However, an examination of the language choice patterns across the different generations tells a different story: while the grandparents' generation uses Teochew with interlocutors from the children's and grandchildren's generations, the shift to significantly less Teochew is apparent in the younger generations (see Table 6.2). Mandarin, in particular mixed with

Teochew, already makes inroads in the parents' generation, and Mandarin and English are dominant in the children's generation, especially when interlocutors are from the parents' and children's generations. This pattern of shift from the other Chinese languages to officially sanctioned Mandarin is also noted in the other Chinese groups (Lim 2010a).

It is illuminating to examine the key factors which contributed to the language shift process in the Teochew community in Singapore, as identified by Li, Saravanan and Ng (1997: 381–2), whose analysis is based on the ethnolinguistic vitality of the community, grouped under four categories – institutional, status, subcultural and sociocultural. Institutional factors include:

i. government policies, such as the demolition of ethnic enclaves through the physical integration of all the ethnic groups in public housing, as well as the government's 'Speak Mandarin Campaign' to promote the use of Mandarin to unify the otherwise fragmented Chinese community, and the promotion of English as the language of wider communication;

ii. mass media support, such as newspapers, television, radio and other communication networks being heavily dominated by the official languages, particularly English;

iii. clan associations, involving the reorientation of roles and activities of the clan associations leading to the promotion of pan-Chinese culture, and the closure of 'dialect' schools and establishment of 'cultural classes' in Mandarin.

Status factors include:

i. sociohistorical and socioeconomic status, viz. the weak economic power and numerical strength of the Teochews, relative to other Chinese groups in Singapore, and the perception that their traditions are more backward;

ii. language status, where theirs is a stigmatised language perceived as having no economic or instrumental value, thus having low prestige and status.

Subcultural factors include:

i. age and generational differences, involving Teochew not being transmitted as the main language to children, and an increasing number of younger speakers shifting to Mandarin and English;

ii. educational level, with better-educated younger generations speaking the national languages and becoming Mandarin–English bilinguals;

   iii. socioeconomic status, with relatively low-income families aspiring
        to speak Mandarin and English instead of Teochew.

Sociocultural factors include:

   i. attitudes, specifically a pragmatic attitude towards the instrumen-
      tal value of English and Mandarin, resulting in the lack of Teochew
      transmission, as well as the separation of language and ethnic
      identity, with Mandarin replacing Teochew as the language for a
      more pan-Chinese identity.

It is clear from this how external factors of the ecology impact on language choice in such a situation of contact. Similar situations abound
in other environments, particularly urban ones, such as with the Hakka,
Hokkien and other Chinese communities in Hong Kong (Lim 2013–2015),
and with urban Taiwanese in Taiwan (Sandel, Chao and Liang 2006).

6.3 LANGUAGE ENDANGERMENT

As is now very well known, the worst-case scenario for the state of languages reads along the following lines: there are some 7,105 known
living languages in the world (as listed in *Ethnologue*, edited by Lewis,
Simons and Fennig 2013). At least half of them, if not 90 per cent of
them, will not exist within the next fifty to a hundred years. Even
though languages have been lost in previous centuries, the demise is
now happening at an unprecedented rate – Table 6.3 shows endangerment in all continents of the world and Table 6.4 provides figures for
Southeast Asia. While there are inconsistencies and limitations in the
various data sets (as critiqued in Bradley 2011: 68), the overall picture is
clear and grim: language endangerment is a major issue in every part
of the world.

The crucial question is, of course, the 'so what?' question. Why should
we worry, why should we care, why should we invest all our energy –
not to mention substantial funds – into some small language no longer
being spoken? After all, there are many other languages that are thriv-
ing in the world, and there are many other perhaps more primary and
pressing issues such as poverty and hunger, universal primary education, maternal health, HIV/AIDS, malaria and other diseases, and challenges of environmental sustainability, as identified, for example, in the
United Nations Millennium Development Goals (United Nations 2013b).

For many linguists, perhaps the central issue is the value of such
languages for linguistic science. While some scholars would have us

Table 6.3 *Degrees of endangerment by continent (adapted from Bradley 2011: 68, with totals corrected)*

	Unsafe	Definitively endangered	Severely endangered	Critically endangered	Extinct
North America	14 / 55	5 / 47	11 / 44	32 / 40	10 / 124
Latin America	82 / 171	11 / 164	46 / 140	130 / 53	36 / 67
Eurasia	45 / –	56 / 93	63 / 43	13 / 28	– / 10
Middle East	15 / –	0 / 3	0 / 3	0 / 2	1 / 0
South Asia	– / 53	– / 150	– / 82	– / 28	– / 1
E/SE Asia	23 / 36	63 / 82	40 / 30	19 / 13	– / 10
Africa	43 / 1	131 / 88	14 / 23	40 / 29	41 / 23
Australia	– / 16	– / 26	– / 30	– / 48	– / 166
Oceania	128 / 121	110 / 106	44 / 40	43 / 44	1 / 55
Total	350 / 453	376 / 759	218 / 435	277 / 285	89 / 456

Note: The numbers to the left of the slash are from chapters in Brenzinger (2007), and those to the right of the slash are from chapters in Moseley (2007). Dashes indicate absence of data, not zero. Eurasia includes Europe plus the nations of the former USSR. Oceania includes insular Southeast Asia, Papua New Guinea and the islands of the Pacific. These totals do not include pidgins which become endangered rather than becoming creolised; they are listed for some areas, but not all.

Table 6.4 *Degrees of endangerment by countries, mainland Southeast Asia (adapted from Bradley 2011: 69, here listed in descending order of numbers reported, and with total added)*

	Unsafe	Definitively endangered	Severely endangered	Critically endangered	Extinct
Laos	4 / 3	21 / 25	5 / 2	0 / 1	0 / 0
Vietnam	6 / 6	10 / 17	7 / 3	0 / 3	0 / 0
Thailand	0 / 0	10 / 8	9 / 7	3 / 5	0 / 1
Myanmar	1 / 2	4 / 8	4 / 5	5 / 0	0 / 4
West Malaysia	0 / 1	4 / 7	10 / 4	0 / 1	0 / 1
Cambodia	1 / 1	1 / 3	4 / 4	1 / 0	0 / 0
Total	12 / 13	50 / 68	39 / 25	9 / 10	0 / 6

Note: The numbers to the left of the slash are from chapters in Brenzinger (2007), and those to the right of the slash are from chapters in Moseley (2007).

believe that it is possible to convey any conceptual meaning in any language, most scholars recognise the myriad ways human beings express themselves. For example, the now extinct Ubykh, a language of the northwest Caucasus whose last speaker passed away in 1992, has eighty-four consonants and two phonemically distinct vowels (compared to, for example, twenty-four consonant phonemes and twenty vowel phonemes in Received Pronunciation for English). That sounds can be produced and perceived at eight or nine different basic places of articulation, each with additional secondary articulation, compels us to view the human phonetic perceptual capacity in a different light. A consideration of a diversity of linguistic systems helps linguists move away from universalising accounts and leads us to a better understanding of language evolution. As the linguist Ken Hale (1998: 204) put it: 'Languages embody the intellectual wealth of the people that speak them. Losing any one of them is like dropping a bomb on the Louvre.' In a charming – non-academic – book on endangered languages, journalist Mark Abley (2003) also wonders whether any other language would be able to convey the kinds of meaning inherent in some of these verbs of Boro (also known as Bodo), a Tibeto-Burman language of northeastern India also found in neighbouring Nepal, Bhutan and Bangladesh, based on his reading of Bhattacharya's (1977) description (see example 6.1).

(6.1)

asusu: to feel unknown and uneasy in a new place
bunhan bunahan: to be about to speak, and about not to speak
gabkhron: to be afraid of witnessing an adventure
serrom: to examine by light pressing
egthu: to create a pinching sensation in the armpit
onsay: to pretend to love

But there has to be more to it. And perhaps there is. Linguistic diversity is now widely recognised as a pillar of cultural diversity – which is a driving force of development – in economic growth, and as a means of leading a more fulfilling intellectual, emotional, moral and spiritual life. Further, the loss of language means loss of cultural traditions, in particular oral literature. This has been recognised not only by linguists but also by supranational bodies such as the United Nations Educational, Scientific and Cultural Organisation (UNESCO), which in 2001 issued a Universal Declaration on Cultural Diversity. This sets out the framework in which the international community is to tackle linguistic diversity, its Action Plan calling for Member States to take the appropriate measures towards:

i. safeguarding the linguistic heritage of humanity and giving support to expression, creation and dissemination in the greatest possible number of languages;

ii. encouraging linguistic diversity – while respecting the mother tongue – at all levels of education, wherever possible, and fostering the learning of several languages from the earliest age;

iii. promoting linguistic diversity in cyberspace and encouraging universal access through the global network to all information in the public domain.

The importance of intangible cultural heritage is now widely recognised; this includes oral traditions, performing arts, social practices, rituals, festive events, knowledge and practices concerning nature and the universe, and the knowledge and skills to produce traditional crafts. Of those that pertain to oral traditions, a fair number have been recognised. Naqqāli is the oldest form of dramatic performance in the Islamic Republic of Iran (UNESCO 2012a), in which performers – functioning both as entertainers and as bearers of Persian literature and culture – need to be acquainted with local cultural expressions, languages and dialects, and traditional music, and are deemed the most important guardians of folktales, ethnic epics and Iranian folk music. A decline in the popularity of coffee houses, one of the traditional venues, and the aging of master performers,combined with an uninterested younger generation, threatens the survival of this dramatic art, and the traditional body of literature and culture with it. In a similar vein, Yimakan storytelling of the Hezhen ethnic minority of northeast China (UNESCO 2012b) is essential to the community's worldview and historical memory. Narrated in the Hezhen language, and taking both verse and prose forms, Yimakan storytelling consists of many independent episodes depicting tribal alliances and battles, and not only highlights the defence of ethnic identity and territorial integrity but also preserves traditional knowledge of shamanic rituals, fishing and hunting. Performers improvise stories and alternate between singing and speaking, making use of different melodies to represent different characters and plots. As the Hezhen have no writing system, Yimakan plays a key role in preserving their mother tongue, religion, beliefs, folklore and customs. The Hezhen vernacular is now endangered, a consequence of the acceleration of modernisation and the standardisation of school education, with only the elders able to speak their native language, and with only five master storytellers currently capable of performing the Yimakan tradition.

Strong correlations have also been recognised between cultural and linguistic diversity on the one hand and biological diversity on the other.

In regions such as Indonesia and Papua New Guinea, where biological diversity is amongst the highest in the world, it has also been found that linguistic and cultural diversity is high, and similar factors that threaten biological ecologies – such as urbanisation – also threaten linguistic ones. In addition, in many cases minority communities are the link to traditional or indigenous knowledge, economies and alternative systems related to biological diversity, and have elaborated complex systems for the natural world, reflecting a profound understanding of and close association with their local environment. Environmental knowledge is embedded in indigenous names, oral traditions and taxonomies, and these stand to be lost if the community shifts to another language. Numerous examples of this have been reported, such as the plants and animals known to the Huichol people of Mexico (Grimes 1980a, 1980b) and Maori ancestral sayings – whakataukī – which embody traditional ecological knowledge concerning plant growth, soils and nutrients, ecological niches and ecological communities, as well as landscape processes (Wehi 2009; Wehi, Whaanga and Roa 2009). In the Peruvian Upper Amazon in the Amuesha tribe, whose language is severely endangered, the loss of speakers and knowledge-keepers has directly and negatively impacted the diversity of crops (Salick, Cellinese and Knapp 1997).

Even in more urban environments one finds the loss of traditional knowledge related to the environment as a consequence of language endangerment. A traditional minority in Hong Kong are the Tanka (*daan6gaa1*) – the community of fisherfolk or boat dwellers – an ethnic group of southern China who are also found in coastal parts of Guangdong, Guangxi, Fujian, Hainan and Zhejiang provinces. The Tanka have historically lived on small boats grouped together to form colonies, inhabiting fishing towns and managing the commerce of the seas in the roles of fishermen, longshoremen, coolies and coxswains. With Qing Dynasty edicts classifying them as being of the mean class, the Tanka were not allowed to settle on shore, and were not recognised as part of Hong Kong by the Chinese government. In Hong Kong they were traditionally found in Aberdeen and Shau Kei Wan on the southwest and northeast of Hong Kong Island respectively, in Tai O on the northwest of Lantau Island, on the island of Cheung Chau and in typhoon shelters in the harbour areas; in the middle of the twentieth century some 200,000 were anchored in Hong Kong. Considered the lowest of classes of the Chinese and outcasts, the Tanka did not intermarry with other Chinese. Their peculiar origins and their exclusion from the mainstream meant that they continued as a group unto themselves until recent times, preserving their own customs and practices. The Tanka language spoken in Hong Kong is considered a subdialect of Yue Chinese, which, because of their involvement in the fishing industry, encompasses special terms as well as knowledge and worldviews related specifically to fishing or more generally to the sea. Tanka terms like *ce4hei3* 'evil air' = 'waterspout', *zam1* 'needle' = 'tail of waterspout', *hoi1saang1* 'sail' – terms which clearly relate to their environment – are not understood by mainstream Hongkongers (Ho et al. 2010). Their 鹹水歌 *haam4 seoi2 go1* 'sea water song' is sung on special occasions such as wedding ceremonies, friends' gatherings and fishing. Particularly important in wedding ceremonies for demonstrating sincerity when bestowing compliments, the lyrics also provide very specific classification of fish, as shown in example 6.2 (Ho et al. 2010).

(6.2)

牙帶出身 游曬白肚
黃花出水 頭帶金銀
立錐出身游作個竇
泥鰍出身就要打番頭

'Largehead hairtail becomes white in colour after death
Yellow croaker has a golden yellow head
Moray eel makes a shelter when it gets older
Weather loach ties itself when it is in danger.'

Intelligible only to the Tanka, the community is not, however, passing such a song down to the next generation, considered as it is old-fashioned. More generally, the Tanka language is not seeing inter-generational transmission, with contemporary times seeing shifts in the community to the dominant Cantonese language and culture. Several factors may be identified that underlie this shift (Ho et al. 2010; Lim 2013–2015).

 i. **Urbanisation and mobility.** While in the past, the Tanka's closed and tightly-knit community – living in close quarters on boats moored together, with dense, multiplex networks – all contributed to maintenance of their vernacular, most of the younger generation have relocated onshore and live in more urbanised areas, for access to modern amenities and better job opportunities.
 ii. **Traditional livelihood.** Much of the language developed around the ecology and practice of fishing, but with such small-scale family-run fishing industry practically obsolete, and the younger generation not continuing in their grandparents' and parents' line of work, such specialised vocabulary and discourse – and the knowledge associated with them – serve little purpose, and start being lost from the community's repertoire.

iii. **New economy.** Even though some older-generation Tanka continue working in a related context – for example, on a sightseeing sampan in Aberdeen Harbour in the south of Hong Kong Island, or as a tour guide in Tai O – the languages used, for better communication with tourists, are Cantonese and English. The specialised Tanka vocabulary and song genres are not practised.

iv. **Attitudes.** Because of discrimination that the Tanka have received in the past, a loss of the language and the associated identity as Tanka is not regarded with regret by the community. Community members also feel that speaking in the Tanka language and singing Tanka songs – such as the Sea Water Song – are practices that are old-fashioned and outdated, and they refuse to do so, even if they may still like their songs.

Also recognised as one of the fundamental reasons for diversity are linguistic human rights – that is, the right to use one's own language in public and private – captured, for example, by Hinton (1999, quoted in Hinton 2001: 4):

> The decline of linguistic diversity in the world is linked to the world political economy which invades and takes over the territories of indigenous peoples, threatens the ecosystems in which they live, wipes out their traditional means of livelihood, and (at best) turns them into low-caste laborers in the larger society in which they must now live on the margins.

The ability of communities to develop their own cultures, traditions and languages free from coercion and outside pressures is now widely understood as a critical human right, and is embodied in the Universal Declaration of Human Rights in several of the articles.

i. Article 2 – all individuals are entitled to the rights declared without discrimination based on language.

ii. Article 10 – individuals are entitled to a fair trial, and this is generally recognized to involve the right to an interpreter if an individual does not understand the language used in criminal court proceedings, or in a criminal accusation. The individual has the right to have the interpreter translate the proceedings, including court documents.

iii. Article 19 – individuals have the right to freedom of expression, including the right to choose any language as the medium of expression.

iv. Article 26 – everyone has the right to education, with relevance to the language of medium of instruction.

The preservation of linguistic diversity thus goes beyond being a desire but becomes a moral obligation.

6.4 THE CASE OF SRI LANKA MALAY

In this section, we present a case study of the Sri Lankan Malay community, introduced in Chapter 4, and here especially revealing in all four facets of repertoire choice, based on research conducted over several years by this book's authors (see e.g. Lim and Ansaldo 2007; Ansaldo 2009a). In the first instance we see how – in spite of their relatively insignificant numbers in the population of the country – because of the social and symbolic capital they possessed, and positive attitudes held towards their culture and language, their linguistic vitality was for the longest time extremely high. Subsequently, as a response to national language policies at independence promoting Sinhala, a shift to English occurs in the urban communities who have the resources, while maintenance of the vernacular – Sri Lanka Malay (SLM) – continues in the more peripheral communities. The revitalisation activities in the SLM speech community highlight the responses of small communities in the diaspora – who speak a restructured variety – to language situations in the homeland, in which the choice of a 'standard' variety over the vernacular may be seen to be motivated by not only economic and cultural capital but also (mis)understanding of linguistic classification of the variety in question. This leads into the perennial questions of the composition and negotiations of identity.

6.4.1 Ethnolinguistic vitality, maintenance and shift

Factors contributing to the ethnolinguistic vitality of the Malays of Sri Lanka have been evaluated by Lim and Ansaldo (2007). From the late 1800s to the present time, the Malays have consistently comprised approximately 0.3 per cent of the population, and are still today a numerical minority in Sri Lanka, with the majority Sinhalese comprising two thirds to three quarters of the population and a significant minority of Tamils comprising a quarter of the population. They are found in several communities located in various parts of the island, such as the more urban community in the capital Colombo, as well as peripheral communities in fishing villages on the south coast, such as Hambantota and Kirinda. They can also be seen to constitute a minority in name as, until recently, they tended to be categorised in official government statistics together with the Sri Lankan Moors (Tamil-speaking people tracing their ancestry to Arab traders who arrived in Sri Lanka between the eighth and fifteenth centuries) and Indian Moors (from India) as 'Moors' or 'Muslims'. On the Sri Lankan government's official website currently Moors, Malays, Burghers and others are indicated as together comprising 7.9 per cent of the population. In spite of the size of the population and proportion within the country and their distribution within the territory, as well as a relatively low symbolic capital within their own country and low institutional support, a number of factors come together to support the maintenance of SLM over the centuries.

The Sri Lankan Malays' status within the country can in fact be seen always to have been quite high. As outlined in Chapter 4, a majority of the ancestors of the Colombo, Kandy and Hambantota communities would have been Javanese nobility exiled during the wars of succession in Java during Dutch rule. Official documents of 1792, for example, list 176 individuals belonging to twenty-three families of royalty and nobility exiled with their families from Java, Batavia and Sumatra to Ceylon. The older Javanese, because of their proficiency in Dutch, were appointed the 'captains' supervising the cinnamon gardens, the spice being one of the most precious commodities during Dutch rule; with increased production of cinnamon, these superior officers would be rewarded with more power, promotions and privileges. Most of the exiles became enlisted in the military and were later retained under the British as members of the Malay Regiment (as well as in the police and the fire brigade, where, although they dropped their royal titles, they nonetheless maintained their status as was the practice of the time. After the disbandment of the regiment in 1873, many of these joined the tea estates and functioned as intermediaries between the English superintendents and the Indian labour force. The Malays' contribution to sports has also been significant: the Colombo Malay Cricket Club, founded in 1872, is the oldest cricket club in the country and has produced numerous cricketers and hockey players who have represented Sri Lanka. In short, although officially symbolic recognition would appear to be low, the Malays have held a status amongst the communities that has been high, in no small part due to their origins and their multilingual linguistic abilities.

While official institutional support is lacking, informal institutional support has been strong and vibrant for decades, in the form of a large number of social and cultural groups. These include, for example, the Sri Lanka Malay Confederation (the umbrella organisation), the Sri Lanka Malay Rupee Fund, the Conference of Sri Lanka Malays, and Malay associations of the communities located around the island, which are all extremely active in the organisation of regular social, cultural, commemorative and fund-raising activities and initiatives.

Even while identification is lacking at the official level, however, the Sri Lankan Malays' own identity has always been extremely vibrant. While there is a strong sense of identity for each of the different communities, they nonetheless all identify themselves as Sri Lankan Malays. This has surely been the case since colonial rule, when this 'Malay' diaspora was testified to being a close-knit community, in which contacts between the different Malay/Indonesian ethnicities, as well as the different social extractions, were maintained through the ranks of the army and through common religious practice. There is also much awareness and expression of the community members' culture and ancestry. Given their dense and multiplex networks, it is not surprising that SLM has been widely spoken as a home language for generations.

In spite of a strong ethnolinguistic vitality, however, the SLM community has not been immune to shift. The first factor that prompted the shift must be the official language policies enacted at the country's independence. In 1956, the new coalition government introduced the Sinhala Only language act, which promised to proclaim Sinhala – the majority native language used by the majority ethnic group – as the sole official language of Sri Lanka (though later revisions made way for Tamil as a co-official language). This was a political move that was seen to be rectifying past injustices – namely that of the minority Tamils perceived as having dominated the old British colonial administrative system through the advantage of their English education. In practice this meant that, amongst other things, Sinhala started to be used as the medium of education in schools, with a reduction in teaching and learning English. Amongst the urban Colombo community's members, whose level of education is high and who are in general English-educated, Sri Lankan Malay parents and grandparents with the resources make the conscious decision to speak to their children in English in the home domain. They do so in order to provide them with a resource recognised as requisite for communication and advancement internationally – recognised by community members as the key to a good job and a comfortable life. The general pattern displayed is a clear shift to English from SLM in the home domain. As a result, the community typically shows strong linguistic vitality in SLM in the oldest to middle generations, and rapidly decreasing linguistic competence to nil in the vernacular in the young generation. SLM is seen now to have a mere fifth position in the community after Sinhala, Tamil, English and Arabic (the last in the religious domain); it is no longer a home language for the younger generation of middle/upper-class Sri Lankan Malays in Colombo.

In sharp contrast to the shift in more urban communities such as Colombo is the language maintenance in the more peripheral communities such as that found in Kirinda, a relatively isolated fishing village on the southeast coast, where 90 per cent of the village are Malay, and they comprise some 4 per cent of the 46,000 SLM population. With a dense and multiplex social network, and limited educational and employment opportunities, they exhibit strong maintenance of the vernacular. Initial investigations (Ansaldo 2005; Ansaldo and Lim 2005) showed the SLM variety of Kirinda to be structurally distinct from other SLM varieties. Ansaldo (2008) describes its nominal case system – a striking feature, considering the rarity of complex morphological marking in contact languages in which a rare case of split is occurring – developing a new coding for object marking from a morpheme originally used for Dative-like functions. Lexically and grammatically, there seems to be a stronger influence of Sinhala and Tamil, and trilingualism in SLM, Sinhala and Tamil is very common in all generations (Ansaldo 2008). The children of Kirinda, numbering about 200, were reported in 2004 to be the only children to be native monolingual speakers of a variety of SLM. There was thus no endangerment of the language here; on the contrary, it was and is still extremely vital – the dominant language of all generations of the community, spoken in all domains, even as the working language in the Tamil-medium *madrasah* (Muslim school). Kirinda at that point in time was viewed as the only fully vital community of Sri Lankan Malays in which a young generation of speakers of a SLM variety as first language (L1) could be found, though some Upcountry communities were later also found to show similar vitality, albeit to a lesser extent.

We can see the explanation for this choice in terms of the capital the various languages possess in the country. In the local linguistic market – of school, profession, politics – Sinhala is recognised as necessary capital and accepted without battle; it has in any case always been in the SLM speakers' repertoire. Similarly, English has been an important variety in their linguistic repertoire: it was a language which allowed the SLM many privileges as colonial subjects. Even in postcolonial Sri Lanka a multilingualism including English is recognised as crucial to the Malays. In fact, scholars such as Thiru Kandiah (1984) note how the English language became even more of a weapon – a *kaduva* 'sword' – dividing the haves and the have-nots in postcolonial Sri Lanka. The politics of English in Sri Lanka is also outlined in Lim (2013). In consequence, SLM which has low capital in the local linguistic market is forfeited, and thus becomes not only minority and marginalised but also endangered.

6.4.2 Endangerment of contact languages

It has been suggested that endangered contact languages are doubly marginalised (Garrett 2006: 177–8): marginalised amongst the world's languages in general, and then marginalised again amongst endangered languages. There are several reasons for this. In general terms, contact languages, like endangered languages, are on the whole oral – that is, unwritten – and spoken by relatively small populations lacking in political and economic power, who inhabit geopolitically remote areas such as small islands and tropical coastlines. Additionally, contact languages have certain other characteristics that render them marginal even amongst the remaining thousands of relatively small, relatively powerless languages, grouped under two related themes: lack of historicity and perceived lack of autonomy. Their relative lack of historicity tends to attenuate their ties to specific geographical territories and to the contemporary inhabitants of those territories. The ethnic identities of such contact language-speaking groups may be less coherent and less robust, in that they are less focused or more diffused – to use the concepts of Le Page and Tabouret-Keller (1985) – and more open to negotiation and contestation. Then, many contact languages are regarded, even by their own speakers, as merely 'broken' or 'corrupted' versions of the lexifier to which they are self-evidently related. We see how this plays out in the situation of SLM.

That SLM had started to become an endangered linguistic variety did not go unnoticed by the urban community, and as a response to this steps in language revitalisation were in fact taken by the SLM community itself in the late twentieth century. As there is no place in the official spheres for addressing and politicking for minority rights, civil society organisations – outside state structures – were the ones to step in and initiate discourse on the issues of their language being a minority and endangered – with interesting consequences. The subaltern publics – i.e. sites formed around social and civil movements – are the SLM groups mentioned earlier, as well as individuals in the SLM community, in particular in the Colombo community, who can be seen to be more linguistically aware and to have the inclination and resources. Their initiation may be seen to be the publication in 1987 of an article in a local newspaper on 'The Sri Lankan Malay Language and its future', followed by a public lecture on the same theme at the Sri Lanka Malay Association. Members of the community under their own steam published books on their identity and language, as well as books comparing SLM with Standard Malay (StdM) and Malay primers. The individuals involved in these activities did not as such have backgrounds in linguistics or language education. What is significant is that the 'revitalisation' taking place was not of SLM itself, due to a combination of two general phenomena.

First is a factor in which linguists have inadvertently played a part, through the practice of analysis and categorisation. An earlier interpretation of the SLM communities as a Tamil-Malay 'hybrid' (for a fuller critique, see Ansaldo 2009a) led to the classification of SLM as a 'creole'. It is referred to as a creole in an early account by a historian (Hussainmiya 1986) and by linguists (see e.g. Smith, Paauw and Hussainmiya 2004), and it is listed as Sri Lankan Creole Malay in *Ethnologue* (Gordon 2005; Lewis, Simons and Fennig 2013). As suggested in Garrett (2006: 180), and as will be seen in the case of SLM, such a classification[1] has a significant impact on the type of shift that may occur, as well as its speed. The awareness of speaking a 'corrupt' or 'broken' variety of some 'standard' language to which it is related, as is often implied in the current definition of creole languages, may lead to a perception of their linguistic variety as not being 'good' enough to maintain, and further strengthens a community's desire to move away to a more standard variety. As a result, the SLM community members' perception of their own language was less positive, as they interpreted 'creole' as an 'imperfect' code and an ungrammatical dialect of Malay. It also later became clear through discussions and discourse that in many cases the community did not make a very clear distinction between SLM and StdM. One of the local publications mentioned above, a textbook presented in StdM with Sinhala, Tamil and English, is intended to 'help Sri Lankan Malays to study their mother tongue in its internationally recognised form'.

Second, in contrast with the status the community has in its own country, greater recognition has been found instead from Malaysia (and also Indonesia) in at least two significant and related thrusts, both clearly seen as arising from scholarly and transnational contexts which have associated symbolic and material markets. Malaysia's Institute of Malay Language and Culture has as one of its objectives 'to get in touch with Malays in different parts of the world and teach them the real Malay'. One of the realisations of this was the organisation by the Institute of language classes in Bahasa Melayu, the StdM of Malaysia. The Malaysian High Commission in Sri Lanka from around the early 2000s demonstrated interest in, and strong support for, the SLM community, and was providing aid in terms of student scholarships for undergraduate and postgraduate studies in Malaysia, as well as job market openings; one of the requirements of the latter is competence in basic Malay.

With these two phenomena working in tandem, it is not surprising that it was with Malaysia that the SLM community aligned itself, in terms of both language and identity. This also resonates with the suggestion that a community that has seen displacement at some point in its history tends to make some identification with a more remote

[1] In addition, such a claim has been analysed as problematic on historical as well as theoretical grounds (Aboh and Ansaldo 2007; Ansaldo and Matthews 2007).

community perceived as from their origins, and has a less coherent and robust identity (Le Page and Tabouret-Keller 1985; Errington 2003). The choice in the revitalisation process was consequently not for SLM, which had so far been seen as an embarrassing, 'bad' or corrupt code and therefore unworthy of any effort of preservation, but for Malaysia's prestigious StdM. In the annual Hari Bahasa Melayu (Malay Language Day) organised by the community in Colombo in August 2006 and 2007, activities such as essay-writing and oratory contests were conducted for both SLM and StdM.

The rationale is not difficult to understand, of course; it repeats itself every day in every minority community that wishes to join the global world. The belief is that the transition from an unworthy 'creole' to a national language such as StdM will provide not only cultural capital such as available written material for education but also, more importantly, increased economic and political capital, to plug into the global economy and direct the community's trajectory in social space upwards.

An alternative view draws on the notion of identity alignment discussed in Chapter 4. The conscious 'shift' in the Sri Lankan Malay community, at least in the urban communities, from SLM to StdM – the latter a variety in which cultural and economic functions of language come together – can be seen as one that was made in appropriate circumstances, and which aids the acquisition of a resource on the semiotic, economic and global fronts. This outcome may thus be seen as a resource, rather than a threat, that enables a minority group to gain access to better education and enhanced political self-representation. In other words, the Malay communities of Sri Lanka could be seen to be achieving two ends (Lim and Ansaldo 2007): they were not only gaining a useful economic tool but also managing to preserve and represent their position through identity alignment, which involves:[2]

i. not contesting their imposed identity, which is not negotiable, of 'Muslim' in the context of the local nation state;
ii. maintaining their presumed ethnic identity as 'Sri Lankan Malays';
iii. aligning themselves with an assumed global 'Malay' identity – that is, one which is accepted and not negotiated.

---

[2] For more on types of identity and ethnic identity, see Pavlenko and Blackledge (2004) and Edwards (1985) respectively. Their assumed identity is one which is recognisable through an empowered linguistic identity, and recognised by the Malay 'homeland'; we also see in this the identification of displaced communities with a more remote community.

6.5 CONCLUDING REMARKS

In situations of shift and endangerment, there are those who believe that 'there is no language for which nothing at all can be done' (Fishman 1991: 12), and revitalisation activities are on the schedule in numerous projects (see also Hinton 2011). Two decades ago Joshua Fishman (1991) outlined a programme for reversing language shift. This involves eight levels corresponding to each of the levels of his Graded Intergenerational Disruption Scale, which outlines specific activities needed if language shift is to be reversed. Several scholars have, however, queried the attention and activities involved in such an endeavour of halting language shift and/or revitalising endangered languages. The late Peter Ladefoged suggested that, since language death is a natural part of the process of human cultural development, linguists should simply document and describe languages scientifically but not interfere with the process of loss and revitalisation. A poignant anecdote provided by Ladefoged (1992: 810–11), often cited but well worth mentioning, is as follows:

> Last summer I was working on Dahalo, a rapidly dying Cushitic language, spoken by a few hundred people in a rural district of Kenya. I asked one of our consultants whether his teen-aged sons spoke Dahalo. 'No,' he said. 'They can still hear it, but they cannot speak it. They speak only Swahili.' He was smiling when he said it, and did not seem to regret it. He was proud that his sons had been to school, and knew things that he did not. Who am I to say that he was wrong?

The very idea that 'all is lost' when a language becomes extinct is often questioned. As Mufwene (2004b, 2007, 2008) argues, the emergence of new languages through contact language formation (CLF) should be viewed as a continuous ongoing process in the cycle of language birth and death. In the rest of this section, we examine two outcomes in situations of language shift which demonstrate how some form of language creation can take place.

First, there may be borrowing of some aspects of the grammar from the language being shifted away from. For example, in China, the northern dialect of Lisu has now almost replaced Anung: there are only about 40 Anung speakers left in China, few of whom are monolingual, amongst the 7,300 Anung who are members of the Nu national minority; and about 6,000 of 10,000 ethnic Anung in Burma speak only Lisu (Bradley 2011: 73). However, the word for the main traditional priest in northern Lisu comes from Anung and, even more extensively, the Anung system of nine male and nine female birth order names has been borrowed into northern Lisu and has replaced the original Lisu birth-order name system that is found in other dialects.[3] This is striking, not only because the two languages are traditionally considered to belong to different branches of the Tibeto-Burman family and thus not to be very closely related but also because it seems odd that the replacing language should adopt certain features of the language it is displacing. Why should it be that, even while becoming imminently obsolete, a less dominant language still leaves its mark on the dominating and overtaking language? External factors of the ecology provide an explanation. Bradley (2011: 72) postulates that it may well be that the incoming Lisu, arriving in the area about 250 years ago, were mainly men who married local Anung women. Northern Lisu, even while it was replacing Anung, thus acquired various culturally important parts of the Anung lexicon, including some entire semantic fields.

In some situations of language shift, the language of wider communication – such as English – with which the vernacular or ancestral language comes into contact is at times adapted ideologically, if not always structurally, to communicative ends which are continuous with those earlier fulfilled by the ancestral language, as observed by Woodbury (2005). An instance discussed by Woodbury is that of Aboriginal communities in southeast Queensland, Australia, studied by Diana Eades (1988: 97, 101), who finds that:

> While many Aboriginal people [in southeast Queensland] may speak English as their first language, the context of conversation has significant Aboriginal cultural and social aspects which lead to distinctively Aboriginal interpretations and meanings. While the chosen language code is frequently English, there are important continuities in the ways language is used . . . The Aboriginal priority on developing, maintaining, and strengthening social relationships is both reflected in, and created by, the way people speak to each other, whether the language variety is English, Aboriginal English, or Lingo [any Aboriginal language].

Similarly, in Koyukon communities in Alaska's interior, studied by Patricia Kwachka (1992: 70, 71), what is found is that, in the rapid shift from Koyukon to English:

> The Koyukon people have been able to transfer and permute a very important cultural pattern at the discourse level, the tradition of narrative . . . Although [stories from a distant time] are rarely told

---

[3] Additionally, northern Lisu clothing is identical to the Anung, in contrast to Lisu clothing elsewhere.

today, the narrative, as a social and rhetorical structure, has not only
persisted but flourished.

In the Peranakan community in Singapore, which, by the middle of
the twentieth century, shifted from their vernacular – the restructured
variety Baba Malay – to English, it is a characteristic Peranakan English
(PerE) that is their code, as documented in Lim (2010b). In written mode,
there are numerous lexical items of Baba Malay and Hokkien origin,
such as terms and phrases for cultural practices (*ronggeng, dondang
sayang* [Malay]), food (*tong poon lady* [Hokkien]; *biji sagar seeds, rempah*
[Malay]), naming and address practices (*kimpoh choh* [Hokkien 'maternal
great great aunt'], exclamations (*kus semangat!* [Malay]), greetings,
wishes and thanks (*apa khabar* [Malay 'how are you']; *May we extend to
all readers a Selamat Tahun Baru* [Malay 'happy new year'] *and may you all
enjoy panjang panjang umor* [Malay 'very long life'] *in the year of the Goat;
The Main Wayang Company would like to say a big KAMSIAH* [Hokkien 'thank
you']). In spoken form, PerE should be viewed, as (Lim 2010b) argues,
as a (single) English-*Baba Malay* code, as illustrated in example 6.3
(Lim 2010b: 336).

(6.3)

Like drugs you know when you're under drugs . . . The babies come out crying
crying *Apa dia mo? mo?* Drugs. *Nanti* alcohol the same. They get into their
system. *Kita semua tak drin[k]* . . . Keep yourself clean and healthy. Don[t] drin[k]
don[t] drin[k].

'Like drugs, you know, when you're under the influence of drugs . . . The babies
are born crying. What do they [the babies] want? Drugs. Then it's the same with
alcohol – it gets into your system. We all didn't drink . . . Keep yourself clean and
healthy. Don't drink.'

Moreover, even with the shift to (Peranakan) English, and Baba Malay
having a role simply as a post-vernacular variety – i.e. not used as
vernacular in everyday communication but only in cultural practices –
the vitality of the Peranakan community is extremely high (Lim 2014a,
forthcoming).

The examples above are important observations for at least three
reasons. First, as mentioned above, they underscore the evolutionary
approach where language birth, language change and language death
are all part of the life cycle of language (Mufwene 2004b, 2008).
Second, as noted by Woodbury (2005: 254), they show concern for
the maintenance of social identity in situations of language shift.

This is very much in line with the central role of identity in the evolutionary approach to CLF outlined in Chapter 4. Finally, they focus on actual language behaviour in contemporary speech communities, highlighting the value of emergent language practice in a community – which in many cases comprises a contact variety – which, in the field of documentary linguistics, needs to be recognised as equally valuable in the enterprise of documentation and description.

DISCUSSION POINTS

1. Identify communities in your nation state or city who may have undergone or be undergoing language shift (though not necessarily language endangerment or language death). Identify the factors leading to language shift. Do you feel that (more) attention needs to be paid to these situations?

2. Do newly formed languages such as creoles and other contact varieties counter the trend of decreasing linguistic diversity? Why or why not?

3. Should we 'save' languages? Despite the growing awareness of endangered languages witnessed in the past decade, not everyone agrees that languages are under threat. Consider the diverse views on maintaining and/or revitalising endangered languages, and provide an informed opinion on what kind of attention, if any, is important to endangered languages.

FURTHER READING

The edited volume by Austin and Sallabank (2011b) provides a very good overview of a wide range of issues involved in the field of language endangerment, documentation and challenges, including areas of new roles for and economic development of endangered languages. For an approach which explores why such linguistic diversity exists in the first place, and what the best response might be to the challenge of recording and documenting oral traditions while they are still with us, see Evans (2010). There are also increasingly numerous online resources, such as Al Jazeera's *Living the Language* (www.aljazeera.com/programmes/livingthelanguage/), a six-part series on indigenous peoples fighting to preserve endangered languages and the cultures at risk of dying with them – which includes episodes on Australia's Aboriginal communities, who have the highest rate of language extinction in the world, and the Maori model for revitalisation – and the episode 'Life and death' in the series *Speaking in Tongues: The History of Language* (www.christenebrowne.com/speaking-in-tongues-educational-sales/ speaking-in-tongues-episode-five-life-and-death/). For an example of work on endangered languages in urban areas, see the online resource Endangered Languages Alliance (elalliance.org).

7   Contact and globalisation

7.1   INTRODUCTION

Globalisation – the process by which regional economies, societies and cultures have become integrated through a global network of trade, communication, immigration and transportation – has, as a word, existed since the 1960s. While in the more recent past globalisation was often primarily focused on the economic side of the world, and was the term initially widely used by economists and other social scientists, it now encompasses a broader range of areas and activities, including culture, media, technology, sociocultural, political and even biological factors, such as climate change. The term achieved such widespread use in the mainstream press by the late 1980s that, in the new millennium, many ask if 'globalisation' has become a global cliché (Lechner and Boli 2004). Nonetheless, even the more critical of observers accept that the processes associated with globalisation, while not new in substance, are certainly new in intensity, scope and scale (Coupland 2010a). And, even if linguists have been 'late getting to the party', as noted by Nikolas Coupland (2003), one of the earlier scholars in language and globalisation, research in the field has certainly burgeoned (see e.g. Coupland 2010b).

Several phenomena associated with the globalised era have been identified by scholars, mentioned in Chapter 1 and reiterated here (from Coupland 2010a: 2–3, excerpted, reordered and numbered here):

  i. the decline of the (British) Establishment;
 ii. national boundaries becoming (perhaps until recently) more permeable;
iii. massively increasing demographic mobility, often for economic reasons;
 iv. developing ethnic pluralism, especially in urban settings;
  v. the proliferation and speeding up of communication technologies;

vi. the growth of the middle class but the accentuation of the rich/
poor divide;

vii. an upsurge in consumer culture and many new forms of
commodification;

viii. greater subservience to global market economics, in the face of its
demerits;

ix. a large shift to service-sector work, globally dispersed.

Each of the above has implications for bringing communities and their
languages into contact with each other in new, contemporary contexts
which, to echo Coupland, are contexts that are distinct from those of
the past in terms of intensity, scope and scale.

Additionally, we feel strongly that the study of language contact in a
globalisation perspective turn its lens particularly to the Asian region
because of two major factors in the ecology in what is largely recognised
in this Asian Century[1] – the term used to describe the belief that, if certain demographic and economic trends persist, the twenty-first century
will be dominated by Asian politics and culture – because of two major
factors in the ecology. The first factor comprises the great shift in the
global economy's centre of gravity from West to East, which entails various phenomena of globalisation and economic growth in Asia, such as
the pursuit of linguistic capital, mobility, trade, communication technology, etc. These all have significant implications for language contact
in terms of bringing together communities and their languages in new
dynamics, providing new sites and potential for consequences of contact. The second factor is Asia's status as the site of the largest and
most quickly growing number of users of English – the only real global
language for the predictable future. The total English-using population
in Asia is some 600 million, far more than English speakers in the
'Inner Circle'. Taken together, it also means that Asian English speakers are interacting with other Asian Englishes or speakers of other New
Englishes – for example, African Englishes – in ways more numerous and
more meaningful than with Inner Circle or 'native' English speakers.
Again, what does this mean for spread, and contact, and change?

In this chapter we outline a number of phenomena that, in this era of
globalisation, involve new dynamics of contact – whether this involves
contact that is even more diverse than before, or sites which by their very

---

[1] The term 'Asian Century' is attributed to a 1988 meeting between People's Republic
of China leader Deng Xiaoping and Indian Prime Minister Rajiv Gandhi; cf. the
preceding 'American Century', as coined by *Time* publisher Henry Luce to describe
the dominance of the US for much of the twentieth century, and the nineteenth
century, known as the 'British Century'.

nature prompt more intense contact than would have occurred under more 'normal' circumstances. In a number of these areas, outcomes of contact are already in evidence and have been documented. In other areas, the sociolinguistic circumstances are fresh, and the linguistic outcomes of contact are yet to manifest themselves in a stable manner; nonetheless, we also include them in this chapter as areas to keep an eye on.

7.2 CONTACT OUTCOMES OF COMPUTER-MEDIATED COMMUNICATION

No-one needs to be convinced of the ubiquity and prominence of electronic communication in this era. Still, some statistics mentioned in Chapter 1 are particularly compelling to reflect on. While some 4.1 billion people – that is, just over 60 per cent of the world's population – had access to a mobile phone in 2009 (United Nations 2009), it is currently estimated that 6 billion out of the world's population of 7 billion now have mobile phones; more significantly, as we will see later, nearly 5 billion of these are in developing countries (World Bank 2012).[2] In Sub-Saharan Africa, while fixed-line phones have a penetration rate of just over 2 per cent – found only in offices and the richest households – the growth of mobile phones has been so explosive that the region is now home to approximately 650 million mobile phone subscribers, a number that surpasses that in the US or the European Union (World Bank and African Development Bank 2013).[3] This makes Sub-Saharan Africa the region with the second largest number of mobile phone users, behind only Asia. Numbering 2.43 billion mobile phone users, the Asia-Pacific comprises 56.3 per cent of mobile phone users in the world (the region was the only one to show growth in mobile phone sales in the first quarter of 2013). A billion of these users are in China and half a billion in India, with India now the fastest growing market in the Asia-Pacific

---

[2] The extent of mobile phone penetration world-wide is especially striking when considered alongside another, more sobering, statistic that far fewer of the world's population – only 4.5 billion people – have access to working toilets (United Nations 2013a). India, which alone is responsible for 60 per cent of the global population that lacks access to basic sanitation, was reported in 2010 to have about half of its 1.2 billion residents as mobile phone subscribers, but only 366 million people – that is, one third of its population – with access to toilets (Wang 2013).

[3] Again, this is an especially striking statistic when considered alongside the fact that, in some African countries, more people have access to a mobile phone than to clean water, a bank account or even electricity (World Bank and African Development Bank 2013).

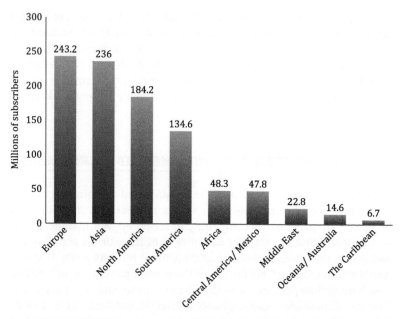

Figure 7.1 Facebook users in the world by regions (September 2012)

with a quarter-on-quarter growth of 27 per cent in the third quarter of 2014 (eMarketer 2013; Gartner 2013; International Data Corporation 2014). A look at Facebook, the largest social network in the world, as an example of the extent to which people are using social media reveals other impressive figures: there are 1.11 billion users world-wide (as of May 2013); notably, Asia comprises the second largest region of users, with 236 million (see Figure 7.1).

Some two decades ago, scholarship started recognising the emergence of new ways of expression as a consequence of the rise of new electronic media. These new literacies, shaped by the opportunities and constraints of the electronic medium, are variously termed Netspeak, netlish, web-lish, internet language, cyberspeak, electronic discourse, computer-mediated communication (CMC), SMS-lingo, etc. (Crystal 2001). Studies have focused on both the diachronic analysis of language change as a consequence of electronic media and the synchronic analysis of lan-guage in all areas of internet activity, including email, chatroom and games interaction, instant messaging and webpages, as well as associ-ated areas of CMC such as SMS messaging (texting). We believe that the area of CMC is a crucial domain for study in which language contact is concerned for a number of reasons, several interrelated.

First, and most obviously, such a widespread and ever-increasing use of the internet and mobile phone technology means – at least in theory – increased opportunities, and opportunities as never before, for communities from different cultural and language backgrounds to communicate, multiplying the contact scenarios exponentially. But let us examine this assumption at the outset: is it really multilingual contact situations that we find in CMC contexts? In 1996, the *New York Times* in an article titled 'World, Wide, Web: 3 English Words' (Specter 1996) rather confidently proclaimed, 'if you want to take full advantage of the Internet, there is only one real way to do it: learn English'. Two decades later, it is clear that English has not, as doomsayers had predicted, taken over the virtual world. About 1500 languages – that is, one quarter of the world's languages – were noted to have web presence a decade ago (Crystal 2001), and the balance is still tipping. While before 1990, 80 per cent of webpages were in English, by the end of the millennium the presence of other languages such as German, Japanese, French and Spanish had been noted to be rising, such that in 2011 only about 56 per cent of webpages are in English. Internet access in non-English-speaking countries is also growing rapidly: it increased twenty-fold from 7 million in 1995 to 136 million in 2000, and internet penetration saw the greatest growth in the decade 2000–2010 in non-English-speaking countries including China, India and Africa. With the current growth rates, the total number of users accessing the internet in Chinese is predicted to overtake those using English in 2015 (Broadband Commission 2012). And what of the languages used online? While the use of English online saw growth of 281 per cent in the past ten years, the growth in the use of other languages has far outstripped this: Chinese grew by 1277 per cent, with Spanish, Russian and Arabic also seeing phenomenal growth in usage by 2011. The opportunities for users of different languages to come into virtual contact are obvious.

CMC involves the interplay between what technology allows and what the communicator brings to technology. As is widely recognised, text messaging involves:

i. brevity and speed, which is less about technology, and more about turntaking and fluidity of social interaction, and which entails the abbreviation of lexical items and minimal use of capitalisation and standard grammatical punctuation;

ii. paralinguistic restitution to redress the loss of such socioemotional or prosodic features, especially for marking emphasis, playfulness and emotional states in general, involving capitalisation, multiple punctuation and emoticons or emojis;

iii. phonological approximations, which also reduce the number of written characters (see e.g. Deumert and Masinyana 2008).

On the one hand, the penetration of English is obvious. Even with increasing multilingualism on the internet, most language influence testifies to the global reach of English. Textisms like *lol, u, brb, ily*, all acronyms from English, are global internet-speak. English letters of the alphabet are adopted in languages that do not have such letters: for example, in Italian, which does not have 'k', texters write *ke* for *che*. English abbreviations are used for parts of a word in another language: instead of writing *morgen* 'tomorrow' and *vandaag* 'today' or some abbreviation of the words, Dutch texters write *2m* and *2d*, clearly closer to abbreviations of English *tomorrow* and *today*. Especially creative examples of contact are found in English approximations via number homophone abbreviations: Japanese texters type *39 [san kyu]* 'three nine' in Japanese for English *thank you* and Hong Kong texters use *88 [bat bat]* 'eight eight' in Cantonese for English *bye bye*, while Chinese texters use *886 [ba ba liu]* 'eight eight six' in Mandarin, which gives the mixed English *bye bye* and Mandarin *le* 'already, completed'. Such practices catch on with other users, with non-Hongkongers in Hong Kong also using *88*.

At the same time, other languages still make their presence felt in multilingual language contact, as seen in text messaging amongst the youth in South Africa. Here, *isiXhosa* is present in various grammatical levels: as phrases, at discourse level in the form of the isiXhosa practice of pre-clausal emphatic pronouns, and down to morphology in the form of the isiXhosa nominal case marker on an English noun, illustrated in examples 7.1, 7.2 and 7.3 respectively (Deumert and Masinyana 2008).[4]

(7.1)

Hulo chom yam ('hi my friend'), I know u graduating, hw ws graduation.im sooo proud of u my friend. Wel dun. I mis u. im in e.c nw needed tym away 4rm c.t take care n njy da holidays.

(7.2)

Hey scramble egg :-) How's Durban? *Mna* ('me'), um so BORED!!! Tis Weds and I actually thought twas Friday . . .

---

[4] The isiXhosa nominal case marker *i-* is a prefix of class 5 that frequently precedes loan words, and its use with an English noun is seen to be a playful technique used by young people and advertisers, sometimes in jest (Rajend Mesthrie, personal communication 2013).

(7.3)

> Why r u down? Hope its nothing serious. I feel lyk dat most of da tym. I swear im going thru *i*depression!

Finally, what is especially significant for language contact and evolution is what occurs in particular in contexts involving different orthographic traditions. Non-Latin alphabetic scripts (such as Arabic, Brahmic and Cyrillic scripts) have keyboards based on the QWERTY layout and can input Latin letters as well as the script of the language by a special key or through some combination of keys. East Asian languages (namely Chinese, Japanese and Korean), on the other hand, require special input methods due to the thousands of possible characters in these languages. While various methods have been invented to fit every possibility into a QWERTY keyboard, there is no one-to-one mapping between keys and characters. Input may be, for example, by entering the desired character's pronunciation and selecting from possibilities, or by giving its component shapes, radicals and stroke count. Even if there is the option of using such character scripts, some users may well prefer to use a Latin-based keyboard and/or English due to the constraints of the keyboard or the comparative efficacy compared to using character keystrokes. Young Hongkongers, for instance, who are normally Cantonese-dominant in non-CMC domains, overwhelmingly agree that English is easier to input (74.3 per cent) than Chinese (25.7 per cent), and report a significant preference for using English, or English and Cantonese (60.6 per cent), rather than Chinese (Lin 2005). Clearly, CMC promotes significantly greater English usage than would be usual for a community dominant in another language. Two major consequences follow on from this, as suggested by Lim (2015). First, because CMC platforms comprise a site quite distinct from the community's usual communicative practices, one in which there is more widespread use of English than in non-CMC contexts, this results in more frequent mixing of codes – in the case of Hong Kong, of Cantonese and English – as well as other outcomes of language contact.

Much evidence of this is found in the online chat of young Hongkongers, illustrated in the following examples (from Wong 2009; layout as in original, headings modified), where a number of linguistic practices clearly demonstrating the outcome of language contact are noted. There is romanisation of Cantonese (sometimes ad hoc) (examples 7.4 and 7.5) and a widespread use of Cantonese exclamations (example 7.4) and particles, as in *ge, ar, la, wor* for *ge2, aa3, laa3, wo5* (example 7.5), as well as regular instances of common Cantonese phrases romanised, such as *mafan* 'troublesome' for 麻煩 *maa4faan4* (example 7.5). (Cantonese phrases and particles in italics in examples 7.4–7.7.)

(7.4)

Romanised	Cantonese	Meaning
wah/wa	嘩 [waa4]	Expresses surprise or wonder (Matthews & Yip 1994: 358)
chur/cher	嗔 [ce1]	Expresses disparagement, like tut-tut in English (Matthews & Yip 1994: 358)
ai	唉 [aai1]	Sigh
ha?	吓 [haa2]	Expresses surprise or shock, like 'what did you?' in English

(7.5)

Texter	Message	Idiomatic gloss
Raymond	head ask you for resume??	the department head asked you for résumé?
Raymond	how come *ge*	how come [ge2]?
Lily	yes *ar*,	yes [aa3]
Lily	he said he ask all people *la wor*	he said he has already asked everyone for résumé already [laa3 wo5]
Raymond	what for	what is that for?
Raymond	*ma fan*	it's so troublesome
Lily	Not my head	he is not my supervisor
Lily	programmer head	my supervisor is the head of the programming department

More radical restructuring also occurs, in the form of direct translation or calqueing of Cantonese expressions into English, such as 'add oil' for Cantonese 加油 *ga1yau4,* literally 'add oil' (example 7.6, in bold), which is a general exhortation to persevere or to work hard. Morpheme-for-morpheme translation, or relexification, also occurs – for example, *gum is you dun ask* and *or... gum you continue lo* (example 7.7, in bold), where the Cantonese item 咁 *gam2* functions as an adverb meaning 'so, then'.

(7.6)

Texter	Message	Idiomatic gloss
Shirley	7:00am...	I have to work at 7:00am
Shirley	Very shit *lei* ~~	It's very bad [ne]
Ellen	ahaha~~~ **add oil!!!!**	(*laugh) work hard!
Ellen	Then goodnight and sweet dreams *la*	goodnight [laa1]
Shirley	talk to u next time!	talk to you next time

(7.7)

Texter	Message*	Idiomatic gloss
Peter	did u ask Wilson to pick you up in the train station?	did u ask Wilson to pick you up in the train station?
Chloe	ah . . . not yet . . . hahaaa	oh, I haven't asked him yet . . . (*laugh)
Peter	***gum is u dun ask . . .*** 咁 係 你 唔 問 gam2 hai6 nei5 ng4 man6	then it's you who don't ask him to pick you up
Peter	dun say wt danger later 唔 好 話 咩 危 ng4hou2 waa6 me1 ngai4 *ar . . . ghaa* 險 一 陣 呀 him2 jat1 zan6 aa3	don't say it is dangerous later (*laugh)
Chloe	I'm doing assignment *ar ma . . . .*	because I am doing assignment [aa1 maa3]
Chloe	forgot *jo*	I forgot about it [zo1]
Chloe	hahaa	(*laugh)
Peter	***or . . . gum u continue lo*** 哦 咁 你 繼 續 囉 ngo4 gam2 nei5 gai3 zuk6 lo1	ok . . . then you continue working on your assignment [lo1]

Note: in the message column, where three lines are provided, the first is the original message and the second and third lines provide for comparison what it has been calqued from in Cantonese, in Chinese characters and in Jyutping Romanisation respectively.

An examination of the calqueing of 'add oil' in recent work by Lim (2015) demonstrates the kind of language evolution that can transpire in such situations of language contact in CMC. Sixty-eight Hong Kong undergraduates, who are bilingual in English but are by and large Cantonese-dominant, reported regular use of Cantonese 加油 when speaking in Cantonese (a score of 2.26, using a three-point scale where 0 = never/rarely and 3 = regularly), but rare use of the English calque 'add oil' whether speaking in Cantonese (0.84), English (0.78) or mixed Cantonese-English (0.87). In CMC, on the other hand, Cantonese 加油 is used less regularly than it is in spoken communication – only relatively often when texting in Cantonese (1.71); however the use of the English calque 'add oil' increases significantly to quite often whether texting in Cantonese (1.33), or in English or Cantonese-English (both 1.72). In fact the overall score for the use of English 'add oil' is higher at 1.59 than the overall score for the use of Cantonese 加油 at 1.33. This is a significant finding in itself – that the CMC platform does indeed prompt the development of a contact variety of English, in this case, in the use of particular Hong Kong English (HKE) phrases, here calqued from Cantonese. In effect, Lim (2015) argues, the increased use of English as a characteristic of the CMC domain comprises a drive in the direction of the community becoming more English dominant, first in that domain and then in others, which is the road to further nativisation of a restructured New English in a contact context. Clearly such an innovation is already widely used in the community, in CMC. Lim's study also highlights a small subset of Hongkongers (numbering four), comprising Hong Kong returnees – i.e. Hongkongers who emigrated several years ago and then returned to Hong Kong – and Hongkongers of mixed parentage who, while still bilingual in Cantonese and English (and other languages), are more English dominant. A different pattern emerges in this group when compared with the linguistic practices of the local Hong Kong group. Cantonese 加油 is used much less regularly when speaking in Cantonese (1.75). English 'add oil' is used more often when texting in any of the languages (1.75 for all). And, perhaps most significantly, English 'add oil' is used significantly more often than the local group when speaking, whether in Cantonese (1.5), in Cantonese-English (1.5) or in English (1.25). By all definitions, this appears to be the start of the spread of the innovation – originally found only in CMC domains – to spoken discourse, possibly catalysed by the more English-dominant members on the periphery (the returnees and mixed-heritage Hongkongers) making the transition from CMC to spoken discourse.

Two more points bear mentioning, as documented in Lim (2015). First, this HKE innovation also appears to be spreading outside the community – that is, to non-Hongkongers with Hong Kong networks. Young Japanese, whose culture also values hard work and whose language also has a similar exhortation 頑張って (がんばって) *ganbatte* (sometimes *gambatte*), are reported to have taken on this Chinese phrase 加油 'add oil' but rendered it as a Japanese, not English, calque (Chie Adachi, personal communication May 2014). Increased mobility, in the form of Japanese and Chinese students on exchange or doing postgraduate study in China and Japan respectively, account for the spread of the term. That the Japanese have English less in their repertoire, and that the Japanese input method for computers and mobile phones is primarily via keyboard keys or numerical keypads corresponding to kana, the syllabic Japanese scripts, would appear to be significant factors for why the English calque has not evolved. Second, a most recent and prominent use of 'add oil' is found in an initiative in the 2014 pro-democracy protests in Hong Kong – 'Stand by you: "Add oil" machine'. This is an online platform that allows messages of support to be sent by anyone in the world; it then displays the messages, in English and Chinese, in a real-time scrolling feed on the website and in projection on buildings near the protests. The phrases 加油 and 'add oil' are frequently included in these messages, as well as in messages posted in other forms (such as banners, posters and post-its) all over the protest sites; the hashtags #加油 and #addoil have also been used even more than before on social media such as Instagram and Twitter as a consequence of the protests.

CMC and social media are identified as some of the forces in the current knowledge economy that can catalyse the evolution of a new variety (Lim 2015). Even more, when politics, social media and technology (and art) come together to put on public display such an innovation of a contact variety, as in the case of 'add oil', this may well lead to a significant increase in its intelligibility and codification, and further stabilisation of an emerging contact variety.

7.3 CONTACT OPPORTUNITIES IN THE GLOBALISED NEW ECONOMY

The emergence of the globalised new economy has, amongst its consequences, new conditions for the production of language practices and forms, and new challenges to current ways of thinking about language. One of the four consequences – the other three outlined in Chapter 1 – that global expansion has for language, as identified by Monica Heller (2010: 349–52), a leading scholar in this field, is the emergence of 'language industries', where language is not only part of the work process but either the product or an important dimension of it. A number of such language industries comprise novel sites of contact – in this section we explore linguistic migration and call centres, and briefly revisit globalised neighbourhoods (this last topic discussed in Chapter 2) – and the implications for the breadth and diversity of contact situations, in combinations not previously attested, are intriguing.

7.3.1 Linguistic capital

Along the classic lines of sociologist Pierre Bourdieu (2001), the principal forms of capital comprise:

   i. economic capital, which creates and maintains wealth and is immediately convertible to money and property;
  ii. cultural capital, which entails accumulated knowledge and skills that are potentially convertible to economic capital – for example, through educational qualifications;
 iii. social capital, which is made up of group membership, social obligations or group connections – also potentially convertible into economic capital;

iv. symbolic capital, which comprises accumulated prestige and
    honour.

While previously the pursuit of capital was directly linked to business
and commerce, in today's new economy capital may be acquired more
indirectly, usually through the prior possession of a premium language,
which is then exchanged for economic capital. In other words, in the
new economy which highlights language as a resource and a commodity
(one manifestation of Coupland's phenomenon vii), language itself may
be regarded as capital, which possesses value and is a means by which
people and nations may achieve varied goals.

An increasingly common manifestation of the acquisition of linguistic capital is 'linguistic migration',[5] when linguistic capital is not usually available in the aspirants' own country and has to be sought elsewhere. In Asia, Korean and mainland Chinese children, accompanied
by their mothers – known as 'wild goose mothers' (Korean 기러기엄
마 kirogi omma) or 'study mothers/mamas' (Mandarin 陪读妈妈 peidu
mama) – are sent to a foreign country such as Singapore, with the main
aim of acquiring linguistic capital unavailable in their home country.
Such a manifestation of language as capital is supported by other factors
of the global era, and Chew (2010) provides an account of the strategies
of the 'buyers' and the 'sellers' in such an exchange. First, there is
the expanded role of transnational corporations with many production
facilities outside the home countries. Two thirds of the top 700 companies in Korea have branches or regional offices abroad; conversely,
most of the world's 500 largest corporations have a foothold in China.
In both cases, employees need to speak English. Second, education is
highly prized in both these Confucian-based societies, with economic
success closely affiliated to educational success, and children regarded
primarily as the wealth of the family and part of the family's economic
capital. However, employment and educational opportunities are vastly
uneven, with a far greater number of graduates than jobs for them. Competition for the best schools and universities is increasingly fierce, with
great investment in linguistic capital via tuition, supplementary classes,
extra books and so forth. In the realm of language, China has made edu-
cating its population in English a priority. Most recently, English has
started to be taught in all kindergartens, is compulsory in all primary

---

[5] 'Linguistic migration' may be seen as a form of economic migration; more common
   types of transnational migrants include 'astronaut husbands' – professional parents
   who seek to relocate their families in safe havens such as Canada and the US – and
   'satellite kids' – children who remain in the host country even when their parents
   have returned to the country of origin.

schools and is one of three core subjects in the secondary school curriculum. All universities use English as the main medium of instruction in information technology, biotech, new-material technology, finance, foreign trade, economics and law. More than 300 million Chinese are studying English – nearly one quarter of the population. Hand in hand with this has been the growth of a new middle-class population with higher disposable income and technical expertise – the result of industrialisation in Korea in the 1960s and in China from the 1980s and, more broadly, a phenomenon of globalisation (Coupland's phenomenon vi). The growth of the middle class has been extraordinary, particularly in China: while as recently as 2000 only 4 per cent of urban households were middle class, by 2012 this had burgeoned to two thirds of the population, with estimates for 2022 reaching 630 million – three quarters of urban households and 45 per cent of the population.[6] The rise of the middle class is correlated with growing demand for education – in particular, English education. However, the number and level of qualified English teachers in both countries is low. And parents seek to give children an edge – by helping them become fluent in English, and sparing them and themselves the stress of studying in their own countries' education systems. Participants in Chew's (2010) study are clear on this, as seen in the commonly held view, expressed by a Chinese parent in example 7.8.

(7.8)

There are too many geniuses in China . . . the only way to compete with them is to learn English.

Finally, we see how transnational mobility (Coupland's phenomenon iii), another luxury of the global era, completes the picture. Asians, who have experienced economic growth in recent years and who value education, in particular in this era of English education, pursue education abroad. The pursuit of higher education abroad is a practice that has been around for decades, but it has certainly been on the rise, reflecting the globalisation of economies and societies and the expansion of tertiary systems and institutions world-wide. The number of students enrolled in higher education programmes outside their country of citizenship has increased five-fold from some 0.8 million in 1975 to 4.1 million in 2010 (OECD 2012). Students from several Asian countries are the most significant consumers. In 2009, for example, in absolute numbers, the largest numbers of international tertiary students were

---

[6] The various population statistics are updated here, as Chew's (2010) article reports statistics and predictions pre-2010.

from China, India and Korea, with Asian students representing 52 per cent of foreign students enrolled world-wide. However, more recently it is younger students who are journeying abroad. A country in the region such as Singapore, well regarded as English-dominant, has taken advantage of this in recent years, profiling itself as a 'Mecca for education'. Traditionally the island republic has drawn students from Malaysia and Indonesia; now the majority of students are from China, numbering some 36,000 in 2008, and a large number are from Korea – to whom Singapore started actively marketing its education system from 2005 – numbering some 6,500 Koreans enrolled in local schools by 2008. The commodification of Singapore's educational system (another manifestation of Coupland's phenomenon vii) to foreign students involved building on four strengths, as identified by Chew (2010):

  i. use of English as a medium of instruction, and also as a primary working language in society;
  ii. widespread use of Mandarin, both taught in school and used in society;
  iii. high academic standards, with Singapore students consistently ranking highly in mathematics and science competitions, reading literacy skills and other international measures;
  iv. an increasingly cosmopolitan nature, which amongst other things includes policies involving immigration of highly skilled foreigners, notably from China and India, and scholarships available for bright foreign students, also notably from China and India.

A cosmopolitan yet still Asian culture that embraces such values, together with modernity, and an academic culture that values hard work (including a lot of homework, as noted favourably by participants) are both certainly important considerations for these ambitious East Asian parents and students. The very significant presence of Mandarin both in education and in society is also important: this needs no explanation where the Chinese are concerned, and for the Koreans it is the other most important foreign language in their country. However, the English language is clearly the raison d'être for this transnational migration in pursuit of linguistic capital, as evidenced in views expressed by the parents, as in example 7.9.

(7.9)

We will get a 'leg up' when my son goes back to Korea.

Other similar phenomena in this global era that are the consequence of increased mobility, investment in and commodification of education – and, of course, the spread and penetration of English – are also worth mentioning here. Notably these again involve movements, whether of people or material, between communities in the Asian region, and a few examples are described here. In the Japan Exchange and Teaching programme, while the majority of participants who are assistant language teachers are from traditionally (native-)English-speaking countries, some are from Jamaica and Singapore. In 2013, 48 out of a total of 4,000 assistant language teachers hailed from Singapore, which – excluding the native English-speaking countries – comprised the second largest proportion of teachers. Educational software from Singapore also finds its way to other Asian countries – for instance, through donations to rural schools in the Philippines. For students of the University of Hong Kong's Faculty of Social Sciences, one of the many summer internships available is the Migrant Outreach Education Initiative (MOEI), already in its sixth year. This provides nine to ten weeks of intensive English-language education for migrant children and adults in Cambodia, Laos, Myanmar, Thailand and China; in 2013 sixty to seventy students participated in MOEI, approximately three quarters of them coming from Hong Kong. Malaysia, building on its state religion of Islam, is home to the International Islamic University Malaysia (IIUM), an international institution for tertiary education based on Islamic principles, sponsored by eight different governments from the Organisation of the Islamic Conference. The institution draws students from across the region and the world: in 2005 it had approximately 20,000 students from over forty Muslim-majority countries, as well as students from non-Muslim-majority countries. IIUM is significant for at least two language-related reasons. Established in 1983, it became the first international university and the first university in Malaysia to have English as its medium of instruction and administration – and with the Malaysian lecturers this is Malaysian English (MalE) (Hannah Chiang, personal communication July 2012). Arabic is used for instruction in courses related to the Islamic sciences; it also acts as another lingua franca within the university.

In the pursuit of linguistic capital in this global era – which more often than not means English – phenomena such as linguistic migration and various English language teaching programmes such as those listed above produce new sites of contact, which notably happen in the Asian sphere and involve Asian Englishes and Asian languages. Several implications follow from this. The reinforcement of common or similar features of the various languages in the ecologies can be expected. To continue the train of thought of Chapter 5, we may make predictions for the features of particles and tone. As most Asian languages – and, increasingly, Asian varieties of English – have particles, contact between these languages would mean particles being extremely salient in the feature pool or, to put it another way, speakers being primed for particles, already having them in their linguistic repertoire. Anecdotal reports indicate the spread of the Singapore English (SgE)/MalE particle *lah* to Filipino children, as they learn English from educational software from Singapore (Aurelio Viliplano, personal communication Oct 2009, cited in Lim 2014b), and to students in IIUM (Hannah Chiang, personal communication July 2012, cited in Lim 2014b). This latter case is an additionally interesting situation, since this is a situation of contact that can be seen to be a result of a global religion. Where tone is concerned, the contexts which bring together speakers of mainland Southeast Asian and Sinitic languages bring more tone languages and thus more tone into the feature pool of the ecologies, thus increasing its frequency. This may well mean a greater likelihood of tone developing in the emerging Englishes, as has been seen in Chapter 5.

Ironically, it is not such products of contact that individuals necessarily seek in their endeavours. Parents of East Asian students studying in Singapore (in Chew's 2010 study) are quite clear on this point, as exemplified in examples 7.10 and 7.11: views from a Korean and a Chinese parent, respectively.

(7.10)

We discourage our children from speaking local forms of English...

(7.11)

We understand the value of Singlish in Singapore but [it is] certainly not what we want.

The outcomes of such new contexts of contact are well worth monitoring.

7.3.2 Call centres

As outlined in Chapter 1, the global workplace has seen tremendous growth in business process outsourcing, where multinationals and UK- and US-based companies outsource services, such as medical and legal transcription, to developing countries like India and the Philippines because of the factors of cheap labour, English fluency and literacy, and fast (overnight) turn-around time. As noted by Heller (2010) as one of the four consequences of global expansion for language (detailed in Chapter 1), in such economic activities that have to deal with globalised forms of exchange, many more social actors than before are now involved, dealing more often with communication across social, cultural and linguistic differences. Communication involving such diversity raises important issues for language contact.

The call centre industry, often held up as an iconic symbol of the new economy, is certainly one of the better-known business process outsourcing thrusts. Comprising centralised offices used for the purpose of receiving and transmitting a large volume of requests by telephone, administering product support, fielding information enquiries from consumers, telemarketing, debt collection, etc., the industry has been around for some two decades and was an especially fast-growing industry in Asia in the early 2000s. In the period 2001–2003, the US lost 250,000 call centre jobs to Asia. Until very recently, India – in particular Bangalore but also Mumbai and Delhi – was the call centre powerhouse, pulling in US$5.3 billion in revenue in 2009, employing some 350,000 workers in 2012, paying salaries at five times the national average. The typical profile of a call centre worker in India comprises males and females in their early 20s, often with tertiary qualifications and good communication skills. They have been considered the cool new generation, symbolic of India's economic growth; they are financially independent, with work-hard-play-hard lifestyles – 'cyber coolies' not in a real job. In 2011, fourteen years after its start in the industry, the Philippines overtook India as the world's call centre capital, with almost 640,000 Filipinos working in the industry, 75 per cent of these located in the capital region of Metro Manila. The industry in the Philippines is expanding even faster than the global rate, growing by an average annual rate of 28 per cent for the past six years, employing (as of 2013) about 420,000 workers – five out of every hundred applicants – with salaries some 40 per cent higher than the country's minimum wage. Between 2009 and 2011 sector-wide revenues doubled, from US$5.5 billion to topping US$11 billion, accounting for about 5 per cent of the country's GDP, and they are projected to grow to US$20 billion by 2016 (McGeown 2012; Njau 2013). A new player in this field is South Africa, where the industry has grown exponentially over the last ten years – including an increase of over 85 per cent from 2007 to 2010 – with some 10,000 people currently employed in this sector, a number expected to rise to 40,000 by 2015.

Language is critically a commodity here – 'at the centre of the commodification process' (Cowie 2007). The rise and fall of these different players in the industry hinges on their accent. All call centres (in India and the Philippines) provide accent training for their agents. A British English or American English accent is the target, depending on the company and clientele, though increasingly there is a preference for a 'neutral' global accent as it allows workers to be shifted around more easily without additional retraining – sometimes referred to as Call Centre English. While India saw great growth in the earlier years, towards the end of the 2000s there was increased dissatisfaction with the 'Indian accent', with customers from the UK and the US finding it unintelligible, while the South African accent – particular that of Durban – is perceived as more 'neutral', such that UK customers are more receptive to it. The great success of the Philippines in the industry is attributed to their well-educated, youthful and service-oriented workforce, but more specifically to their American colonial past and cultural affinity with the US, where many of the calls originate. Young Filipino call centre workers are steeped in American pop culture and speak English with an accent that is more American and 'more pleasing to North Americans', as claimed by the president of Telus International's Philippines operations.

Scholars working in the field have examined the issue of accent training that call centre workers have to undergo (Cowie 2007, 2010; Rahman 2009), which involves disguising their origins by eliminating stigmatised local features and adapting to American or British norms; this has been couched as cultivating a 'neutralised international accent'. Others have raised the issue of whether this is hegemony or linguistic imperialism (Phillipson 1992) – the dominance asserted and retained by the establishment and continuous reconstitution of structural and cultural inequalities between English and other languages or, in this case, between 'native' and 'non-native' varieties of English, involving the imposition of 'native-speaker' English accents and the corresponding loss of identity. The attempt at or act of accent neutralisation by call centre workers has also been explored along the lines of crossing – that is, the use of a linguistic variety that in one way or another feels anomalously 'other' – or passing, where the speaker is taken for an authentic speaker of that linguistic variety (Rampton 1999). Scholars such as Chand (2009a, 2009b) and Rahman (2009) argue that as passing practices constitute a temporary performance, context-specific in that it is typical of first encounters – often service encounters – designed for a particular audience (Chand 2009a: 80), call centre workers who use native-speaker English are indexing group membership or social identity (Rahman 2009: 326). Identity is thus constantly being created and performed – the conscious creation of a linguistic voice called forth by context and facilitated by the Asian bilingual's linguistic creativity. Language varieties or accents are indeed commodities in this age and, with Asia drawing the call centre jobs, a significant question is whether the world is getting 'flat(ter)' – as journalist-columnist-author Thomas Friedman (2005) suggests has been happening in the sense of the levelling of the global playing field – through the spread of (varieties of the) English language.

In relation to language contact, one of the issues that bears further thought and research is the following. In the call centre industry, there is greater and more intensive contact with Inner Circle English varieties – not under colonial or postcolonial conditions but in the global arena and economy where, more critically perhaps, the differential value of different varieties, such as 'native' versus 'non-native' accents of English, is so clearly commodified. The question arises then whether the varieties involved, such as Indian English and Philippine English, will see a shift towards – a reinforcing, focusing or adopting of – features of more 'native speaker' or 'standard' varieties of English, particularly some American English variety; or whether, conversely, the currency of such varieties will spread, with certain features becoming more widely known in other communities and potentially adopted.

7.3.3 Sino-African relations

Since the medieval age there has been contact between China and the African continent, notably the journeys to China in the fourteenth century of Ibn Battuta, Moroccan scholar and traveller, and Sa'id of Mogadishu, Somali scholar and explorer, and the Ming Dynasty voyages of Chinese Admiral Zheng He and his fleet, which rounded the coast of Somalia and followed it down to the Mozambique Channel. The twenty-first century has witnessed increasingly strong economic ties between the two parties, through Sino-African trade relations, investments and aid on the African continent. China is currently Africa's largest trade partner and the biggest investor in Africa. A million Chinese citizens reside in Africa, and some 500,000 Africans work in China, with the largest African diaspora found in Guangzhou, the commercial and trading centre of south China; it is estimated that some 100,000 Africans are living and doing business in Guangzhou (Bodomo 2010). Only very recently has some research been conducted on language use in these communities. In a survey of 120 Africans and Chinese in Guangzhou, the most frequently used language between the two communities is overwhelmingly English (88.3 per cent), with the majority saying they use English most or all of the time (50 per cent and 35 per cent) (Liu 2013). More pertinently, it is African and Chinese varieties of English that are used (Bodomo 2010, 2012; Liu 2013), as shown in the following examples (A: African interlocutor; C: Chinese interlocutor) of Guangzhou traders. Amongst the linguistic features observed is reduplication – of adjectives or prenominal modifiers to serve emphatic or intensive functions, as in example 7.12, and of verbs to indicate repetition, as in example 7.13

(Liu 2013: 31, 34) – which is common cross-linguistically and is certainly found in African and Sinitic languages.

(7.12)

A: ɛː   *big-big modau,* ɛː
   PRT big-big model PRT
   'Really big model, OK?'

(7.13)

C: you talk-talk-talk too much and push the price.
   'You keep on talking too much and push the price very low.'
A: No, me talk-talk I pay.
   'No, I keep on talking but I pay.'

(7.14)

A: Here, chop-chop-chop-chop-chop-chop-chop...
   'Here, eat eat eat...' [imitating action of eating]
C: Ah I know, chop-chop-chop...
   'Yes, I know, eat eat eat...'
A: Dis means aha finish.
   'This means I don't have any more money.'
C: We we oso need chop-chop.
   'We also need to eat.'

Abbreviation: PRT: particle.

The instance of *chop-chop* in example 7.14 warrants discussion. This reduplicated phrase has long been accepted in English, meaning 'quickly', and is well known to have its origins in Chinese Pidgin English meaning 'quick' (Holm 1988: 516), from Cantonese 急急 *gāpgāp* 'quick'. In the contemporary linguistic practices observed amongst the traders in Guangzhou, however, it is used – by Africans and Chinese alike – to mean 'to eat' (Liu 2013). In various West African Pidgin English varieties, such as Nigerian Pidgin English, Ghanaian Pidgin English and Pichi, the meaning of (non-reduplicated) *chop* is 'to eat, food' (Faraclas 1996; Blench 2006; Yakpo 2009), whose origin is suggested to lie in the obsolete English verb *chap* or *chop* 'to take in the chops and eat' (Huber 1999: 99). It would appear that in the contemporary contact situation, the more stabilised African English varieties may exert more influence. Indeed, this is what seems to be the perception amongst the communities themselves, where the Chinese comment on picking up linguistic patterns such as *now-now* from the Africans (see example 7.15) and, more generally, that 'some Chinese follow African speaking' (Liu 2013).

(7.15)

> The Africans use repetition phrases first and we pick up this expression from them... they say 'now now', 'money money', 'last last'. Sometimes they also say it in Chinese, like when you ask them 'how many', they answer 'henduo henduo' [many many]. They like to use repetition. I asked my coworkers before, I ask 'why did you say "now now"?' My coworker said 'they say it like this, so I also say it in this way'. The Africans bring this expression. They like repetition. You ask them how many and they say 'many many'. They also use 'last last'.

In the opposite direction, accommodation strategies are also observed in the linguistic practices, with Africans (A) exhibiting accommodation towards Chinese (C), as seen with *pieces > piece* in example 7.16 (Liu 2013).

(7.16)

> A: Kilo is how many pieces?
> C: Ten piece.
> A: Oh, ten piece.

The implications for what this means for the feature pool and the resultant restructured variety/ies and mixing of codes are exciting and call for further study.

7.4 CONTACT IN GLOBALISED URBAN AND RURAL POPULATIONS

Globalisation and economic growth are not limited to metropolitan centres but also entail empowering rural populations, and the English language is seen as a crucial key in this process. A striking example can be found in Bangladesh, where a new service, BBC Janala ('window' in Bangla), was launched in 2009. This was part of a nine-year (2008–2017) English in Action language education programme aiming to develop communicative English language skills for 25 million people in Bangladesh, with the goal of contributing to the economic growth of the country by providing communicative English language as a tool for better access to the world economy. The service is available on multiple platforms including mobile phones, the internet, television and print, thus comprising the largest multiplatform innovation to improve English language skills anywhere in the developing world. Apart from being in itself an impressive initiative for affording access to English language learning in Bangladesh, it is worth noting that one of the platforms comprises mobile phones – this is not an insignificant aspect because some 95 million mobile phones are in use in Bangladesh, used by two thirds of the population, notably including the poorer, rural communities.

Another example of the impact of globalisation in rural communities is observed in Lim (2013) of Sri Lanka. At the ceremonial launch of the country's Year of English and Information Technology in 2009 – which also marked the end of the country's twenty-six-year civil war – the Sri Lankan president Mahinda Rajapaksa committed his government to developing English as a tool for rural empowerment, to be delivered to the children of Sinhala- and Tamil-speaking homes. To this end, Sri Lanka looked to India for models and expertise. For example, in September 2009 the Sri Lanka India Centre for English Language Training (SLICELT) was established, comprising collaboration with the English and Foreign Languages University (EFLU) in Hyderabad, India, in a programme for the retraining of teachers in the delivery of 'spoken English' to schools. These 'master trainers' of the Presidential Initiative of English as a Life Skill, who received training from EFLU and, crucially, who come from Sinhala- and Tamil-speaking rural homes, have subsequently trained teachers of the country's elite urban schools to teach spoken English to their students.

Efforts to reach the rural populations have also intensified: 605 cadet officers with the Defence Ministry have trained as English teachers and have been assigned to teach English at schools in remote areas such as Moneragala, Batticoloa, Ampara, Anuradhapura and Polonnaruwa. In rural areas of the country, where the linguistic landscape comprises signage almost exclusively in Sinhala and/or Tamil, advertisements for English classes (in English) can be found displayed along the roads (Lisa Lim, field notes). And external initiatives in the country include the following. In the 'Rural Voices Unlimited' project, funded by the US Embassy in Sri Lanka and promoted through the Rotary Club of Colombo West, toastmasters conduct programmes in five outstation (rural) cities in English communication and leadership skills. A postwar Trincomalee-based project, funded by the German government and in collaboration with the Northern and Eastern Provincial Councils, focuses on public servants and locals working in NGOs. It brings together people from diverse backgrounds – from Sinhala, Tamil and Muslim communities, rural and urban districts, central and devolved government and from different age groups – to provide English language training as a link language and a tool for conflict transformation. Such policies and practice mean a shift in users and competence in English, beyond the exonormative, elite minority of about 10 per cent of the population to a larger community of speakers with some other language(s) in their repertoire.

As argued for what has been transpiring in Sri Lanka (Lim 2013), but as is also the case for Bangladesh, what this holds for the communities in terms of contact is two-fold. On the one hand, there is a great likelihood of the development of a mixed code involving speakers' dominant and/or regularly used language(s) and English, akin to the plurilingual practices described in Chapter 2, which will evolve to become more prominent and widespread in the country than at present. On the other hand, this spread of English to the broader society – in particular the more rural, multilingual and non-English-dominant communities – will certainly result in the evolution and spread of a variety showing increased restructuring and more contact features from the various communities' dominant languages than at present. In Sri Lanka this will include features from Sinhala and Tamil (and note that these two languages have seen typological convergence in Sri Lanka); in the Bangladesh lowlands certainly Bengali, spoken by the majority of the country's inhabitants, as well as other closely related varieties such as Assamese and Urdu; and in the mountainous regions various Tibeto-Burman, Austroasiatic and Dravidian languages. This latter outcome will take some time, of course, perhaps in one or two generations. The increase in the use of such a variety will serve to stabilise it, as the number of its users reaches a critical mass.

7.5 CONTACT IN POPULAR CULTURE

A prominent area in globalisation studies is popular culture – cultural forms that have wide public appeal – in particular popular music, and the global, transcultural identifications that are made possible by global popular cultures and languages. Alastair Pennycook, an early, prominent scholar in this area, points out how the ease of cultural movement in this era is made possible by the transnational role of major languages – such as English, French, Chinese and Arabic – plus new digital media, which together allow popular culture to traverse the globe with speed and gregarity (Pennycook 2010). As a counterpoint to earlier sections in this chapter, here we consider his argument that viewing culture and language in terms only of reflections of the economic actually misses the point that new technologies and communications are enabling immense and complex flows of people, signs, sounds and images across multiple borders in multiple directions. More specifically, Pennycook highlights the significance of the language of popular music in involving the construction, performance and confirmation of cultural identities. Focusing in particular on hip-hop music outside African American culture (2007, 2010) – since, in rap, Pennycook holds, lyrics are more central than in other forms of popular culture – he considers what goes on with language use in 'global music' that is adopted in local contexts. First, since many hip-hoppers come from marginalised communities where linguistic normativity has had much less effect, their mixed-code language will likely reflect local language use (Pennycook 2007: 137). Then, rather than the view that hip-hop and rap are just expressions of African American culture, and that all forms of rap and hip-hop elsewhere are therefore derivative of these origins, he argues that hip-hop has become a vehicle through which local identity is reworked. He suggests that there are not just new possible alignments along old linguistic lines, but rather new possibilities of local/global affiliation, which have not been imagined before; and further, that new identifications made possible through popular cultures are never stable or permanent, but are always in flux.

Pennycook illustrates his points using the hip-hop of, amongst others, Malaysian and Japanese hip-hop groups, in which 'flows' between different codes are observed. There are borrowings and imitations of African American English, for instance in Malaysian Too Phat's *hip-hop be connectin' Kuala Lumpur with LB* in example 7.17 and in Japanese hip-hop group Rip Slyme's *yo bring that, yo bring your style.*

(7.17)

Hip-hop be connectin' / Kuala Lumpur with LB / Hip-hop be rockin' up towns / Laced with LV /

Ain't necessary to roll / In nice rimmed M3's / And be blingin' / Hip-hop be bringin' together emcees /

Y'all askin' who that kid / With a flow that's sick / It's Flizzow / And who's Malique / On this Qumran tip /

Now follow / We Too Phat

Hip-hop be runnin' thru our veins / It gets us up in the morning / Hip-hop keeps me sane /

Wherever you rappin' / It's embraced across the globe / It's truly amazing / How it gives people hope / That beat is dope

There are also complex mixes of English with local languages, clearly seen in the Japanese artistes' work. Japanese DJ Tonk in example 7.18 uses the English word 'listen' written in katakana as *rissun*, followed by 2, for 'to', and 'our blues moonlight' in katakana as *buruusu muunraito*, juxtaposed with traditional-sounding Japanese in kanji *tsukiakari no shita* for 'under the moonlight'. Example 7.19 illustrates how Japanese performer Zeebra plays with different rhymes in katakana – *dynamic, Titanic* – producing a final, mixed rhyme with Japanese *dai* 'big' and English *panikku* 'panic' for *daipanikku* 'big panic', to rhyme with *dainamikku* 'dynamic'. Pennycook draws our attention to how separating English and Japanese becomes an impossibility, and the very notion of whether English is invading Japanese culture or being used to represent Japanese culture can no longer be asked (2007: 126–7). Indeed, it is worth noting not only how both the codes – English and Japanese – and the scripts – kanji and katakana – are so mixed, akin to the mixing of codes discussed in Chapter 2, but also how meaning is dependent on such mixtures. (Examples 7.17–7.19 are from Pennycook 2007: 1, 127.)

(7.18)

Lyrics	Transliteration	Translation
リッスン2 俺達の ブルース ムーンラ イト月明かりの下	*rissun* two *oretachino buruusu muunraito tsukiakari no shita*	Listen to our blues moonlight under the moonlight

(7.19)

Lyrics	Transliteration	Translation
のっけからダイナミック まるでタイタニック 想像を超える大パニック	*nokkekara dainamikku marude taitanikku souzouwo koeru dai panikku*	From the very beginning, it was dynamic, just like Titanic, and an unimaginable big panic

At the other end of the spectrum of popular music is a very local genre – Cantopop – which saw its genesis in the mid-1970s as a lyrical mass-appeal style developed through the rise of Cantonese cinema and television, around which the music scene in Hong Kong has centred. While primarily in Cantonese, Cantopop also involves the mixing of English with Cantonese, usually in the salient position of the chorus, to highlight the 'punchlines' or carry the thrust of the song in expressing the singer's requests, as in example 7.20 (Chan 2012: 47). As seen in Chapter 2, a mixed Cantonese-English code rather than a single language – that is, Cantonese or English alone – is increasingly associated with a local 'Hong Kong Chinese' identity. Chan hypothesises that such a mixing of codes in Cantopop and other popular culture media serves to reinforce this association and contributes to positioning Hong Kong Chinese as modern, 'global' people who are less bound by Chinese culture and traditions.

(7.20)

1 See me fly, I'm proud to fly up high
2 不 因 氣 壓 搖 擺, 只 因 有 你 擁 戴
   bat1 jan1 hei3-ngat3 jiu4-baai2, zi5 jan1 jau5 nei5 jung2-daai3
   'Not wavering from side to side amidst different air pressure because of your love'
3 Believe me I can fly, I'm singing in the sky
4 假 使 我 算 神 話, 因 你 創 更 愉 快
   gaa2-si2 ngo5 syun3 san4-waa2, jan1 nei5 cong3 gang3 jyu6-faai3
   'If I were a myth, it'd be a pleasant one because you made it.'
   [Chorus II]
5 Let me fly, I'm proud to fly up high
6 不 因 氣 壓 搖 擺, 只 因 有 你 擁 戴
   bat1jan1 hei3-ngat3 jiu4-baai2, zi5 jan1 jau5 nei5 jung2-daai3
   'Not wavering from side to side amidst different air pressure because of your love'
7 Believe me I can fly, I'm singing in the sky
8 假 使 愛 有 奇 跡, 跟 你 創 最 愉 快
   gaai2-si2 oi3 jau5 kei4-zik1, gan1 nei5 cong3 zeoi3 jyu6-faai3
   'If miracle is borne out of love, it'd be a pleasant one because I made it with you.'

Cantopop is by definition largely in a high variety of Cantonese or written Mandarin lyrics sung in Cantonese. In contrast, the hip-hop music scene which emerged in Hong Kong in the mid-1990s used (low) Cantonese and English, with a third language also at times included in the mix – Mandarin (known as Putonghua in Hong Kong), which has become an important political language in the city since its handover back to Chinese rule in 1997. In example 7.21, Hong Kong hip-hop group 456 Wing, Fama (Six-Wing and C-gwan) draws on Mandarin for an enhanced rhyming resource (Lin 2012: 67–8).

(7.21)

別人笑我瞓街邊 (*gaai-bin*) 我比他人更開心 (*kai xin*)
'Other people laugh at my sleeping on the street; I'm actually more happy than many people'

The rap is primarily in Cantonese, but only works if the final two characters of the sentence are pronounced in Mandarin as *kai xin*, rather than Cantonese *hoi sam*, such that this rhymes with Cantonese *gaai-bin* 'street-side'.

Especially significant for the study of language and contact is the use of creoles in rap, including Jamaican patwa in the UK, Haitian Creole in Montreal, Cabo Verde in the Netherlands and African American English, seen above in example 7.17, as well as Aboriginal English. This, as Pennycook (2007: 130) underlines, can be a sign of street credibility and local authenticity, which also provides an avenue for an oppositional stance in terms of language use rather than lyrical intent. Example 7.22 is an example of hip-hop in the Philippines (Pennycook 2007: 129–30), from the group GHOST 13 (Guys Have Own Style to Talk, 1 group, 3 rappers), who use a mixed code – what they call *halo-halong lenguaje* 'mixed language'. This not only brings together several languages of the community's multilingual repertoire, including English, Tagalog, Visaya and Tausug, but also includes a contact language Chavacano,[7] a Spanish-based creole from Zamboanga in western Mindanao (English; *Tagalog; Chavacano (Zamboangueño)*).

(7.22)

Now lisnen up *por pabor makinig* 2004 rap *sa Pinas yumayanig lalong lumalakas* never *madadaig*
'Now listen to 2004 Philippines rap getting stronger and never beaten'

Making a connection with creole studies, in particular the 'creole exceptionalism' debate (as discussed in Chapter 4), Pennycook goes on to suggest that 'the transgressive language use of rap, mixing and borrowing, using language from wherever, changing the possibilities of language use and language combinations, should be seen as a creolising force' (2007: 132). He claims that this applies whether it involves a variety accepted as a creole such as Chavacano or the mix of Turkish, German and American English used by Turkish youths in their hip-hop culture in Berlin. It is indeed a point worth noting, as put forward by Pennycook (2007: 131), that creole languages, cultures and ways of being should be the model for a new era of globalisation, with hip-hop a driving force not only for the use of creoles but for their creation.

7.6 REFLECTIONS ON GLOBALISATION AND CONTACT

This chapter is by necessity exploratory in nature. Many of the research thrusts presented here are very recent and still being developed. However, what should be clear is that the various contexts of contact – in today's globalised, transnational, transient societies, as well as in rapidly growing urban sprawls – are certainly hothouses for language contact and the emergence of new varieties. We expect to see a growing body of work in these areas in future years. Our conclusions to this as well as the rest of the book are presented in the next, final chapter.

---

[7] The word *Chabacano* is derived from Spanish, meaning 'poor taste, vulgar'.

DISCUSSION POINTS

1. Examine the various phenomena associated with globalisation outlined in this chapter and consider how they play out with regard to the position and use of languages in the nation state or community you live in.

2. Examine your linguistic practices in the CMC you partake in – SMS, email, social networking such as Facebook, Instagram or Twitter – and try to evaluate the impact of a global language such as English, or some other global language dominant in your part of the world – perhaps Mandarin or Spanish – coming into contact with other languages you use. Also try to identify other outcomes of contact that would appear to be accelerated by virtue of the CMC platform being used.

3. If you listen to popular music such as hip-hop, see if you find mixing of codes and/or the use of creoles. What does the use of English alongside the local language in popular music by local musicians mean for the expression of culture and identity? Does the platform of popular music – and, often, the associated urban youth culture – afford greater creativity and thus greater opportunities for innovation in contact situations, including the creation of new creoles?

FURTHER READING

A comprehensive collection of language and globalisation studies – the first volume to assemble leading scholarship in the rapidly developing field – covering topics such as tourism, language teaching, social networking, and markets, is Coupland (2010b). For an account of some of the catalysts for language contact and evolution in the current knowledge economy, see Lim (2015). For the spread of popular culture and language, see Pennycook (2007).

8 Reflections and future directions

8.1 THE STATE OF OUR FIELD

In conceptualising and developing the themes of our book, we have made an effort to be forward looking, as well as eastward minded, in order to present fresh – at times challenging – theoretical views and offer novel empirical content. It seems therefore apt at this point to look back and ask ourselves where we have come to in the field of contact linguistics.

The study of language contact can hardly ever be dissociated from one thinker in particular who, in a short lifespan, made impressive contributions: Uriel Weinreich, mentioned at the outset of this book. Credited by many as the father of modern contact linguistics, his views have time and again proven to be some of the most insightful of our field. As we are now six decades beyond the date of his most influential publication, *Languages in Contact* (1953), we take Weinreich's legacy as the benchmark for our field and for the contributions of this very volume. From a methodological point of view, Weinreich had already established a tradition that continues to this date – namely an intimate relationship between contact and sociolinguistics. His work was to be of great influence for William Labov (Kim 2011) and established early on an important fact: that solid contact linguistics must be closely related to the study of social, cultural and political issues. The outcomes of language contact, which Weinreich calls 'interference', were to be in large part understood on the basis of social variables, demographic as well as historical factors, gender and race, and institutional as well as political functions. In this respect, Thomason and Kaufman's (1988) model of contact, while paying close attention to structural issues in language contact, also reinforces the notion of sociohistorical dynamics as the fundamental explanatory dimension in the study of borrowing and shift.

Thomason and Kaufman also argue against the possibility of structural constraints as an explanatory dimension. Following in these eminent footsteps, our own contribution can be seen as basically a work

187

of sociolinguistic nature, albeit focused on contact. In our analysis of
contact dynamics, we stress that it is ultimately speakers, and speakers'
conscious and less conscious motivations, that determine the outcomes
of contact. This is most clearly seen in the field of language genesis,
which we explain on the basis of identity alignment – namely the construction of a new sociocultural entity of which a new variety is an
essential part (see Chapters 3 and 4). And we find no counterevidence
to Thomason and Kaufman's skeptical view of structural constraints.
As shown in our study of Sri Lanka Malay (SLM), for example, even the
most unexpected developments occur at the grammatical level, when
the ecology – i.e. the typological, social and cognitive dimensions – is
taken into account. The explanatory dimension in contact linguistics
remains, in our view sixty years on, strongly 'external' to structural
dynamics. We see a future in which this intimate bond between contact and sociolinguistics will be strengthened and integrated further, in
particular with the developing joint efforts in the fields of second and
third language acquisition. This has proven to be a rewarding approach
as shown, for example, in the work on relexification and metatypy. Important contributions in which bi/multilingualism and language contact come together have increased in recent years, as can be seen in Yip
and Matthews (2007) for the field of Cantonese–English bilingualism
and Siegel's work on pidgin and creoles (2010).

It is perhaps less familiar to many that Weinreich's work derived in
large part from his dissertation completed two years earlier (Kim 2011:
103). In that work we can distinguish an approach that today would
easily come under the field of 'language documentation', inclusive of
anthropological field annotations and documentary material. Kim goes
so far as to liken him to a scholar-explorer of a previous century in his
attention to tradition and beliefs. This is a very welcome dimension
from our point of view; we see the documentation paradigm as something that goes beyond the concern with minority and endangered
languages. The approach of language description and documentation
is, in our minds, a very promising one in contemporary linguistics,
and brings us back to the very origins of our field as a subfield of
anthropology. Documentation means careful attention to the context
in which language develops; this applies just as much to the study of
contact. As mentioned above, that context includes everything from
history to typological inventory. Beyond that, it also implies looking at
language *use* rather than languages as isolated structural systems. We
believe that in many multilingual contexts language contact means
more than a mere contact between two well-defined varieties. It means
looking at patterns of mixing as communicative practices in their own

right and dealing with varying degrees of competence in the different varieties in contact. It also forces us to consider blurred and transient linguistic practices such as 'crossing' and 'styling' (e.g. Rampton 1995) – the use of linguistic varieties of a community of which the speaker is not considered a member, thus blurring the relation between language use and community belonging – as part and parcel of what defines languages in contact. In this sense, the field has come a long way from the study of straightforward bilingual situations such as those that typify western European standardised linguistic societies, and we have tried to shift the agenda from the more 'static' to the more 'dynamic' types of multilingual contexts, following Weinreich's classification. It is on the understanding of the latter, we believe, that much future research should focus.

Where we see ourselves making a step forward is indeed in moving the notion of the dynamic ecology even further. The range of contexts studied in this book marks a departure from classic studies such as French–German or even German–Romansch bilingualism. These contexts that have for so long dominated the agenda of contact linguistics share a number of common traits.

   i. Typologically, they centre on grammars of the Standard Average European type – i.e. they present us with a tiny subset of structural features amongst the world's linguistic diversity.
  ii. Sociolinguistically, they offer rather clean objects of investigation, with simple standardised varieties and often clearly outlined dynamics of prestige, as well as political functions.
 iii. Most often we are looking at bilingual rather than trilingual or multilingual encounters.

The contexts we have primarily focused on in this book share the following features.

   i. They involve typologically diverse and distant languages in contact, introducing in the contact arena Sinitic, Austronesian, Dravidian and other non-Indo-European varieties.
  ii. They involve varieties in contact that range from national language to minor dialects, pidgins, creoles and other complex objects of linguistic enquiry, from a sociolinguistic, cultural and political/ideological perspective.
 iii. They tend to involve three or more varieties in contact – i.e. they focus more on multilingual rather than bilingual contexts. We believe the former to be a somewhat more common state of affairs in present as well as past societies.

In these respects, then, we hope to have succeeded in offering fresh and challenging ideas.

8.2 ONGOING DEBATES

In this final chapter, we highlight two areas in scholarship on language contact that have attracted – or continue to attract – much interest and research: the notions of universality and exceptionalism, and the debate on simplicity and complexity in languages.

8.2.1 Universality and exceptionalism

In discussing categorisation in scientific thought, the philosopher Paul Feyerabend (1987: 111–12) points out that 'different forms of knowledge engender different ordering schemes...Lists classify in one dimension...[Other] classificatory schemes...may be multidimensional, but static'. Further, classification is a product of certain theories, worldviews and agendas, and serves particular purposes. As outlined in Chapter 1, in the realm of contact linguistics the traditional literature has identified typologies that distinguish between different types of contact languages. The literature to this day compartmentalises pidgins, creoles, mixed languages and – on occasion – New Englishes, and explains how they can be distinguished on (a) structural, (b) developmental and/or (c) sociohistorical grounds.

In the view held by us and a number of scholars before us – most eminently Mufwene and DeGraff – informed by lessons drawn from contact languages of non-European heritage, argument (a) largely fails to deliver a clear typology. As argued repeatedly by Mufwene (1997, 2001), we find that how varieties are named 'has to do more with who has appropriated and speaks them than with how they developed, how different they are structurally from each other, hence how mutually intelligible they are' (Mufwene 1997: 82). Those varieties spoken by descendants of European speakers of English are considered 'legitimate offspring' of the English language, while its 'illegitimate offspring' are the varieties spoken by those who are not, with the more extreme group of 'illegitimate offspring' being the English-based pidgins and creoles. In fact, what are considered 'legitimate' varieties of English have all seen language contact in their development. For example, Irish and Scot-Irish Englishes were influenced by contact with Gaelic, but because these are spoken by communities of 'native speakers' of English, even in their most non-standard forms, they are not termed creoles, in spite of the contact involved in their development. Using a range of examples of Englishes,

Mufwene goes on to illustrate how 'if mutual intelligibility were such a critical criterion over sharing an identifiable ancestor, there would be more reasons for treating Modern English varieties and creoles as dialects of the same language than for lumping the former together with Old English while excluding creoles' (1997: 190).

Neither is there much substance behind argument (b), if for no other reason than that – as long as we maintain the assumption of language transmission being a universal cognitive endowment of humans – there cannot be but one path to acquisition. There are, though, correlations between language type and social context, and these still require explanation. This further justifies the slant of this book, since (c) can only be understood through proper sociohistorical work.

To date, attempts to construct typologies of exceptionality when it comes to contact languages, and in particular creoles, still fall short of the mark. The two proposals that have gone beyond the trivial – Bickerton's Language Bioprogram Hypothesis (LBH), which can be credited with having launched decades of challenging and innovative research, and McWhorter's Creole Prototype (CP), which may be seen as a new incarnation of the LBH – we explored in some detail in Chapters 3 and 4. Even with all the debate and discussion invested in these approaches over the years, the major limitations of both approaches still stand. These are (a) the absence of historical realism, (b) a lack of thorough typological grounding required for any sound theory of language evolution to really work and (c) an account – whether on generative or any other theoretical lines – of why non-creole languages would choose to abandon such an ideal functional state in their lifespans. As discussed in Chapters 3 and 4, the LBH has not only failed to account for the evolution of a number of typical creoles, it has even been proven inappropriate to fully account for the development of Hawai'i Creole English (HCE) (Roberts 1998; Siegel 2007b), the variety on which it was first developed. The CP, despite its many incarnations and fierce defences against the criticism received, still fails to address the basic observation made four decades ago (Givón 1979): that typical creole traits can by and large be derived from the substrate typologies. Indeed, this applies to all other attempts (see e.g. Bakker et al. 2011) to construct contact languages as a class apart from other natural languages. The existence of a single-digit number of features that at times marginally diverge from the typologies of the substrates is typologically and diachronically largely irrelevant.

In scholarship on English varieties too, the concept of vernacular universals has attracted a great deal of attention especially amongst variationist linguists in recent years. As conceived by Jack Chambers

(2004: 128), vernacular universals are 'a small number of phonological and grammatical processes [that] recur in vernaculars wherever they are spoken', which includes vernaculars of all kinds: (non-standard) social and regional dialects, child language, pidgins, creoles and interlanguage varieties. Chambers argues that their ubiquity cannot have been due to diffusion by the founder of the dialect because of geographical spread and diversity of occurrence, and concludes that they must represent 'natural' features of the human language faculty (Chambers 2004: 128–30), and they are thus not restricted to English.

A related approach affords some nuance by identifying cross-dialectal patterns, not merely on an undifferentiated concept of vernaculars but on the basis of a typology of vernaculars according to the nature of the speakers' social networks. As mentioned in Chapter 4, Trudgill (1995, 1996, 2002 and others) identifies 'low contact' versus 'high contact' varieties as a principal factor along which features vary in characteristic ways. With the aim of exploring quantitatively structural complexity and identifying vernacular universals or angloversals, Bernd Kortmann and Benedikt Szmrecsanyi (2004 and others) have examined large-scale patterns of morphosyntactic variation in English varieties. They argue that variety type – comprising high-contact first language (L1) (which includes modern urban and standard varieties as well as overseas varieties with significant mixed settler input), traditional or low-contact L1 (which includes traditional rural dialects), second language (L2) varieties, and pidgins and creoles – is a better predictor of a variety's overall morphosyntactic profile than geographical provenance. This suggests that there is some basis for such typologies. Such an approach – a highly abstracted aggregation of varieties in the search for universals – may, however, obscure the sources of the presence or absence of a particular feature. In particular for bilingual varieties of English, it is imperative, as Devyani Sharma (2009) argues, first to investigate substrate explanations. More specifically, she contends that it is inadequate to define a feature as broadly as 'zero past tense forms of regular verbs', 'wider range of uses of the progressive' or 'deletion of *be*', as in Kortmann and Szmrecsanyi's features #40, #21, and #57 – all amongst their 'candidates for universals of New Englishes', described as shared across a number of regions, including Asian Englishes (2004: 1193). Sharma shows how, although at face value features #40 (past tense use) and #21 (progressive use) can be found in both Indian English and Singapore English (SgE), the actual distribution and use of the former is strikingly parallel in both varieties, while the use of the latter is strikingly different. Significantly, the use of the former feature in the substrate systems is found to be parallel as well, while the use of the latter feature in the substrate systems is different. In other words, Sharma concludes, the degree and distribution of a given feature in a contact variety must be understood in relation to the substrate before any universal claims can be made.

8.2.2 Complexity

The evolutionary approach, as outlined in Chapter 4, has the appeal of being able to account for language evolution within a uniformitarian framework, which we believe is a theoretical advantage. In this approach, the output of any contact situation is directly related to the input languages. For example, if salient morphological paradigms are found in one or more of the dominant input languages, the prediction would be for such morphological patterns to be found in the new grammar. At the same time the CP, in spite of various criticisms directed at it, also has an extremely strong appeal in offering a possible explanation of why languages show markedly different morphological typologies. In this view, morphological abundance is a direct outcome of a language's history. Following the idea of a CP, while continuous and uninterrupted transmission leads naturally to morphological elaboration in mature languages, transmission in contact scenarios, which as we will recall is seen as deficient for optimal learning, is linked to morphological simplification. In other words, strong L1 transmission results in agglutinative or fusional languages, while L2-based transmission yields analytic types. This dialogue is still very much ongoing – for example, in the very recent exchanges on the CP and the evolutionary approach between McWhorter (2012, 2013, 2014) and Mufwene (2014) – and questions of complexity have become important to the field of linguistics in general (see chapters in Miestamo, Sinnemäki and Karlsson 2008; Sinnemäki 2011; Good 2012). Our views on the matter can be articulated as follows.

If we assume that morphological complexity is an appropriate indicator of overall linguistic complexity, we need to think beyond creoles and look at isolating languages overall. One of the early views on the nature of analytic languages can be found in the work of Wilhelm von Humboldt. Humboldt was a keen student of Chinese because the language was essential in the development of his morphological typology. Chinese was, after all, the champion of isolation – especially since Humboldt was familiar with older texts, which tend to be even more analytic in nature that contemporary ones. Humboldt correctly observed that Chinese lacks morphology but relies on other syntactic means for grammatical functions, including word order and particles. But Humboldt was also a believer in the fact that some languages were superior to others in their power of expression and in the way in which they could capture complex concepts. This, to be sure, had nothing to do with more or less sophisticated civilisations. In Humboldt's view, it was almost accidental: some languages, like the Indo-European ones, were fortunate enough to have reached higher stages of sophistication; others, like Chinese, were unfortunate in not having attained the proper structure (i.e. inflection) (Yao 2011). While acknowledging that Chinese syntax is often 'hidden', Humboldt still took a clearly Eurocentric position: lack of morphological material was an indication of a 'simpler' form. We could propose ways to turn this logic on its head. One could argue that overt categories, especially when redundant, move a grammar away from its optimal or 'pure' form. This would make analytic languages the purest type, and consequently label other types of grammar as 'corrupt'. But this is not particularly revealing either. The interesting question, rather, is: can morphological type really be related to language development?

Today we know enough of languages of the isolating type to point out, conversely, that there are of course many areas of alleged complexity that inflecting languages lack. Many strongly isolating languages – think of Chinese and Thai, as well as Kwa in West Africa – display tone systems with lexical and grammatical function. Such suprasegmental complexity is not commonly found in morphologically rich languages. We also know that pragmatic (or utterance) particles play a significant grammatical role in the marking of mood in these languages – again something lacking in, say, Indo-European languages altogether. Would it thus be fair to say that Chinese is suprasegmentally and pragmatically more complex than other languages? Are these types of complexity also linked to language development?

Recall that, according to McWhorter (2005, 2011), 'normal' languages are highly complex. If languages simplify, that is an indication of adult second language acquisition (SLA) at some stage, which, in his view, applies to creoles, Mandarin, Indonesian, English and others alike. McWhorter argues that if your language does not have allomorphy, fine-grained syntactic and semantic distinctions and irregularity, it could belong to one of two groups: non-hybrid conventionalised second-language varieties (NHCSLV) or creoles. The difference between the two is that creoles are even simpler than NHCSLV.

This thesis causes a lot of discomfort for a number of reasons. Here, we focus on the most fundamental one – namely the fact that the concepts of 'linguistic simplicity' and 'complexity' are used in a pre-scientific manner – with 'unscientific or unproven prejudice' (Giuffrè 2013). McWhorter's classification is clearly Eurocentric in its inter-pretation of these notions, when you consider that simple = of little value; complex = not possessing a general harmony; and intermediate = good, balanced (Giuffrè 2013). Be that as it may, we can give part of McWhorter's claim the benefit of the doubt, in particular because it is reinforced by the observations on the issue of 'maturation'. Let us assume, along with Dahl (2004), that some languages, in their history, accumulate morphology. This could be accidental, as indeed suggested by Dahl. It may be that other languages accumulate a different type of complexity, or that they remain the same, for no apparent reason. Following McWhorter, however, we would have to say that languages without complexity (still to be narrowly defined) have lost it due to suboptimal SLA. This is still problematic. Within an evolutionary framework we can show that SLA can also lead to morphological complexity, as shown by the paramount case of SLM. As suggested in Chapter 4, in the case of SLM, complexification happens, undoubtedly due to typological pressure in the contact situation. In this case, originally isolating varieties of Malay acquire robust nominal morphology and develop tense categories under the influence of Lankan languages (Sinhala and Tamil). Crucially, it is not relevant that SLM does not display all the morphological abundance of either Sinhala or Tamil, as McWhorter would want it. What is crucial is that the ancestral varieties of Malay acquire a lot of alleged signs of complexity and maturation. SLM is a clear case of contact-induced complexification in SLA, which goes against orthodox positions on simplification. Whether we posit a Malay pidgin as the ancestral language or – more realistically – various Malay vernacular varieties, the general observation remains that morphological material can develop under radical contact.

We believe that there is a conceptual mistake in comparing a creole grammar to its substrate or its lexifier in order to determine its degree of complexity. In order to illustrate this, let us use the following story. There is a rich, happy child who owns three bicycles: a red, a blue and a yellow one. He likes taking turns riding them around his yard but one day he tires of changing between bikes and decides he wants one of all three colours. So he cleverly disassembles them and rebuilds a new bike out of the selected parts: he wants yellow wheels, a red frame and all mechanical parts in blue. Now he is riding his new tri-colour bike proudly and his father comes out into the garden. What should a proud, wise father think: that his boy is amazing in having been able to create such a splendid new bike, or that the new bike is defective because it lacks the pieces of the other bikes left out on the side? As with all stories, it is just a simple way to visualise a problem. In a multilingual ecology, with many competing languages in use, a newly created contact language will never have all the structural features of each single contributing language. If it did, there would be too many redundant features. It must therefore have a subset of features of each.

As such, at the same time, it also has 'more' than any of those individual languages. So even from a purely structural point of view, our feeling is that the idea of creole simplicity does not hold.

As discussed in Chapter 4, however, the correlation between morphological type and sociodemographic factors has indeed been established in a scientific manner in Lupyan and Dale (2010). In their study the authors show a tendency for small languages spoken in relatively isolated niches ('esoteric') to show rich inflectional morphology, while large speech communities in contact with neighbours ('exoteric') tend towards more analytic morphology. If this correlation stands the test of time, we clearly have something to explain. What we believe needs explanation is why in certain communities morphological elaboration occurs. If morphology is redundant or even difficult for the adult's language faculty, it strikes us as problematic to suggest it may develop in order to facilitate acquisition in the child (see Lupyan and Dale 2010).

8.3 CURRENT AND FUTURE DIRECTIONS

To round off this book, in this final section we identify a number of topics that we believe are pertinent to our world today and should receive more attention in current and future studies of language contact.

8.3.1 Broadening the typological scope

As pointed out in Chapter 1, the majority of published research on contact languages, in particular pidgins and creoles, has grown out of Western scholarship and has focused on contact languages that developed as a consequence of European expansion into Africa and the Caribbean. With the resulting varieties predominantly based on lexifiers such as English, French, Dutch, Portuguese and Spanish, and on West African substrates such as Akan, Wolof and Ewe, our hypothesising about the emergence and typology of the world's pidgin and creole languages tends to be influenced by a Eurocentric view and a typological bias. Recent decades have seen a mustering of effort to redress this bias, in the work of scholars that shifts the focus of pidgin and creole studies from the better-known Atlantic and Caribbean contexts to those of the Indian Ocean, the South China Sea and the Middle East, such as the Indo-Portuguese creoles, Mindanao Chabacano, Makista, China Coast Pidgin, Chinese Pidgin Russian, Bazaar Malay and Gulf Pidgin Arabic (see e.g. articles in Ansaldo 2010b; Cardoso, Baxter and Pinharanda Nunes 2012; Buchstaller, Holmberg and Almoaily 2014; Manfredi and Tosco

2014). The recently published *Atlas of Pidgin and Creole Language Structures* (*APiCS*) (Michaelis et al. 2013), as noted in Chapter 3, is successful in having about one quarter of the seventy-six languages in its data set non-Indo-European-based languages, and about one fifth of them found in Asia. Similarly, the *Electronic World Atlas of Varieties of English* (*eWAVE*) (Kortmann and Lunkenheimer 2013), an interactive database on morphosyntactic variation in spontaneous spoken English, includes fifty varieties of English (traditional dialects, high-contact mother-tongue Englishes and indigenised L2 Englishes) and twenty-six English-based pidgins and creoles in eight Anglophone world regions (Africa, Asia, Australia, the British Isles, the Caribbean, North America, the Pacific and the South Atlantic). Such corpora offer a more extensive platform to test hypotheses on language contact on a more diverse collection of languages. Work that looks at diverse contexts, before and after Western colonial expansion, contributes insights into language contact in historical settings and with empirical features substantially different from those that have thus far shaped the theory of the field. Future research will need to continue expanding the study of non-Indo-European, non-West African contact languages.

An approach to contact language formation (CLF) that encompasses varieties that are traditionally categorised as New Englishes is also important. New Englishes traditionally developed in classroom acquisition contexts, and it has been held that New Englishes and creoles are prototypically clearly differentiable in their social circumstances and linguistic forms (Mesthrie and Bhatt 2008: 183). Mesthrie and Bhatt note that some 'language shift' varieties do show overlaps with creoles (Irish English, South African Indian English, SgE) but overall the varieties surveyed (Nigerian English (NigE), Indian English) are clearly differentiable in their multilingual ethos and structural outcomes. At the same time, such Englishes have been evolving through successive generations who are L1 speakers of the varieties but are also using the English variety in a multilingual contact setting. We hope to have shown that studying New Englishes with an eye on contact dynamics (e.g. Lim and Gisborne 2009, 2011), which includes creating corpora that recognise the multilingual ecology and repertoire of the speakers, can highlight the common processes that such contact Englishes and creole varieties undergo, as well as the structural outcomes.

8.3.2 Contact languages in national language policy and planning ■

With the development and stabilisation in communities of vernacular languages including contact languages – such as creoles – and minority varieties – such as African American Vernacular English – an issue that has come to the fore in recent years is their place in national language planning in general and, more specifically, in the implementation of such varieties in education. Tok Pisin is often viewed as a success story in this dimension. What developed as an English-based trade pidgin evolved and stabilised, becoming the L1 of communities in Papua New Guinea, and became one of the three official languages of the country alongside English and Hiri Motu. Tok Pisin is frequently the language of debate in the national parliament and is often used in broadcasting. In addition, while most government documents are produced in English, public information campaigns are often partially or entirely in Tok Pisin. Until recently, English was the official language of education in Papua New Guinea, and used in all government schools (although Tok Pisin was widely used in community and church-run pre-schools and vocational schools). However, with the recent education reform, communities can choose the language to be used in the first three years of elementary education, and many have chosen Tok Pisin.

The situation of Tok Pisin is the exception rather than the rule; the majority of vernacular languages, such as contact languages, tend to be marginalised and even stigmatised in their societies. They are rarely considered viable options in official language and education policy, considered as they are as the greatest barrier to the acquisition of the standard language, and academic and economic success. Few formal educational programmes actually make use of vernaculars; Siegel's (2007c) overview identifies just three creoles in four countries or territories that are officially used in a nationwide instrumental programme – that is, as a medium of instruction in primary school for teaching literacy and content subjects such as mathematics. These are Seselwa in the Sechelles, Haitian Creole in Haiti and Papiamentu in the Netherlands Antilles and Aruba.

Several other projects exist around the world, with varying degrees of success, such as Jamaican Creole (JC) in Jamaica, French Creole in St Lucia, Papiamentu in the Netherlands Antilles, Lesser Antilles French Creole or Kwéyòl in Saint Lucia and Chabacano in Chabacano communities in the Philippines (see chapters in Migge, Léglise and Bartens 2010; St-Hilaire 2011). Following on the thrusts in such research, further study needs to compare different kinds of educational activities involving creoles, with a view to identifying the sociolinguistic, educational and ideological contexts. It should also investigate the factors and procedures necessary for successfully developing, evaluating and reforming educational activities that aim to integrate creole languages in a viable and sustainable manner into formal education.

8.3.3 Computer-mediated communication ▬▬▬▬▬▬

As mentioned in Chapter 7, computer-mediated communication (CMC) comprises a platform where, in certain contexts, users privilege a language that they would not normally use, such as Cantonese-dominant Hongkongers employing English on CMC. This leads to greater opportunities for the mixing of codes as well as for the evolution of a restructured variety (Lim 2015). In fact, as demonstrated in other contexts, the stabilisation of contact varieties and the emergence of norms may well take place on CMC platforms. For example, Kreol, the French-lexified creole and non-standardised L1 of the majority of Mauritians, is now gaining ground as a written language in the specific context of CMC, which has led to the emergence of writing norms (Rajah-Carrim 2009). Similarly, the standardisation of orthography taking place in JC is not the result of centralised expert language planning but of grassroots activity in CMC (Hinrichs 2004).

Furthermore, web-based communication is particularly significant because it comprises a platform that may be used by communities beyond the original, 'local' context – primarily communities of the diaspora. As observed for users of JC by Christian Mair, diasporic web-based communities of practice use JC forms far more commonly than in traditional writing – an expected result – but also more frequently than in spoken face-to-face interaction (Mair 2011: 234). Such patterns were also noted, for instance, in the case of Hong Kong Cantonese–English bilinguals in CMC (Chapter 7). The reason, Mair goes on to explain, for this readiness to use a stigmatised variety in the new medium is that the covert prestige associated comes for free – that is, users do not run the risk of being categorised as uneducated or lower-class (as they would be in face-to-face encounters) but are able to mobilise the linguistic resources of JC for self-stylisation, the creation or atmosphere and the construction of identity. CMC certainly affords increased opportunity for speakers of contact languages: since the advent of social media, numerous Facebook groups, for example, have been created. These include the groups *Palé kréyòl èvè frazé! Apprenons, parlons Créole!, Annou aprann matjé kréyol, Pwezi Kreyòl /Haitian Creole Poetry, Learn Jamaican Patois, Dóci Papiaçám di Macau, Sri Lanka Malay memes, We Facebook in Nyonya-Baba Peranakan patois*, to name just a selection – which afford a site for communities to interact in – or learn – a particular contact language.

Even more significantly, the CMC platform contributes to further evolution of a variety. The usage of JC by the diaspora, notes Mair (2011), would be seen as incoherent if judged by the norms of face-to-face interaction. Mair argues, however, that JC is no longer the 'local' language that it used to be in earlier stages of its development, firmly rooted in its community of speakers and largely confined to use in face-to-face interaction. Rather, it is a vernacular which is regularly heard on the media, has gone on the move and become a globally available linguistic resource, and includes a specific mix of Jamaican English and JC in web-based communication in no way less real than the different one spoken on the island. Similar patterns are found for Nigerian Pidgin, which is transformed but remains a powerful resource for constructing authentic group membership (Mair 2011: 226; Mair and Heyd 2011). In short, CMC is thus a further context for further, ongoing evolution of language varieties.

As noted by Mair (2011: 226), the world-wide web has not only become linguistically heterogeneous in recent years but has also become a repository of substantial amounts of non-standard English. Studying language contact on the web, from the perspective of the sociolinguistics of globalisation, affords an arena for the world-wide spread of originally highly localised vernacular, and for contact between non-standard varieties of English beyond the sphere of face-to-face interaction in physical space.

8.3.4 Urban linguistic diversity and urban vernaculars ▬▬▬▬

As outlined in Chapter 1, a significant development in this era, particularly in Europe, is the changing patterns and itineraries of migration from the outside into Europe and continued migration by the same people inside Europe, with 'more people . . . now moving from more places, through more places, to more places' (Vertovec 2010: 86). They bring with them vastly more numerous and diverse resources and experiences, leading to the notion of superdiversity – which Vertovec (2006) defines as a diversification of diversity, as diversity can no longer be understood in terms of multiculturalism alone in the sense of the presence of multiple cultures in one society. This encompasses the vastly increased range of resources – linguistic, religious, ethnic, cultural in the widest sense – that characterise late modern societies.

The increasingly multilingual composition of the population of modern urban areas and the consequent linguistic diversity has been garnering particular attention, from both political and scholarly parties, in western Europe. Blommaert (e.g. in Blommaert 2007 and Blommaert and Dong 2010), for example, illustrates what transpires under such conditions in the form of what he terms 'globalised neighbourhoods'. In such contexts, new migrants settle in older immigrant neighbourhoods, which thus develop into a layered immigrant space, with older immigrants renting spaces to newer, more temporary, more transient groups, and new segments of the labour market emerging. The newer immigrants live in economically and legally precarious circumstances, and are strongly dependent on informal employment and solidarity networks. Globalised neighbourhoods appear chaotic; common assumptions about the national, regional, ethnic, cultural or linguistic status of inhabitants do not hold. Migrants maintain intensive contacts with networks elsewhere (telephone resources); they follow and are involved in events in their country of origin (internet). This means that their spatial organisation is local as well as trans-local, real as well as virtual, and has effects on the structure and development of language repertoire and patterns of language use. In a small neighbourhood of Berchem in Antwerp, Belgium, for instance, recent West African immigrants would use one or more African languages, plus a heavily accented vernacular variety of West African English, in the neighbourhood and church. In the Turkish bakery, though, a strongly accented and limited variety of local vernacular Dutch – mixed with some English/German words – would be used, and in phone shops typically run by Indians or Pakistanis, or in their child's school, various vernacular Englishes would be relied on, very likely with help from the child's English and Dutch. TV channels (BBC World, MTV; children's programmes) are in English and Dutch. Telephone contacts with home or fellow migrants from the same area occur in African languages. Visits imply a return to African regional language. The picture that is painted is one of extreme linguistic diversity, comprising complex multilingual repertoires. Several fragments of 'migrant' languages and of lingua franca are combined – fragmented and 'truncated' ('incomplete') repertoires: spoken, vernacular and accented varieties of different languages, as well as differentially developed literacy skills in one or some languages. Collaborative work is also prominent, such as translating or assisting in communication. This is certainly the multilingual portrait of today's multicultural urban centres which is worth continued scholarly attention.

In multicultural cities too one finds the development of urban vernaculars or multi-ethnolects, such as Rinkebysvenska in Stockholm, straattaal in the Netherlands, Kiezdeutsch in Berlin, Jallanorsk in Oslo, Københavnsk multietnolekt in Copenhagen, Multicultural London English and Multicultural Paris French. In recent years these have received increased attention from sociolinguists and contact linguists (see e.g. Cheshire et al. 2011; Rampton 2011; Duarte and Gogolin 2013; Gogolin et al. 2013; Nortier and Dorleijn 2013; Siemund et al. 2013). These have for the most part been considered highly specific slang-like linguistic styles or varieties that have emerged amongst multi-ethnic, primarily adolescent groups – part of the linguistic practices of speakers of more than two different ethnic and (by consequence) linguistic backgrounds, containing an unusually high number of features from more than one language, but with one clear base-language, generally the dominant language of the society where the multi-ethnolect is in use (Nortier and Dorleijn 2013: 229). However, scholars are increasingly recognising them as stabilised contact languages (e.g. Nortier and Dorleijn 2013), worth observing both in their development and in scholarship. The use of such urban vernaculars in global popular music such as hip-hop, as discussed in Chapter 7, is also an area worthy of attention.

Finally, the growth of urban areas also involves the absorption of a diverse population of migrants from rural areas around the globe, many of them speakers of endangered languages. While the pragmatic needs of global urban cultures often trigger rapid language shift and loss, it is also often in the diaspora that ancestral language practices are maintained. Multicultural urban centres are thus valuable centres for identifying and studying minority and/or endangered languages (see e.g. Endangered Language Alliance 2012; Lim 2013–2015).

8.4 CONCLUDING REMARKS

In March 2014, in an interview on Nigeria's Wazobia FM, the first radio station in Nigeria to broadcast in Nigerian Pidgin, the US Ambassador to Nigeria, James F. Entwistle, was asked about Nigeria's controversial new anti-gay legislation and whether the US might impose sanctions. His reply was: 'The US government no say sanction go dey for Nigeria, because of same-sex palava-o'. In other words, the US is not going to impose sanctions on Nigeria for passing a law criminalising same-sex marriages. Another question about next year's much-anticipated elections in Nigeria got this reply: 'Make I tell you say US no get any candidate for mind. The only ting wey go sweet us be say make the election dey transparent, credible and concluded. Make Nigerians pick candidates wey go sweet their belle, wey go do well well for them.' That is to say, 'Washington does not have a preferred presidential candidate. Just let Nigeria's elections be transparent and credible, and Nigerians should choose a candidate who will do them proud.' The Ambassador's efforts to use Pidgin were widely appreciated at the radio station and in the country.

This may perhaps be considered a vignette of the way forward for language contact. The linguistic outcomes of language contact, whether mixed codes or restructured varieties, may be recognised for being the code of a community and appreciated for the linguistic structure that has evolved. In addition, such varieties may not remain confined in the periphery – as unofficial language, only used in informal domains, stigmatised – but may, if their speakers so wish, become increasingly embraced – by the local community, the diaspora and, as in the anecdote of Pidgin above, even beyond. The opportunities for contact in today's world, as outlined in these last two chapters, that are afforded by national and transnational mobility, communication on the worldwide web and the global spread of popular culture and music, mean opportunities for increased, diverse and novel language evolution on both structural and social dimensions. For scholars of language contact, there is much to look forward to.

DISCUSSION POINTS

1. Having seen the development in scholarship over the decades on the issues of universality and (creole) exceptionalism, and the related issue of complexity, how would you evaluate the arguments?

2. Consider the various areas identified in this chapter as current and future directions for research, such as language contact in CMC, and contact languages as used by the diaspora: do you agree that these are significant issues for contact linguistics?

3. Consider some cases of creoles and minority varieties in education. Identify the factors that have led to their successful recognition and implementation or that have impeded progress in the field.

FURTHER READING

For recent work that shifts the focus of pidgin and creole studies from the better-known Atlantic and Caribbean contexts to those of the Indian Ocean, the South China Sea and the Middle East, see the articles in Ansaldo (2010b); Cardoso, Baxter and Pinharanda Nunes (2012); Buchstaller, Holmberg and Almoaily (2014); and Manfredi and Tosco (2014). Similarly, *APiCS* (Michaelis et al. 2013), and *eWAVE*

(Kortmann and Lunkenheimer 2013) are recent interactive online corpora comprising more diverse collections of languages, on which hypotheses on language contact may be tested. Explorations into the question of complexity in the field of linguistics in general can be found in Miestamo, Sinnemäki and Karlsson (2008); Sinnemäki (2011); and Good (2012). For recent work on the position of various contact languages in language policy and education, see the chapters in Migge, Léglise and Bartens (2010). For examples of research on minority and endangered languages and contact in multicultural urban areas, see the online resources Endangered Languages Alliance (elalliance.org) and LinguisticMinorities.HK (linguisticminorities.hk).

References

Abazov, Rafis. 2013. Globalisation of migration: What the modern world can learn from nomadic culture. *UN Chronicle* I(3). http://unchronicle.un.org/article/globalization-migration-what-modern-world-can-learn-nomadic-cultures/.

Abley, Mark. 2003. *Spoken Here*. New York, NY: Houghton Mifflin Books.

Aboh, Enoch O. 2006. The role of the syntax-semantics interface. In Claire Lefebvre, Lydia White and Christine Jourdan (eds.), *L2 Acquisition and Creole Genesis: Dialogues*. (Language Acquisition and Language Disorders 42.) Amsterdam/Philadelphia, PA: John Benjamins, 253–75.

2009. Competition and selection: That's all! In Enoch O. Aboh and Norval Smith (eds.), *Complex Processes in New Languages*. (Creole Language Library 35.) Amsterdam/Philadelphia, PA: John Benjamins, 317–44.

2015. *The Emergence of Hybrid Grammars: Language Contact and Change*. (Cambridge Approaches to Language Contact.) Cambridge: Cambridge University Press.

and Umberto Ansaldo. 2007. The role of typology in language creation: A descriptive take. In Umberto Ansaldo, Stephen Matthews and Lisa Lim (eds.), *Deconstructing Creole*. (Typological Studies in Language 73.) Amsterdam/Philadelphia, PA: John Benjamins, 39–66.

Adelaar, K. Alexander and David J. Prentice. 1996. Malay: Its history, role and spread. In Stephen A. Wurm, Peter Mühlhäusler and Darrel T. Tryon (eds.), *Atlas of Languages of Intercultural Communication in the Pacific, Asia and the Americas, vol. II*. Berlin: Mouton de Gruyter, 6736–93.

Aikhenvald, Alexandra Y. 2002. *Language Contact in Amazonia*. Oxford: Oxford University Press.

2008. Multilingual imperatives: The elaboration of a category in Northwest Amazonia. *International Journal of American Linguistics* 74(2): 189–225.

Alsagoff, Lubna. 2010. Hybridity in ways of speaking: The glocalization of English in Singapore. In Lisa Lim, Anne Pakir and Lionel Wee (eds.), *English in Singapore: Modernity and Management*. Hong Kong: Hong Kong University Press, 109–30.

Andersen, Roger W. 1983. A language acquisition interpretation of pidginization and creolization. In Roger W. Andersen (ed.), *Pidginization and Creolization as Language Acquisition*. Rowley, MA: Newbury House, 1–59.

Annamalai, E. 2001. *Managing Multilingualism in India*. New Delhi: Sage.

Ansaldo, Umberto. 2004. The evolution of Singapore English: Finding the matrix. In Lisa Lim (ed.), *Singapore English: A Grammatical Description*. (Varieties of English around the World G33.) Amsterdam/Philadelphia, PA: John Benjamins, 127–49.

2005. Typological admixture in Sri Lanka Malay: The case of Kirinda Java. Unpublished manuscript. University of Amsterdam.

2008. Revisiting Sri Lanka Malay: Genesis and classification. In K. David Harrison, David Rood and Arianne Dwyer (eds.), *A World of Many Voices: Lessons from Documenting Endangered Languages*. (Typological Studies in Language.) Amsterdam/Philadelphia, PA: John Benjamins, 13–42.

2009a. *Contact Languages: Ecology and Evolution in Asia*. (Cambridge Approaches to Language Contact.) Cambridge: Cambridge University Press.

2009b. Contact language formation in evolutionary terms. In Enoch O. Aboh and Norval Smith (eds.), *Complex Processes in New Languages*. (Creole Language Library 35.) Amsterdam/Philadelphia, PA: John Benjamins, 265–91.

2010a. Identity alignment and language creation in multilingual communities. *Language Science* 32(6): 615–23.

(ed.). 2010b. Pidgins and creoles in Asia. *Journal of Pidgin and Creole Linguistics* 25(1).

2011. Metatypy in Sri Lanka Malay. In Rajendra Singh and Ghanshyam Sharma (eds.), *Annual Review of South Asian Languages and Linguistics 2011*. Berlin: Mouton de Gruyter, 3–16.

and Lisa Lim. 2005. The KirJa collection: A corpus of Kirinda Java, a vital variety of Sri Lanka Malay. Unpublished manuscript. University of Amsterdam.

and Lisa Lim. forthcoming. Citizenship theory and fieldwork practice in Sri Lanka Malay communities. In Lisa Lim, Christopher Stroud and Lionel Wee (eds.), *The Multilingual Citizen: Towards a Politics of Language for Agency and Change*. (Encounters.) Bristol: Multilingual Matters.

Lisa Lim and Salikoko S. Mufwene. 2007. The sociolinguistic history of the Perankans: What it tells us about 'creolization'. In Umberto Ansaldo, Stephen Matthews and Lisa Lim (eds.), *Deconstructing Creole*. (Typological Studies in Language 73.) Amsterdam/Philadelphia, PA: John Benjamins, 203–26.

and Stephen Matthews. 2001. Typical creoles and simple languages: The case of Sinitic. *Linguistic Typology* 5: 311–26.

and Stephen Matthews. 2004. The origins of Macanese reduplication. In Geneviève Escure and Armin Schwegler (eds.), *Creoles, Contact and Language Change: Linguistic and Social Implications*. (Creole Language Library 27.) Amsterdam/Philadelphia, PA: John Benjamins, 1–19.

and Stephen Matthews. 2007. Deconstructing creole: The rationale. In Umberto Ansaldo, Stephen Matthews and Lisa Lim (eds.), *Deconstructing*

Creole. (Typological Studies in Language 73.) Amsterdam/Philadelphia, PA: John Benjamins, 1–18.

Ansaldo, Umberto, Stephen Matthews and Lisa Lim (eds.). 2007. *Deconstructing Creole.* (Typological Studies in Language 73.) Amsterdam/Philadelphia, PA: John Benjamins.

Ansaldo, Umberto, Stephen Matthews and Geoff Smith. 2010. China Coast Pidgin: Texts and contexts. In Umberto Ansaldo (ed.), *Pidgins and Creoles of Asia,* Special issue, *Journal of Pidgin and Creole Languages* 25(1): 63–94.

Ansaldo, Umberto, Stephen Matthews and Geoff Smith. 2012. China Coast Pidgin: Texts and contexts. In Umberto Ansaldo (ed.), *Pidgins and Creoles of Asia.* Amsterdam/Philadelphia, PA: John Benjamins, 59–90.

and Sebastian Nordhoff. 2009. Complexity and the age of languages. In Enoch O. Aboh and Norval Smith (eds.), *Complex Processes in New Languages.* (Creole Language Library 35.) Amsterdam/Philadelphia, PA: John Benjamins, 346–63.

Appel, René and Pieter Muysken. 1987. *Language Contact and Bilingualism.* London: Edward Arnold.

Arends, Jacques. 1989. *Syntactic developments in Sranan.* Unpublished PhD thesis, University of Nijmegen.

1995. Demographic factors in the formation of Sranan. In Jacques Arends (ed.), *The Early Stages of Creolization.* (Creole Language Libarary 13.) Amsterdam/Philadelphia, PA: John Benjamins, 233–85.

and Adrienne Bruyn. 1994. Gradualist and developmental hypotheses. In Jacques Arends, Pieter Muysken and Norval Smith (eds.), *Pidgins and Creoles: An Introduction.* Amsterdam/Philadelphia, PA: John Benjamins, 111–20.

Arends, Jacques, Pieter Muysken and Norval Smith (eds.). 1994. *Pidgins and Creoles: An Introduction.* Amsterdam/Philadelphia, PA: John Benjamins.

Asmah, Haji Omar. 1986. Sociolinguistic varieties of Malay. In Joshua Fishman, Andrée Tabouret-Keller, Michael Clyne, B. Krishnamurti and M. Abdulaziz (eds.), *The Fergusonian Impact: In Honor of Charles A. Ferguson,* vol. 2 : *Sociolinguistics and the Sociology of Language.* (Contributions to the Sociology of Language 42.) Berlin/New York, NY: Mouton de Gruyter, 191–206.

Auer, Peter (ed.). 1998. *Code-Switching in Conversation: Language, Interaction, and Identity.* London: Routledge.

1999. From code-switching via language mixing to fused lects: Towards a dynamic typology of bilingual speech. *International Journal of Bilingualism* 3: 309–32.

Austin, Peter K. and Julia Sallabank. 2011a. *Introduction.* In Peter K. Austin and Julia Sallabank (eds.), *The Cambridge Handbook of Endangered Languages.* Cambridge: Cambridge University Press, 1–24.

(eds.). 2011b. *The Cambridge Handbook of Endangered Languages.* Cambridge: Cambridge University Press.

Bailey, Richard W. and Manfred Görlach. 1982. *English as a World Language.* Ann Arbor, MI: University of Michigan Press.

Baker, Philip. 1995. Some developmental inferences from the historical studies of pidgins and creoles. In Jacques Arends (ed.), *The Early Stages of Creolization.* (Creole Language Libarary 13.) Amsterdam/Philadelphia, PA: John Benjamins, 1–24.

   and Anand Syea (eds.). 1996. *Changing Meanings, Changing Functions. Papers Relating to Grammaticalization in Contact Languages.* London: University of Westminster Press.

Bakker, Peter. 1994. Pidgins. In Jacques Arends, Pieter Muysken and Norval Smith (eds.), *Pidgins and Creoles: An Introduction.* Amsterdam/Philadelphia, PA: John Benjamins, 25–39.

   1997. *A Language of Our Own: The Genesis of Michif, the Mixed Cree-French Language of the Canadian Métis.* New York, NY: Oxford University Press.

   2008. Pidgins versus creoles and pidgincreoles. In Silvia Kouwenberg and John V. Singler (eds.), *The Handbook of Pidgin and Creole Studies.* Oxford: Wiley-Blackwell, 130–57.

Bakker, Peter, Aymeric Daval-Markussen, Mikael Parkvall and Ingo Plag. 2011. Creoles are typologically distinct from non-creoles. *Journal of Pidgin and Creole Languages* 21(1): 5–42.

   and Yaron Matras (eds.). 2013. *Contact Languages: A Comprehensive Guide.* Berlin/New York, NY: Mouton de Gruyter.

   and Maarten Mous (eds.). 1994. *Mixed Languages: 15 Case Studies in Language Intertwining.* (Studies in Language and Language Use 13.) Amsterdam: Institute for Functional Research into Language and Language Use.

   and Pieter Muysken. 1994. Mixed languages and language intertwining. In Jacques Arends, Pieter Muysken and Norval Smith (eds.), *Pidgins and Creoles: An Introduction.* Amsterdam/Philadelphia, PA: John Benjamins, 41–52.

Bakker, Peter, Marike Post and Hein van der Voort. 1994. TMA particles and auxiliaries. In Jacques Arends, Pieter Muysken and Norval Smith (eds.), *Pidgins and Creoles: An Introduction.* Amsterdam/Philadelphia, PA: John Benjamins, 247–58.

Bao, Zhiming. 2005. The aspectual system of Singapore English and the systemic substratist explanation. *Journal of Linguistics* 41: 237–67.

   2015. *The Making of Vernacular Singapore English.* (Cambridge Approaches to Language Contact.) Cambridge: Cambridge University Press.

Baskaran, Loga. 1994. The Malaysian English mosaic. *English Today* 37(10): 27–32.

   2008. Malaysian English: Phonology. In Rajend Mesthrie (ed.), *Varieties of English, vol. 4: Africa, South and Southeast Asia.* Berlin: Mouton de Gruyter, 278–91.

Baskaran, Lohanayahi. 1988. *Aspects of Malaysian English Syntax.* Unpublished PhD thesis, University College London.

Bautista, Maria Lourdes S. and Andrew B. Gonzales. 2009. Southeast Asian Englishes. In Braj Kachru, Yamuna Kachru and Cecil L. Nelson (eds.), *The Handbook of World Englishes*. Oxford: Wiley-Blackwell, 130–44.

Besemeres, Mary and Anna Wierzbicka. 2003. The meaning of the particle *lah* in Singapore English. *Pragmatics and Cognition* 11(1): 3–38.

Bhattacharya, Pramod Chandra. 1977. *A Descriptive Analysis of the Boro Language*. Gauhati: Department of Publication, Gauhati University.

Bickerton, Derek. 1981. *Roots of Language*. Ann Arbor, MI: Karoma.

1984. The Language Bioprogram Hypothesis. *Behavioral and Brain Sciences* 7: 173–221.

Blench, Roger. 2006. *Archaeology, Language, and the African Past*. Lanham, MD: AltaMira Press.

Blom, Jan-Petter and John Gumperz. 1972. Social meaning in linguistic structures: Code switching in northern Norway. In J.J. Gumperz and D. Hymes (eds.), *Directions in Sociolinguistics: The Ethnography of Communication*. New York, NY: Holt, Rinehart, and Winston, 407–34.

Blommaert, Jan. 2007. Sociolinguistic scales. *Intercultural Pragmatics* 4(1): 1–19.

2010. *The Sociolinguistics of Globalization*. Cambridge: Cambridge University Press.

and Jie Dong. 2010. Language and movement in space. In Nikolas Coupland (ed.), *The Handbook of Language and Globalisation*. Malden, MA/Oxford: Wiley-Blackwell, 366–85.

Bloomberg. 2012. China's urban population exceeds countryside for first time. *Bloomberg*, 17 January. www.bloomberg.com/news/articles/2012-01-17/china-urban-population-exceeds-rural.

Bodman, Nicholas Cleaveland. 1987. *Spoken Amoy Hokkien, vol. I*. New York, NY: Spoken Language Services.

Bodomo, Adams. 2010. The African trading community in Guangzhou: An emerging bridge for Africa–China relations. *China Quarterly* 203: 693–707.

2012. *Africans in China: A Sociocultural Study and Its Implications for Africa–China Relations*. Amherst, NY: Cambria Press.

Bourdieu, Pierre. 2001. The forms of capital. In Mark Granovetter and Richard Swedberg (eds.), *The Sociology of Economic Life*. Oxford: Westview Press, 29–51.

Bourhis, Richard, Howard Giles and Doreen Rosenthal. 1981. Notes on the construction of a 'subjective vitality questionnaire' for ethnolinguistic groups. *Journal of Multilingual and Multicultural Development* 2: 144–55.

Bowden, John. 2005. Language contact and metatypic restructuring in the directional system of North Maluku Malay. *Concentric: Studies in Linguistics* 31: 133–58.

Bradley, David. 2011. A survey of language endangerment. In Peter K. Austin and Julia Sallabank (eds.), *The Cambridge Handbook of Endangered Languages*. Cambridge: Cambridge University Press, 66–77.

Brenzinger, Matthias. 2007. *Language Diversity Endangered*. Berlin: Mouton de Gruyter.

Broadband Commission for Digital Development. 2012. *The State of Broadband 2012: Achieving Digital Inclusion for All*. Geneva: International Telecommunication Union and UNESCO. www.broadbandcommission .org/Documents/bb-annualreport2012.pdf.

Buchstaller, Isabelle, Anders Holmberg and Mohammad Almoaily (eds.). 2014. *Pidgins and Creoles beyond Africa-Europe Encounters*. (Creole Language Library 47.) Amsterdam/Philadelphia, PA: John Benjamins.

Canagarajah, A. Suresh. 1995a. The political-economy of code choice in a revolutionary society: Tamil/English bilingualism in Jaffna. *Language in Society* 24(2): 187–212.

1995b. Functions of code-switching in the ESL classroom: Socialising bilingualism in Jaffna. *Journal of Multilingual and Multicultural Development* 16: 173–96.

2007. Lingua Franca English, multilingual communities, and language acquisition. *Modern Language Journal* 91(5): 921–37.

2009. The plurilingual tradition and the English language in South Asia. In Lisa Lim and Ee-Ling Low (eds.), *Multilingual, Globalising Asia: Implications for Policy and Education, AILA Review* 22: 5–22.

Cardoso, Hugo, Alan Baxter and Mário Pinharanda Nunes (eds.). 2012. *Ibero-Asian Creoles*. (Creole Language Library 46.) Amsterdam/Philadelphia, PA: John Benjamins.

Chambers, Jack. 2004. Dynamic typology and vernacular universals. In Bernd Kortmann (ed.), *Dialectology meets Typology*. Berlin/New York, NY: Mouton de Gruyter, 127–45.

Chan, Brian Hok-Shing. 2012. English in Cantopop: Code-switching, pop songs and the local identity of Hong Kong Chinese. In Jamie Shinhee Lee and Andrew Moody (eds.), *English in Asian Popular Culture*. (Asian Englishes Today.) Hong Kong: Hong Kong University Press, 35–57.

Chan, Kam Wing. 2012. Migration and development in China: Trends, geography and current issues. *Migration and Development* 1(2): 187–205.

Chand, Vineeta. 2009a. *Who owns English? Political, social and linguistic dimensions of Urban Indian English language practices*. Unpublished PhD thesis, University of California, Davis.

2009b. [V]hat is going on? Local and global ideologies about Indian English. *Language in Society* 38(4): 393–419.

Chaudenson, Robert. 1979. *Les Créoles Français*. Paris: F. Nathan.

1992. *Des Iles, des Hommes, des Langues: Essais sur la Créolisation Linguistique et Culturelle*. Paris: L'Harmattan. Revised English edition: *Creolization of Language and Culture*. London: Routledge.

2000. Créolisation du français et françisation du créole: Le cas de Saint-Barthélemy et de la Réunion. In I. Newmann-Holzschuh and E.W. Schneider (eds.), *Degrees of Restructuring in Creole Languages*. Amsterdam/ Philadelphia, PA: John Benjamins, 361–81.

2001. *Creolization of Language and Culture*. London: Routledge.

2003. *La Créolisation: Théorie, Applications, Implications*. Paris: L'Harmattan.

Chen, Charles C. Jr. and Ching-Pong Au. 2004. Tone assignment in second language prosodic learning. Speech Prosody 2004 Conference. Nara, Japan, 23–26 March. www.isca-speech.org/archive/sp2004/sp04_091.html.

Chen, Katherine Hoi Ying. 2008. Positioning and repositioning: Linguistic practices and identity negotiation of overseas returning bilinguals in Hong Kong. *Multilingua* 27:57–75.

Cheshire, Jenny, Paul Kerswill, Susan Fox and Eivind Torgersen. 2011. Contact, the feature pool and the speech community: The emergence of Multicultural London English. *Journal of Sociolinguistics* 15(2): 151–96.

Chew, Phyllis Ghim-Lian. 2010. Linguistic capital, study mothers and the transnational family in Singapore. In Viniti Vaish (ed.), *Globalisation of Language and Culture in Asia*. London/New York, NY: Continuum, 82–105.

Coupland, Nikolas (ed.). 2003. *Sociolinguistics and Globalisation*, Thematic issue, *Journal of Sociolinguistics* 7(4).

2010a. Introduction: Sociolinguistics in the global era. In Nikolas Coupland (ed.), *The Handbook of Language and Globalisation*. Malden, MA/Oxford: Wiley-Blackwell, 1–27.

(ed.). 2010b. *The Handbook of Language and Globalisation*. Malden, MA/Oxford: Wiley-Blackwell.

Cowie, Claire. 2007. The accents of outsourcing: The meanings of 'neutral' in the Indian call centre industry. *World Englishes* 26(3): 316–30.

2010. The demand and supply of accents in the Indian call centre industry: 'Anyone doing something phonetic can attract business these days'. In Helen Kelly-Holmes and Gerlinde Mautner (eds.), *Language and the Market*. Basingstoke: Palgrave-Macmillan, 33–43.

Croft, William. 2000. *Explaining Language Change: An Evolutionary Approach*. Edinburgh: Longman.

Crystal, David. 2000. *Language Death*. Cambridge: Cambridge University Press.

2001. *Language and the Internet*. Cambridge: Cambridge University Press.

Curnow, Timothy Jowan. 2001. What language features can be 'borrowed'? In Alexandra Y. Aikhenvald and Robert M.W. Dixon (eds.), *Areal Diffusion and Genetic Inheritance: Problems in Comparative Linguistics*. Oxford: Oxford University Press, 412–36.

Dahl, Östen. 2004. *The Growth and Maintenance of Linguistic Complexity*. Amsterdam/Philadelphia, PA: John Benjamins.

David, Maya Khemlani. 2001. *The Sindhis of Malaysia: A Sociolinguistic Study*. London: Asean.

David, Maya Khemlani, Ibtisam M.H. Naji and Sheena Kaur. 2003. Language maintenance or language shift among the Punjabi Sikh community in Malaysia? *International Journal of the Sociology of Language* 161: 1–24.

Decamp, David. 1971. Introduction: The study of pidgin and creole languages. In Dell Hymes (ed.), *Pidginization and Creolization of Languages*. Cambridge: Cambridge University Press, 13–39.

Dediu, Dan, Michael Cysouw, Stephen C. Levinson, Andrea Baronchelli, Morten H. Christiansen, William Croft, Nicholas Evans, Simon Garrod, Russell D. Gray, Anne Kandler and Elena Lieven. 2013. Cultural evolution of language. In Peter J. Richerson and Morten H. Christiansen (eds.), *Cultural Evolution : Society, Technology, Language, and Religion*. Cambridge, MA: MIT Press, 303–32.

DeGraff, Michel. 2000. À propos des pronoms object dans le créole d'Haïti: Regards croisés de la morphologie et de la diachronie. *Langages* 138: 89–113.

2001a. Morphology in creole genesis: Linguistics and ideology. In Michael Kenstowicz (ed.), *Ken Hale: A Life in Language*. Cambridge, MA: MIT Press, 53–121.

2001b. On the origins of creoles: A Cartesian critique of Neo-Darwinian linguistics. *Linguistic Typology* 5(2/3): 213–310.

2003. Against creole exceptionalism. *Language* 79(2): 391–410.

2004. Against creole exceptionalism (redux). *Language* 80: 834–9.

2005a. Linguists' most dangerous myth: The fallacy of creole exceptionalism. *Language in Society* 34: 533–91.

2005b. Morphology and word order in 'creolization' and beyond. In Guglielmo Cinque and Richard S. Kayne (eds.), *The Oxford Handbook on Comparative Syntax*. Oxford: Oxford University Press, 293–372.

Department of Census and Statistics Sri Lanka. 2014. *Census of Population and Housing 2012: Provisional Information based on 5% Sample*. Colombo: Department of Census and Statistics, Ministry of Finance and Planning. www.statistics.gov.lk/PopHouSat/CPH2011/Pages/Activities/Reports/CPH_2012_5Per_Rpt.pdf.

Deumert, Ana and Sibabalwe Oscar Masinyana. 2008. Mobile language choices: The use of English and isiXhosa in text messages (SMS). *English World-Wide* 29(2): 117–47.

Dillard, J.L. 1970. Principles in the history of American English: Paradox, virginity, cafeteria. *Florida FL Reporter* 7: 32–3.

Djité, Paulin G. 2006. Shifts in linguistic identities in a global world. *Language Problems and Language Planning* 30(1): 1–20.

Duarte, Joana and Ingrid Gogolin (eds.). 2013. *Linguistic Superdiversity in Urban Areas: Research Approaches*. (Hamburg Studies on Linguistic Diversity.) Amsterdam/Philadelphia, PA: John Benjamins.

Eades, Diana. 1988. They don't speak in an Aboriginal language, or do they? In Ian Keen (ed.), *Being Black: Aboriginal Cultures in 'Settled' Australia*. Canberra: Aboriginal Studies Press, 97–115.

Edwards, John. 1985. *Language, Society and Identity*. Oxford: Blackwell.

1994. *Multilingualism*. London: Routledge.

Elgibali, Alaa. 1988. The language situation in Arabic-speaking nations. In Christina Bratt Paulston (ed.), *International Handbook of Bilingualism and Bilingual Education*. New York, NY/Westport, CT/London: Greenwood Press, 47–62.

eMarketer. 2013. *The Global Media Intelligence Report.* New York, NY: eMarketer.

Endangered Language Alliance. 2012. *Endangered Language Alliance.* elalliance.org

Enfield, Nicholas J. 2005. Areal linguistics and mainland Southeast Asia. *Annual Review of Anthropology* 34: 181–206.

Errington, Joseph. 2003. Getting language rights: The rhetorics of language endangerment and loss. *American Anthropologist* 105(4): 723–32.

Evans, Nicholas. 2010. *Dying Words: Endangered Languages and What They Have to Tell Us.* Chichester: Wiley-Blackwell.

    and Steven C. Levinson. 2009. The myth of language universals: Language diversity and its importance for cognitive science. *Behavioral and Brain Sciences* 32: 429–92.

Faraclas, Nicholas. 1996. *Nigerian Pidgin.* London: Routledge.

Fasold, Ralph W. 1984. *The Sociolinguistics of Society.* Oxford: Blackwell.

Ferguson, Charles A. 1959. Diglossia. *Word* 15: 325–40.

Feyerabend, Paul. 1987. *Farewell to Reason.* London: Verso/New Left Books.

Fishman, Joshua. 1964. Language maintenance and language shift as a field of inquiry. *Linguistics* 9: 32–70.

    1965. Who speaks what to whom and when? *Linguistique* 2: 67–88.

    1972. Domains and the relationship between micro- and macrosociolinguistics. In John J. Gumperz and Dell Hymes (eds.), *Directions in Sociolinguistics: The Ethnography of Communication.* New York, NY/Oxford: Basil Blackwell, 435–53.

    1991. *Reversing Language Shift: Theoretical and Empirical Foundations of Assistance to Threatened Languages.* Clevedon: Multilingual Matters.

Friedman, Thomas L. 2005. *The World is Flat: A Brief History of the 21st Century.* New York, NY: Farrar, Straus and Giroux.

Gal, Susan. 1979. *Language Shift: Social Determinants of Linguistic Change in Bilingual Austria.* New York, NY: Academic Press.

García, Ofelia. 2009. *Bilingual Education in the 21st Century: A Global Perspective.* Oxford: Wiley-Blackwell.

Garrett, Paul. 2006. Contact languages as 'endangered' languages: What is there to lose? *Journal of Pidgin and Creole Languages* 21(1): 175–90.

Gartner. 2013. Gartner says Asia/Pacific led worldwide mobile phone sales to growth in first quarter of 2013. Announcement, 14 May. www.gartner.com/newsroom/id/2482816.

Gensler, Orin and David Gil (eds.). forthcoming. *Malay/Indonesian Linguistics.* London: Curzon Press.

GfK Asia. 2012. Southeast Asia's mobile phones market grew by 24 percent in volume over the last 12 months. Press release, 17 September 2012. www.gfk.com/news-and-events/press-room/press-releases/pages/gfk%20asia%20-%20southeast%20asias%20mobile%20phones%20market%20grew%20by%2024%20percent%20in%20volume%20over%20the%20last%2012%20months.aspx.

Gibbons, John. 1979. U-gay-wa: A linguistic study of the campus language of students at the University of Hong Kong. In Robert Lord (ed.), *Hong Kong Language Papers*. Hong Kong: Hong Kong University Press, 3–43.

1987. *Code-Mixing and Code-Choice: A Hong Kong Case Study*. Clevedon: Multilingual Matters.

Giles, Howard, Richard Bourhis and Douglas Taylor. 1977. Towards a theory of language in ethnic group relations. In Howard Giles (ed.), *Language, Ethnicity and Intergroup Relations*. London: Academic Press, 307–44.

Giuffrè, Mauro. 2013. Review of *Linguistic Simplicity and Complexity*. *LINGUIST List*. http://linguistlist.org/pubs/reviews/get-review.cfm?SubID= 10438241.

Givón, Talmy. 1979. *On Understanding Grammar*. New York, NY: Academic Press.

Goddard, Cliff. 1994. The meaning of *lah*: Understanding 'emphasis' in Malay (Bahasa Melayu). *Oceanic Linguistics* 33: 145–65.

Goedemans, Rob and Ellen van Zanten. forthcoming. In Orin Gensler and David Gil (eds.), *Malay/Indonesian Linguistics*. London: Curzon Press, 35–62.

Gogolin, Ingrid, Peter Siemund, Monika Schulz and Julia Davydova. 2013. Multilingualism, language contact and urban areas: An introduction. In Peter Siemund, Ingrid Gogolin, Monika Edith Schulz and Julia Davydova (eds.), *Multilingualism and Language Diversity in Urban Areas: Acquisition, Identities, Space, Education*. Amsterdam/Philadelphia, PA: John Benjamins, 1–15.

Good, Jeff. 2004a. Tone and accent in Saramaccan: Charting a deep split in the phonology of a language. *Lingua* 114: 575–619.

2004b. Split prosody and creole simplicity: The case of Saramaccan. *Journal of Portuguese Linguistics* 3: 11–30.

2006. The phonetics of tone in Saramaccan. In Ana Deumert and Stephanie Durrleman (eds.), *Structure and Variation in Language Contact*. Amsterdam/ Philadelphia, PA: John Benjamins, 9–28.

2012. Typologizing grammatical complexities, or: Why creoles may be paradigmatically simple but syntagmatically average. *Journal of Pidgin and Creole Languages* 27(1): 1–47.

Gordon, Raymond G. Jr. (ed.) 2005. *Ethnologue: Languages of the World*, 15th edition. Dallas, TX: SIL International.

Greenfield, Lawrence. 1972. Situational measures of normative language view in relation to person, place, and topic among Puerto Rican bilinguals. In Joshua Fishman (ed.), *Advances in the Sociology of Language, vol. II*. The Hague: Mouton, 17–35.

Grenoble, Lenore A. 2011. Language ecology and endangerment. In Peter K. Austin and Julia Sallabank (eds.), *The Cambridge Handbook of Endangered Languages*. Cambridge: Cambridge University Press, 27–44.

Grimes, Joseph E. 1980a. Huichol life form classification I: Animals. *Anthropological Linguistics* 22(5): 187–200.

1980b. Huichol life form classification II: Plants. *Anthropological Linguistics* 22(6): 264–74.

Gumperz, John J. 1982. *Discourse Strategies*. Cambridge: Cambridge University Press.

Gupta, Anthea Fraser. 1989. Singapore Colloquial English and Standard English. *Singapore Journal of Education* 10: 33–9.

1992. The pragmatic particles of Singapore Colloquial English. *Journal of Pragmatics* 18: 31–57.

1994. *The Step-Tongue: Children's English in Singapore*. Clevedon: Multilingual Matters.

2006. Epistemic modalities and the discourse particles of Singapore. In Kerstin Fischer (ed.), *Approaches to Discourse Particles*. Amsterdam: Elsevier, 244–63.

Gussenhoven, Carlos. 2004. *The Phonology of Tone and Intonation*. Cambridge: Cambridge University Press.

Gut, Ulrike. 2005. Nigerian English prosody. *English World-Wide* 26: 153–77.

2007. First language influence and final consonant clusters in the New Englishes of Singapore and Nigeria. *World Englishes* 26: 346–59.

Gutiérrez, Kris D., Patricia Baquedano-López, Héctor Alvarez and Ming Ming Chiu. 1999. Building a culture of collaboration through hybrid language practices. *Theory into Practice* 38(2): 87–93.

Hagège, Claude. 1993. *The Language Builder: An Essay on the Human Signature in Linguistic Morphogenesis*. Amsterdam/Philadelphia, PA: John Benjamins.

Hale, Ken. 1998. On endangered languages and the importance of linguistic diversity. In L.A. Grenoble and L.J. Whaley (eds.), *Endangered Languages: Current Issues and Future Prospects*. Cambridge: Cambridge University Press, 192–216.

Hall, Robert A. 1966. *Pidgin and Creole Languages*. Ithaca, NY: Cornell University.

Harbert, Wayne. 2011. Endangered languages and economic development. In Peter K. Austin and Julia Sallabank (eds.), *The Cambridge Handbook of Endangered Languages*. Cambridge: Cambridge University Press, 403–22.

Harris, Alice C. and Lyle Campbell. 1995. *Historical Syntax in Cross-Linguistic Perspective*. Cambridge: Cambridge University Press.

Haspelmath, Martin. 2001. The European linguistic area: Standard Average European. In Martin Haspelmath, Ekkehard König, Wulf Oesterreicher and Wolfgang Raible (eds.), *Language Typology and Language Universals: An International Handbook, vol. 2.* (Handbücher zur Sprach- und Kommunikationswissenschaft 20.2.) Berlin/New York, NY: Walter de Gruyter. 1492–510.

Haugen, Einar. 1971. The ecology of language. *The Linguistic Reporter*, Supplement 25: 19–26.

Hauser, Marc D., Noam Chomsky and W. Tecumseh Fitch. 2002. The faculty of language: What is it, who has it, and how did it evolve? *Science* 298: 1569–79.

Heller, Monica. 2010. Language as resource in the globalised new economy. In Nikolas Coupland (ed.), *The Handbook of Language and Globalisation.* Malden, MA/Oxford: Wiley-Blackwell, 349–63.

Hesseling, Dirk Christiaan. 1897. Het Hollandsch in Zuid-Afrika. *De Gids* 60(1): 138–62. [Reprinted in English: Hesseling, Dirk. 1979. *On the Origin and Formation of Creoles: A Miscellany of Articles.* Ann Arbor, MI: Karoma.]

Hinrichs, Lars. 2004. Emerging orthographic conventions in written Creole: Computer-mediated communication in Jamaica. *Arbeiten aus Anglistik und Amerikanistik* 29(1): 81–109.

Hinton, Leanne. 1999. Teaching endangered languages. In Bernard Spolsky (ed.), *Concise Encyclopedia of Educational Linguistics.* Oxford: Elsevier.

2001. Language revitalization: An overview. In Leanne Hinton and Ken Hale (eds.), *The Green Book of Language Revitalization in Practice.* Leiden: Brill, 3–18.

2011. Revitalisation. In Peter K. Austin and Julia Sallabank (eds.), *The Cambridge Handbook of Endangered Languages.* Cambridge: Cambridge University Press.

Hjelmslev, Louis. 1938. Essai d'une théorie des morphèmes. In *Essais linguistiques.* Copenhagen: Nordisk Sprog-og Kulturforlag, 152–64.

Ho, Wing Lun Vienna, Carrie Lam Ka Yee, Jerome Ng Tik Lun and Phyllis Wong Wing Sui. 2010. *Tanka Community.* http://tanka-community .blogspot.hk/2010/02/what-is-tanka-community.html.

Holm, John. 1988. *Pidgins and Creoles, vol. 1: Theory and Structure.* Cambridge: Cambridge University Press.

1989. *Pidgins and Creoles, vol. 2: A Reference Survey.* Cambridge: Cambridge University Press.

Huber, Magnus. 1999. *Ghanaian Pidgin English in its West African Context.* (Varieties of English around the World G24.) Amsterdam/Philadelphia, PA: John Benjamins.

Hussainmiya, Bachamiya A. 1986. Melayu Bahasa: Some preliminary observations on the Malay creole of Sri Lanka. *Sari* 4(1): 19–30.

Hymes, Dell. 1971. *Pidginisation and Creolisation of Languages.* Cambridge: Cambridge University Press.

International Data Corporation. 2014. IDC announces India as the fastest growing smartphone market in Asia/Pacific in Q3 2014. *International Data Corporation*, 26 November. www.idc.com/getdoc.jsp?containerId= prIN25276014.

James, Gregory. 2001. Cantonese particles in Hong Kong students' emails. *English Today* 17(3): 9–16.

Jespersen, Otto. 1922. *Language: Its Nature, Development, and Origin.* London: Allen and Unwin.

Kachru, Braj B. (ed.). 1982. *The Other Tongue: English across Cultures.* Urbana, IL: University of Illinois Press.

1986. *The Alchemy of English: The Spread, Function and Models of Non-Native Englishes.* Urbana, IL: University of Illinois Press.

(ed.). 1992. *The Other Tongue: English across Cultures*, 2nd edition. Urbana, IL: University of Illinois Press.

Kachru, Yamuna and Cecil L. Nelson. 2006. *World Englishes in Asian Contexts*. Hong Kong: Hong Kong University Press.

Kandiah, Thiru. 1984. 'Kaduva': Power and the English language weapon in Sri Lanka. In Percy Colin-Thomé and Ashly Halpé (eds.), *Honouring E.F.C. Ludowyk: Felicitation Essays*. Colombo: Tisara Prakasakayo, 117–54.

Khin Khin Aye. 2005. *A Grammar of Singapore Bazaar Malay*. Unpublished PhD thesis, National University of Singapore.

Khubchandani, Lachman M. 1997. *Revisualising Boundaries: A Plurilingual Ethos*. New Delhi: Sage.

Killingley, Siew-Yue. 1972. Clause and sentence types in Malayan English. *Orbis* 21(2): 537–48.

Kim, Ronald I. 2011. Uriel Weinreich and the birth of modern contact linguistics. In Piotr P. Chruszczewski and Zdzisław Wąsik (eds.), *Languages in Contact 2010*. Wrocław: Philological School of Higher Education in Wrocław Publishing, 99–111.

Kortmann, Bernd and Kerstin Lunkenheimer 2013. *The Electronic World Atlas of Varieties of English 2.0*. [eWAVE 2.0]. Leipzig: Max Planck Institute for Evolutionary Anthropology. http://ewave-atlas.org.

and Benedikt Szmrecsanyi. 2004. Global synopsis: Morphological and syntactic variation in English. In Bernd Kortmann and Edgar W. Schneider (eds.), *A Handbook of Varieties of English, vol. 2: Morphology, Syntax*. Berlin/New York, NY: Mouton de Gruyter, 1142–202.

Kouwenberg, Silvia. 2004. The grammatical function of Papiamentu tone. *Journal of Portuguese Linguistics* 3: 55–69.

and John V. Singler (eds.). 2009. *The Handbook of Pidgin and Creole Studies*. New York, NY: Wiley-Blackwell.

Kulick, Don and Bambi Schieffelin. 2007. Language socialization. In Alessandro Duranti (ed.), *A Companion to Linguistic Anthropology*. Malden, MA: Blackwell, 347–68.

Kwachka, Patricia. 1992. Discourse structures, cultural stability, and language shift. *International Journal of Society and Language* 93: 67–73.

Kwan-Terry, Anna. 1978. The meaning and source of the 'la' and the 'what' particles in Singapore English. *RELC Journal* 9(2): 22–36.

1992. Towards a dictionary of Singapore English: Issues relating to making entries for particles in Singapore English. In Anne Pakir (ed.), *Words in a Cultural Context*. Singapore: UniPress, 62–72.

Kwek, Melody Y.P. 2005. *English teachers using Singapore Colloquial English: An examination of two secondary school teachers' lessons*. Unpublished BA Academic Exercise, National Institute of Education, Nanyang Technological University, Singapore.

Kwok, Helen. 1984. *Sentence Particles in Cantonese*. Hong Kong: Centre of Asian Studies, University of Hong Kong.

Ladefoged, Peter. 1992. Another view of endangered languages. *Language* 68(4): 809–11.

Lange, Claudia. 2009. 'Where's the party yaar!': Discourse particles in Indian English. In Thomas Hoffmann and Lucia Siebers (eds.), *World Englishes: Problems, Properties and Prospects*. (Varieties of English Around the World G40.) Amsterdam/Philadelphia, PA: John Benjamins, 207–26.

Lechner, Frank J. and John Boli (eds.). 2004. *The Globalization Reader*, 2nd edition. Malden, MA: Blackwell.

Lefebvre, Claire. 2004. *Issues in the Study of Pidgin and Creole Languages*. (Studies in Language Companion Series 70.) Amsterdam/Philadelphia, PA: John Benjamins.

Le Page, Robert B. and Andrée Tabouret-Keller. 1985. *Acts of Identity: Creole-based Approaches to Language and Ethnicity*. Cambridge: Cambridge University Press.

Ler, Soon Lay Vivien. 2006. A relevance-theoretic approach to discourse particles in Singapore English. In Kerstin Fischer (ed.), *Approaches to Discourse Particles*. Amsterdam: Elsevier, 149–66.

Lewis, M. Paul, Gary F. Simons and Charles D. Fennig (eds.). 2013. *Ethnologue: Languages of the World*, 17th edition. Dallas, TX: SIL International. www.ethnologue.com.

Li, Charles N. and Sandra A. Thompson. 1981. *Mandarin Chinese: A Functional Reference Grammar*. Berkeley, CA: University of California Press.

Li, Wei. 1998. Banana split? Variations in language choice and code-switching patterns of two groups of British-born Chinese in Tyneside. In Rodolfo Jacobson (ed.), *Codeswitching Worldwide*. (Trends in Linguistics: Studies and Monographs 106.) Berlin/New York, NY: Mouton de Gruyter, 153–75.

Vanithamani Saravanan and Julia Ng Lee Hoon. 1997. Language shift in the Teochew community in Singapore: A family domain analysis. *Journal of Multilingual and Multicultural Development* 18(5): 364–84.

Lim, JooHyuk and Ariane M. Borlongan. 2011. Tagalog particles in Philippine English: The cases of *ba, na, 'no*, and *pa. Philippine Journal of Linguistics* 42: 59–74.

Lim, Lisa. 2004. Sounding Singaporean. In Lisa Lim (ed.), *Singapore English: A Grammatical Description*. (Varieties of English around the World G33.) Amsterdam/Philadelphia, PA: John Benjamins, 19–56.

2007. Mergers and acquisitions: On the ages and origins of Singapore English particles. *World Englishes* 26(4): 446–73.

2008. Dynamic linguistic ecologies of Asian Englishes. *Asian Englishes* 11(1): 52–5.

2009a. Revisiting English prosody: (Some) New Englishes as tone languages? In Lisa Lim and Nikolas Gisborne (eds.), *The Typology of Asian Englishes*, Special issue, *English World-Wide* 30(2): 218–39.

2009b. Beyond fear and loathing in SG: The real mother tongues and language policies in multilingual Singapore. In Lisa Lim and Ee-Ling Low (eds.), *Multilingual Globalizing Asia: Implications for Policy and Education, AILA Review* 22: 52–71.

2009c. Not just an 'Outer Circle', 'Asian' English: Singapore English and the significance of ecology. In Thomas Hoffmann and Lucia Siebers (eds.), *World Englishes: Problems, Properties, Prospects.* (Varieties of English around the World G40.) Amsterdam/Philadelphia, PA: John Benjamins, 179–206.

2010a. Migrants and 'mother tongues': Extralinguistic forces in the ecology of English in Singapore. In Lisa Lim, Anne Pakir and Lionel Wee (eds.), *English in Singapore: Modernity and Management.* (Asian Englishes Today.) Hong Kong: Hong Kong University Press, 19–54.

2010b. Peranakan English in Singapore. In Daniel Schreier, Peter Trudgill, Edgar W. Schneider and Jeffrey P. Williams (eds.), *The Lesser-Known Varieties of English: An Introduction.* (Studies in English Language.) Cambridge: Cambridge University Press, 327–47.

2011a. Tone in Singlish: Substrate features from Sinitic and Malay. In Claire Lefebvre (ed.), *Creoles, Their Substrates and Language Typology.* (Typological Studies in Language 95.) Amsterdam/Philadelphia, PA: John Benjamins, 271–87.

2011b. Revisiting English prosody: (Some) New Englishes as tone languages? In Lisa Lim and Nikolas Gisborne (eds.), *The Typology of Asian Englishes.* (Benjamins Current Topics 33.) Amsterdam/Philadelphia, PA: John Benjamins.

2013. *Kaduva* of privileged power, instrument of rural empowerment? In Lionel Wee, Robbie B.H. Goh and Lisa Lim (eds.), *The Politics of English: South Asia, Southeast Asia and the Asia Pacific.* Amsterdam/Philadelphia, PA: John Benjamins, 61–80.

2013–2015. *LinguisticMinorities.HK.* http://linguisticminorities.hk/.

2014a. Yesterday's founder population, today's Englishes: The role of the Peranakans in the (continuing) evolution of Singapore English. In Sarah Buschfeld, Thomas Hoffmann, Magnus Huber and Alexander Kautzsch (eds.), *The Evolution of Englishes.* (Varieties of English around the World G49.) Amsterdam/Philadelphia, PA: John Benjamins, 401–19.

2014b. Southeast Asia. In Markku Filppula, Juhani Klemola and Devyani Sharma, (eds.) *The Oxford Handbook of World Englishes.* Oxford: Oxford University Press.

2015. Catalysts for change: On the evolution of new contact varieties in the multilingual knowledge economy. Unpublished manuscript. The University of Hong Kong.

2016. Multilingual mediators: The role of the Peranakans in the contact dynamics of Singapore. In Li Wei (ed.), *Multilingualism in the Chinese Diaspora World-Wide.* New York/Abingdon: Routledge.

forthcoming. The art of losing: Beyond *java, patois* and postvernacular vitality – Repositioning the periphery in global Asian ecologies. In Martin Pütz and Luna Filipović (eds.), *Endangered Languages: Issues of Ecology, Policy and Documentation*. Amsterdam/Philadelphia, PA: John Benjamins.

and Umberto Ansaldo. 2007. Identity alignment in the multilingual space: The Malays of Sri Lanka. In Eric Anchimbe (ed.), *Linguistic Identity in Postcolonial Multilingual Spaces*. Cambridge: Cambridge Scholars Publishing. 218–43.

and Umberto Ansaldo. 2012. Contact in the Asian arena. In Terttu Nevalainen and Elizabeth C. Traugott (eds.), *The Oxford Handbook of the History of English*. New York, NY: Oxford University Press, 560–71.

and Joseph A. Foley. 2004. English in Singapore and Singapore English: Background and methodology. In Lisa Lim (ed.), *Singapore English: A Grammatical Description*. (Varieties of English around the World G33.) Amsterdam/Philadelphia, PA: John Benjamins, 1–18.

and Nikolas Gisborne (eds.). 2009. *The Typology of Asian Englishes*, Special issue, *English World-Wide* 30(2).

and Nikolas Gisborne (eds.). 2011. *The Typology of Asian Englishes*. (Benjamins Current Topics 33.) Amsterdam/Philadelphia: John Benjamins.

Lim, Lisa, Anna Karregat and Wu Yuncang. 2009. Once isolated; now multilingual? Language practices, attitudes and identity in Volendam and Inner Mongolia compared. Multilingualism, Regional and Minority Languages: Paradigms for 'Languages of the Wider World' Conference. School of Oriental and African Studies, University of London, 16–17 April.

and Tan Ying Ying. 2001. How are we stressed?! Phonetic correlates and stress placement in Singaporean English. In John A. Maidment and Eva Estebas Vilaplana, (eds.), *Proceedings of PTLC 2001: Phonetics Teaching and Learning Conference 2001*. London: University College London, 27–30.

Lim, Sonny. 1988. Baba Malay: The language of the 'Straits-born' Chinese. In Hein Steinhauer (ed.), *Papers in Western Austronesian Linguistics* No. 3. (Pacific Linguistics Series A, No. 78.) Canberra: Department of Linguistics, Research School of Pacific Studies, The Australian National University.

Lin, Angel M.Y. 2005. Gendered, bilingual communication practices: Mobile text-messaging among Hong Kong college students *Fibreculture* 6. journal.fibreculture.org/issue6/index.html.

2012. The hip hop music scene in Hong Kong: Hybridity and identity in youth culture. In Jamie Shinhee Lee and Andrew Moody (eds.), *English in Asian Popular Culture*. (Asian Englishes Today.) Hong Kong: Hong Kong University Press.

Liu, Yucong. 2013. *Marketplace communication between Africans and Chinese in Guangzhou: An emerging pidgin?* Unpublished MPhil thesis, The University of Hong Kong.

Lock, Graham. 1988. *Variation, norms and prescribed standard in the Mandarin Chinese spoken in Singapore.* Unpublished PhD thesis, University of Sydney.

Low, Ee-Ling. 2000. Is lexical stress placement different in Singapore English and British English? In Adam Brown, David Deterding and Ee-ling Low (eds.), *The English Language in Singapore: Research on Pronunciation.* Singapore: Singapore Association of Applied Linguistics, 22–34.

Luke, Kang-kwong. 2000. Phonological re-interpretation: The assignment of Cantonese tones to English words. Ninth International Conference on Chinese Linguistics. National University of Singapore, June.

2008. Stress and intonation in Hong Kong English. Fourteenth Conference of the International Association for World Englishes (IAWE). Hong Kong, 1–5 December.

Lunden, S.S. 1978. Tracing the ancestry of Russenorsk. *Slavia Orientalis* 27(2): 213–17.

Lupyan, Gary and Rick Dale. 2010. Language structure is partly determined by social structure. *PLoS1* 5(1): 1–10.

Mackey, William F. 1986. The polyglossic spectrum. In Joshua Fishman, Andrée Tabouret-Keller, Michael Clyne, B. Krishnamurti and M. Abdul-Aziz (eds.), *The Fergusonian Impact. In Honour of Charles A. Ferguson, vol. I : From Phonology to Society; vol. II: Sociolinguistics and the Sociology of Language.* Berlin: Mouton de Gruyter, 237–43.

Maddieson, Ian. 2013. Tone. In Matthew S. Dryer and Martin Haspelmath (eds.), *The World Atlas of Language Structures Online.* Leipzig: Max Planck Institute for Evolutionary Anthropology. http://wals.info/chapter/13.

Mair, Christian. 2011. Corpora and the New Englishes: Using the 'Corpus of Cyber-Jamaican' to explore research perspectives for the future. In Fanny Meunier, Sylvie De Cock, Gaëtanelle Gilquin and Magali Paquot (eds.), *A Taste for Corpora: In Honour of Sylviane Granger.* Amsterdam/Philadelphia, PA: John Benjamins, 209–36.

and Theresa Heyd. 2011. 'I hardly speak pidgin – I just type it on the computer': Displaced and mediated vernaculars as a challenge to research on World Englishes. Indexing Authenticity: Perspectives from Linguistics and Anthropology. University of Freiburg, Germany, 25–27 November.

Makoni, Sinfree. 2002. From misinvention to disinvention: An approach to multilingualism. In Sinfree Makoni, Geneva Smitherman, Arnetha F. Ball and Arthur K. Spears (eds.), *Black Linguistics: Language, Society and Politics in Africa and the Americas.* London: Routledge, 132–53.

Manfredi, Stefano and Mauro Tosco (eds.). 2014. *Arabic-based Pidgins and Creoles,* Special issue, *Journal of Pidgin and Creole Languages* 29(2).

Matras, Yaron. 2000. How predictable is contact-induced change in grammar? In Colin Renfrew, April McMahon and Larry Trask (eds.), *Time Depth in Historical Linguistics, vol. II.* Oxford: MacDonald Institute for Archaeological Research, 563–83.

2009. *Language Contact*. Cambridge: Cambridge University Press.

2010. Contact, convergence and typology. In Raymond Hickey (ed.), *The Handbook of Language Contact*. Malden, MA/Oxford: Wiley-Blackwell, 66–85.

and Peter Bakker (eds.). 2003. *The Mixed Language Debate: Theoretical and Empirical Advances*. Berlin/New York, NY: Mouton de Gruyter.

Matthews, Stephen and Virginia Yip. 1994. *Cantonese: A Comprehensive Grammar*. London: Routledge.

McFarland, Curtis D. 2009. Linguistic diversity and English in the Philippines. In Maria Lourdes S. Bautista and Kingsley Bolton (eds.), *Philippine English: Linguistic and Literary Perspectives*. (Asian Englishes Today.) Hong Kong: Hong Kong University Press, 131–55.

McGeown, K. 2012. Call me: Tech powers Philippine call centre success. *NNC News: Business*, 14 May. www.bbc.co.uk/news/business-18061909.

McWhorter, John. 1998. Identifying the creole prototype: Vindicating a typological class. *Language* 74(4): 788–818.

2000. Defining 'creole' as a synchronic term. In Ingrid Neumann-Holzschuh and Edgar Schneider (eds.), *Degrees of Restructuring in Creole Languages*. Amsterdam/Philadelphia, PA: John Benjamins, 85–123.

2005. *Defining Creole*. New York, NY: Oxford University Press.

2011. *Linguistic Simplicity and Complexity: Why Do Languages Undress?* Berlin/New York, NY: Mouton de Gruyter.

2012. Case closed? Testing the feature pool hypothesis. *Journal of Pidgin and Creole Languages* 27(1): 171–82.

2013. It's not over: Why it matters whether there is such thing as a creole. *Journal of Pidgin and Creole Languages* 28(2): 409–23.

2014. A response to Mufwene. *Journal of Pidgin and Creole Languages* 29(1): 172–6.

Meakins, Felicity. 2011. *Case-marking in Contact: The Development and Function of Case Morphology in Gurindji*. Amsterdam/Philadelphia, PA: John Benjamins.

2013. Mixed languages. In Peter Bakker and Yaron Matras (eds.), *Contact Languages: A Comprehensive Guide*. Berlin/New York, NY: Mouton de Gruyter, 159–228.

Meeuwis, Michael and Jan Blommaert. 1998. A monolectal view of code-switching: Layered code-switching among Zairians in Belgium. In Peter Auer (ed.), *Code-Switching in Conversation: Language, Interaction and Identity*. London: Routledge, 76–99.

Meillet, Antoine. 1921. *Linguistique Historique et Linguistique Générale*. Paris: E. Champion.

1929. Le développement des langues. In Jacques Chevalier, Louis de Broglie, Maurice Hauriou, Georges Urbain, Edouard Le Roy, Paul Archambault, Jacques Nanteuil and Rene Aigrain (eds.), *Continu et Discontinu*. Paris: Bloud & Gay, 119ff. [Reprinted in Meillet 1951: 71–83.]

1951. *Linguistique Historique et Linguistique Générale, vol. II*. Paris: Klincksieck.

Mesthrie, Rajend and Rakesh M. Bhatt. 2008. *World Englishes: The Study of New Linguistic Varieties.* (Key Topics in Sociolinguistics.) Cambridge: Cambridge University Press.

and Clarissa Surek-Clark. 2013. Fanakalo. In Susanne Maria Michaelis, Philippe Maurer, Martin Haspelmath and Magnus Huber (eds.), *Contact Languages Based on Languages from Africa, Asia, Australia, and the Americas.* Oxford: Oxford University Press, 34–41.

Michaelis, Susanne Maria, Philippe Maurer, Martin Haspelmath and Magnus Huber (eds.). 2013. *The Atlas of Pidgin and Creole Language Structures.* Oxford: Oxford University Press.

Miestamo, Matti, Kaius Sinnemäki and Fred Karlsson (eds.). 2008. *Language Complexity: Typology, Contact, Change.* (Studies in Language Companion Series 94.) Amsterdam/Philadelphia, PA: John Benjamins.

Migge, Bettina, Isabelle Léglise and Angela Bartens (eds.). 2010. *Creoles in Education: An Appraisal of Current Programs and Projects.* (Creole Language Library 36.) Amsterdam/Philadelphia, PA: John Benjamins.

Milroy, Lesley and Pieter Muysken (eds.). 1995. *One Speaker, Two Languages: Cross-Disciplinary Perspectives on Code-Switching.* Cambridge: Cambridge University Press.

Moore, Leslie. 1999. Language socialization research and French language education in Africa: A Cameroonian case study. *Canadian Modern Language Review/La Revue Canadienne des Langues Vivantes* 56(2): 329–50.

Moseley, Christopher J. (ed.). 2007. *Encyclopedia of Endangered Languages.* London: Routledge.

Mufwene, Salikoko S. 1986. Les langues créoles peuvent-elles être définies sans allusion à leur histoire? *Etudes Créoles* 9: 135–50.

1990. Creoles and Universal Grammar. *Linguistics* 28(4): 783–807.

1991. Pidgins, creoles, typology, and markedness. In Francis Byrne and Thom Huebner (eds.), *Development and Structures of Creole Languages: Essays in Honor of Derek Bickerton.* Amsterdam/Philadelphia, PA: John Benjamins, 123–43.

1992. Why grammars are not monolithic. In Diane Brentari, Gary N. Larson and Lynn A. MacLeod (eds.), *The Joy of Grammar: A Festschrift in Honor of James D. McCawley.* Amsterdam/Philadelphia, PA: John Benjamins, 225–50.

1996a. Creole genesis: A population genetics perspective. In Pauline Christie (ed.), *Caribbean Language Issues Old and New.* Kingston, Jamaica: University of the West Indies Press, 168–209.

1996b. The founder principle in creole genesis. *Diachronica* 13:83–134.

1997. The legitimate and illegitimate offspring of English. In Larry E. Smith and Michael L. Forman (eds.), *World Englishes 2000.* Mānoa: College of Languages, Linguistics, and Literature, University of Hawai'i and the East-West Center, 182–203.

1998. What research on creole genesis can contribute to historical linguistics. In Monica S. Schmid, Jennifer R. Austin and Dieter Stein (eds.),

Historical Linguistics 1997. Amsterdam/Philadelphia, PA: John Benjamins, 315–38.

2000. Creolization is a social, not a structural, process. In Ingrid Neumann-Holzschuh and Edgar W. Schneider (eds.), *Degrees in Restructuring in Creole Languages*. Amsterdam/Philadelphia, PA: John Benjamins, 65–84.

2001. *The Ecology of Language Evolution*. (Cambridge Approaches to Language Contact.) Cambridge: Cambridge University Press.

2004a. Multilingualism in linguistic history: Creolization and indigenization. In Tej K. Bhatia and William C. Ritchie (eds.), *The Handbook of Bilingualism*. Oxford: Blackwell, 460–88.

2004b. Language birth and death. *Annual Review of Anthropology* 33: 201–22.

2007. Population movements and contacts: Competition, selection, and language evolution. *Journal of Language Contact* 1: 63–91.

2008. *Language Evolution: Contact, Competition and Change*. New York, NY: Continuum.

2014. The case was never closed: McWhorter misinterprets the ecological approach to the emergence of creoles. *Journal of Pidgin and Creole Languages* 29: 157–71.

Mühlhäusler, Peter. 1985. Syntax of Tok Pisin. In Stephen A. Wurm and Peter Mühlhäusler (eds.), *Handbook of Tok Pisin (New Guinea Pidgin)*. Canberra: Australian National University, 341–412.

1986. *Pidgin and Creole Linguistics*. Oxford: Blackwell.

1996. *Linguistic Ecology: Language Change and Linguistic Imperialism in the Pacific Region*. (The Politics of Language.) London: Routledge.

Muysken, Pieter 1981. Halfway between Quechua and Spanish: The case for relexification. In Arnold R. Highfield and Albert Valdman (eds.), *Historicity and Variation in Creole Studies*. Ann Arbor, MI: Karoma, 52–78.

1997. Code-switching processes: Alternation, insertion and congruent lexicalisation. In Martin Pütz (ed.), *Language Choices: Conditions, Constraints, and Consequences*. Amsterdam/Philadelphia, PA: John Benjamins, 361–80.

2000. *Bilingual Speech: A Typology of Code-Mixing*. Cambridge: Cambridge University Press.

and Paul Law. 2001. Creole studies: A theoretical linguists' field guide. *Glot International* 5(2): 47–57.

and Norval Smith. 1994. The study of pidgin and creole languages. In Jacques Arends, Pieter Muysken and Norval Smith (eds.), *Pidgins and Creoles: An Introduction*. Amsterdam/Philadelphia, PA: John Benjamins, 3–14.

Myers-Scotton, Carol. 1988. Swahili/English Nairobi corpus. Unpublished raw data.

1993. *Social Motivations for Codeswitching: Evidence from Africa*. Oxford: Clarendon Press.

2006. *Multiple Voices: An Introduction to Bilingualism*. Oxford: Blackwell.

Nadkarni, Mangesh V. 1975. Bilingualism and syntactic change in Konkani. *Language* 51: 672–83.

Nettle, Daniel. 1998. *Linguistic Diversity*. Oxford: Oxford University Press.

and Suzanne Romaine. 2000. *Vanishing Voices: The Extinction of the World's Languages*. Oxford: Oxford University Press.

Ng, E-Ching. 2008. Malay meets Chinese meets English: Where does colloquial Singaporean English word-level tone come from? Language Contact Workshop. Bristol, 11 July.

2012. Chinese meets Malay meets English: Origins of Singaporean English word-final high tone. *International Journal of Bilingualism* 16(1): 83–100.

Njau, Barbara. 2013. Can the Philippines keep BPO crown? *fDiIntelligence*. www.fdiintelligence.com/Sectors/Business-Services/Can-the-Philippines-keep-BPO-crown.

Nordhoff, Sebastian. 2009. *A Grammar of Upcountry Sri Lanka Malay*. PhD thesis. Utrecht: LOT.

Nortier, Jacomine and Margreet Dorleijn. 2013. Multi-ethnolects: Kebabnorsk, Perkerdansk, Verlan, Kanakensprache, Straattaal, etc. In Peter Bakker and Yaron Matras (eds.), *Contact Languages: A Comprehensive Guide*. Berlin/New York, NY: Mouton de Gruyter, 229–72.

OECD. 2012. *Education at a Glance 2012: OECD Indicators*. Paris: OECD Publishing.

Ochs, Elinor. 1988. *Culture and Language Development: Language Acquisition and Language Socialization in a Samoan Village*. Cambridge: Cambridge University Press.

Pakir, Anne.1992. Dictionary entries for discourse particles. In Anne Pakir (ed.), *Words in a Cultural Context*. Singapore: UniPress, 143–52.

Patrick, Peter. 2004. Jamaican Creole: Morphology and syntax. In Bernd Kortmann, Edgar W Schneider, Clive Upton, Rajend Mesthrie and Kate Burridge (eds.), *A Handbook of Varieties of English, vol. 2: Morphology and Syntax*. (Topics in English Linguistics.) Berlin/New York, NY: Mouton de Gruyter, 407–38.

Pavlenko, Aneta and Adrian Blackledge. 2004. *Negotiation of Identities in Multilingual Contexts*. Clevedon: Multilingual Matters.

Pennycook, Alastair. 2007. *Global Englishes and Transcultural Flows*. London: Routledge.

2010. Popular cultures, popular languages, and global identities. In Nikolas Coupland (ed.), *Handbook of Language and Globalisation*, Malden, MA/Oxford: Wiley-Blackwell, 592–607.

Phillipson, Robert. 1992. *Linguistic Imperialism*. Oxford: Oxford University Press.

Platt, John T. 1975. The Singapore English speech continuum and its basilect: 'Singlish' as a 'creoloid'. *Anthropological Linguistics* 17: 363–74.

1977. A model for polyglossia and multilingualism (with special reference to Singapore and Malaysia). *Language in Society* 6(3): 361–78.

1980. Multilingualism, polyglossia and code selection in Singapore. In Evangelos A. Afendras and Eddie C.Y. Kuo (eds.), *Language and Society in Singapore*. Singapore: Singapore University Press, 63–83.

1987. Communicative functions of particles in Singapore English. In Ross Steele and Terry Threadgold (eds.), *Language Topics: Essays in Honour of Michael Halliday*, vol. I. Amsterdam/Philadelphia, PA: John Benjamins, 391–401.

and Mian Lian Ho. 1989. Discourse particles in Singaporean English: Substratum influences and universals. *World Englishes* 8(2): 215–21.

and Heidi Weber. 1980. *English in Singapore and Malaysia – Status, Features, Functions*. Kuala Lumpur: Oxford University Press.

Platt, John T., Heidi Weber, Heidi Weber and Mian Lian Ho. 1983. *Singapore and Malaysia*. Amsterdam/Philadelphia, PA: John Benjamins.

Platt, John T., Heidi Weber and Mian Lian Ho. 1984. *The New Englishes*. London: Routledge and Kegan Paul.

Poplack, Shana. 1980. Sometimes I'll start a sentence in English y terminó en Español: Toward a typology of code-switching. *Linguistics* 18: 581–618.

Post, Marike. 1994. Fa d'Ambu. In Jacques Arends, Pieter Muysken and Norval Smith (eds.), *Pidgins and Creoles: An Introduction*. Amsterdam/Philadelphia, PA: John Benjamins, 191–204.

Pride, John (ed.). 1982. *New Englishes*. Rowley, MA: Newbury House.

Rahman, Tariq. 2009. Language ideology, identity and the commodification of language in the call centres of Pakistan. *Language in Society* 38: 233–58.

Rajah-Carrim, Aaliya. 2009. Use and standardisation of Mauritian Creole in electronically mediated communication. *Journal of Computer-Mediated Communication* 14(3): 484–508.

Rampton, Ben. 1995. *Crossing: Language and Ethnicity among Adolescents*. London: Longman.

1999. Sociolinguistics and cultural studies: New ethnicities, liminality and interaction. *Social Semiotics* 9(3): 355–73.

2011. From 'Multi-ethnic adolescent heteroglossia' to 'contemporary urban vernaculars'. *Language and Communication* 31: 276–94.

Ramsay, Robert. 2001. Tonogensis in Korean. In Shigeki Kaji (ed.), *Cross-Linguistic Studies of Tonal Phenomena: Tonogenesis, Japanese Accentology, and Other Topics*. Tokyo: Institute for the Study of Languages and Cultures (ILCAA), 3–17.

Remijsen, Bert. 2001. *Word Prosodic Systems of Raja Ampat Languages*. Utrecht: LOT.

and Vincent J. van Heuven. 2005. Stress, tone and discourse prominence in Curaçao Papiamentu. Unpublished manuscript. Leiden University.

Renfrew, Colin, April McMahon and Larry Trask (eds.). 2000. *Time Depth in Historical Linguistics*. 2 volumes. Cambridge: McDonald Institute for Archaeological Research.

Richards, Jack C. and Mary W.J. Tay. 1977. The *la* particle in Singapore English. In William Crewe (ed.), *The English Language in Singapore*. Singapore: Eastern University Press, 141–56.

Rivera-Castillo, Yolanda and Lucy Pickering. 2004. Phonetic correlates of stress and tone in a mixed system. *Journal of Pidgin and Creole Languages* 19: 261–84.

Roberts, Sarah J. 1998. The role of diffusion in the genesis of Hawaiian creole. *Language* 74: 1–39.

2000. Nativization and genesis of Hawaiian Creole. In John McWhorter (ed.), *Language Change and Language Contact in Pidgins and Creoles*. Amsterdam/Philadelphia, PA: John Benjamins, 257–300.

2004. The emergence of Hawai'i Creole English in the early 20th century: The sociohistorical context of creole genesis. Unpublished PhD thesis, Stanford University.

Romaine, Suzanne. 1989. *Bilingualism*. Oxford: Blackwell.

Römer, Raúl. 1992. *Studies in Papiamentu Tonology.* (Caribbean Culture Studies 5.0.) Amsterdam and Kingston: University of Amsterdam and University of the West Indies.

Ross, Malcolm. 1996. Contact-induced change and the comparative method: Cases from Papua New Guinea. In Mark Durie and Malcolm Ross (eds.), *The Comparative Method Revisited: Regularity and Irregularity in Language Change*. New York, NY: Oxford University Press, 180–217.

2001. Contact-induced change in Oceanic languages in North-West Melanesia. In Alexandra Y. Aikhenvald, R.M.W. Dixon (eds.), *Areal Diffusion and Genetic Inheritance*. Oxford: Oxford University Press, 134–66.

2006. Metatypy. In Keith Brown (ed.), *Encyclopedia of Language and Linguistics, vol. VIII*. Oxford: Elsevier, 95–9.

2007. Calquing and metatypy. *Journal of Language Contact* 1(1): 116–43.

Rountree, S. Catherine. 1972. Saramaccan tone in relation to intonation and grammar. *Lingua* 29: 308–25.

Rubin, Joan. 1968. *National Bilingualism in Paraguay*. Asunción: Mouton and Company.

Saghal, Anju. 1991. Patterns of language use in a bilingual setting in India. In Jenny Cheshire (ed.), *English Around the World: Sociolinguistic Perspectives*. Cambridge: Cambridge University Press, 299–307.

Sakoda, Kent and Jeff Siegel. 2003. *Pidgin Grammar: An Introduction to the Creole Language of Hawai'i*. Honolulu: Bess Press.

Salick, Jan, Nicoletta Cellinese and Sandra Knapp. 1997. Indigenous diversity of Cassava: Generation, maintenance, use and loss among the Amusha of the Peruvian Upper Amazon. *Economic Botany* 51(1): 6–19.

Sandel, Todd L., Wen-Yu Chao and Chung-Hui Liang. 2006. Language shift and language accommodation across family generations in Taiwan. *Journal of Multilingual and Multicultural Development* 27(2): 126–47.

Sasse, Hans-Jurgen. 1985. Sprachkontakt und Sprachwandel: Die Grazisierung der albanischen Mundarten Griechenlands. *Papiere zur Linguistik* 32: 37–95.

1990. Language decay and contact-induced change: Similarities and differences. *Arbeitspapier (Institut für Sprachwissenschaft, Universität zu Köln)* 12 (Neue Folge): 30–56.

Sebba, Mark. 1997. *Contact Languages: Pidgins and Creoles*. Basingstoke: Macmillan.

Selbach, Rachel, Hugo C. Cardoso and Margot van den Berg (eds.). 2009. *Gradual Creolization: Studies Celebrating Jacques Arends*. (Creole Language Library 34.) Amsterdam/Philadelphia, PA: John Benjamins.

Seuren, Pieter. 1998. *Western Linguistics: A Historical Introduction*. Oxford: Blackwell.

Shapiro Roman. 2010. Chinese Pidgin Russian. In Umberto Ansaldo (ed.), *Pidgins and Creoles in Asian Contexts*, Special issue, *Journal of Pidgin and Creole Languages* 25(1): 5–62.

Sharma, Devyani. 2009. Typological diversity in New Englishes. In Lisa Lim and Nikolas Gisborne (eds.), *The Typology of Asian Englishes*, Special issue, *English World-Wide* 30(2): 170–95.

Siegel, Jeff. 1997. Mixing, levelling, and pidgin/creole development. In Arthur K. Spears and Donald Winford (eds.), *The Structure and Status of Pidgins and Creoles*. (Creole Language Library 19.) Amsterdam/Philadelphia, PA: John Benjamins, 111–50.

1999. Transfer constraints and substrate influence in Melanesian Pidgin. *Journal of Pidgin and Creole Languages* 14: 1–44.

2000. Substrate influence in Hawai'i Creole English. *Language in Society* 29: 197–236.

2004. Morphological elaboration. *Journal of Pidgin and Creole Languages* 19(2): 333–62.

2006. Links between SLA and creole studies: Past and present. In Claire Lefebvre, Lydia White and Christine Jourdan (eds.), *L2 Acquisition and Creole Genesis: Dialogues*. Amsterdam/Philadelphia, PA: John Benjamins, 15–49.

2007a. Transmission and transfer. In Umberto Ansaldo, Stephen Matthews and Lisa Lim (eds.), *Deconstructing Creole*. Amsterdam/Philadelphia, PA: John Benjamins, 167–201.

2007b. Recent evidence against the Language Bioprogram Hypothesis: The pivotal case of Hawai'i Creole. *Studies in Language* 31(1):51–88.

2007c. Creole and minority dialects in education: An update. *Language and Education* 21(1): 66–86.

2008a. In praise of the cafeteria principle: Language mixing in Hawai'i Creole. In Susanne Michaelis (ed.), *Roots of Creole Structures: Weighing the Contribution of Substrates and Superstrates*. Amsterdam/Philadelphia, PA: John Benjamins, 59–82.

2010. Pidgins and creoles. In Nancy H. Hornberger and Sandra Lee McKay (eds.), *Sociolinguistics and Language Education*. Bristol: Multilingual Matters, 232–62.

Siemund, Peter, Ingrid Gogolin, Monika Edith Schulz and Julia Davydova (eds.). 2013. *Multilingualism and Language Diversity in Urban Areas: Acquisition, Identities, Space, Education*. Amsterdam/Philadelphia, PA: John Benjamins.

Silver, Rita Elaine and Wendy Bokhorst-Heng. 2013. Linguistic hybridity in student peer talk. International Symposium on Bilingualism (ISB9). Singapore, 10–13 June.

Silverstein, Michael. 1996. Monoglot 'standard' in America: Standardisation and metaphors of linguistic hegemony. In Donald Brenneis and Ronald Macaulay (eds.), *The Matrix of Language: Contemporary Linguistic Anthropology*. Boulder, CO: Westview Press, 284–306.

Singler, John. 1986. Remarks in response to Derek Bickerton's 'Creoles and Universal Grammar: The unmarked case?' *Journal of Pidgin and Creole Languages* 1: 141–5.

1990. The impact of decreolization upon T-M-A: Tenselessness, mood, and aspect in Kru Pidgin English. In John Singler (ed.), *Pidgin and Creole Tense-Mood-Aspect Systems*. Amsterdam/Philadelphia, PA: John Benjamins, 203–30.

Sinnemäki, Kaius. 2011. *Language universals and linguistic complexity: Three case studies in core argument marking*. Unpublished PhD thesis, University of Helsinki.

Smith, Geoff P. 2002. *Growing Up with Tok Pisin: Contact, Creolization, and Change in Papua New Guinea's National Language*. London: Battlebridge.

Smith, Ian, Scott Paauw and B.A. Hussainmiya 2004. Sri Lanka Malay: The state of the art. In Rajendra Singh (ed.), *The Yearbook of South Asian Languages and Linguistics 2004*. Berlin/New York, NY: Mouton de Gruyter, 197–215.

Snow, Don. 2010. Hong Kong and modern diglossia. *International Journal of the Sociology of Language* 206: 155–79.

Sorensen, A.P. 1971. Multilingualism in the northwest Amazon. *American Anthropologist* 69: 670–84.

Specter, Michael. 1996. Computer speak: World, wide, web: 3 English words. *The New York Times*, 14 April. www.nytimes.com/1996/04/14/weekinreview/computer-speak-world-wide-web-3-english-words.html.

Spolsky, Bernard. 2011. Ferguson and Fishman: Sociolinguistics and the sociology of language. In Ruth Wodak, Barbara Johnstone and Paul E. Kerswill (eds.), *The SAGE Handbook of Sociolinguistics*. London: SAGE Publications Ltd, 11–23.

Sridhar, S.N. and Kamal K. Sridhar. 1980. The syntax and psycholinguistics of bilingual code-mixing. *Canadian Journal of Psychology* 34(4): 407–16.

St-Hilaire, Aonghas. 2011. *Kwéyòl in Postcolonial Saint Lucia: Globalisation, Language Planning and National Development*. (Creole Language Library 40.) Amsterdam/Philadelphia, PA: John Benjamins.

Stell, Gerald and Kofi Yakpo (eds.). 2015. *Code-Switching between Structural and Sociolinguistic Perspectives*. (Linguae and Litterae 43.) Berlin/Munich/Boston, MA: Walter de Gruyter.

Svantesson, Jan-Olof. 2001. Tonogenesis in South East Asia: Mon-Khmer and beyond. In Shigeki Kaji (ed.), *Proceedings from the Symposium Cross-Linguistic Studies of Tonal Phenomena: Historical Development, Phonetics of*

Tone, and Descriptive Studies. Tokyo: Tokyo University of Foreign Studies, Institute for Language and Cultures of Asia and Africa, 45–58.

Tay, Mary W.J. 1968. *A phonological study of Hokkien*. Unpublished PhD thesis, University of Edinburgh.

Thomason, Sarah G. 2001. *Language Contact: An Introduction*. Washington DC: Georgetown University Press.

and Terrence Kaufman. 1988. *Language Contact, Creolisation and Genetic Linguistics*. Berkeley, CA: University of California Press.

Thurgood, Graham. 1999. *From Ancient Cham to Modern Dialects: Two Thousand Years of Language Contact and Change*. (Oceanic Linguistics Special Publications 28.) Hawai'i: University of Hawai'i Press.

Thurston, William R. 1994. Renovation and innovation in the languages of North-western New Britain. In Tom Dutton and Darrell Tryon (eds.), *Language Contact and Change in the Austronesian World*. Berlin: Mouton de Gruyter, 573–609.

Tomasello, Michael 2003. *Constructing a Language: A Usage-Based Theory of Language Acquisition*. Cambridge, MA/London: Harvard University Press.

2005. Beyond formalities: The case of language acquisition. *The Linguistic Review* 22: 167–81.

Tongue, Ray K. 1974. *The English of Singapore and Malaysia*, 1st edition. Singapore: Eastern Universities Press.

Tordesillas, Ellen. 2013. Gazmin makes the Philippines look pathetic. *Yahoo! News Philippines*, 30 June. http://news.yahoo.com/blogs/the-inbox/ gazmin-makes-philippines-look-pathetic-163745294.html.

Trudgill, Peter. 1995. Grammaticalisation and social structure: Nonstandard conjunction-formation in East Anglian English. In Frank R. Palmer (ed.), *Grammar and Meaning: Papers in Honour of Sir John Lyons*. Cambridge: Cambridge University Press, 136–47.

1996. Dialect typology: Isolation, social network and phonological structure. In Gregory R. Guy, Crawford Feagin, Deborah Schiffrin and John Baugh (eds.), *Towards a Social Science of Language, vol. 1: Variation and Change in Language and Society*. Amsterdam/Philadelphia, PA: John Benjamins, 3–22.

2001. Contact and simplification: Historical baggage and directionality in linguistic change. *Linguistic Typology* 5: 371–4.

2002. Linguistics and social typology. In Jack Chambers, Peter Trudgill and Natalie Schilling-Estes (eds.), *The Handbook of Language Variation and Change*. Oxford: Blackwell, 707–28.

2010. *Investigations in Sociohistorical Linguistics: Stories of Colonization and Contact*. Cambridge: Cambridge University Press.

and Jean Hannah. 1982. *International English: A Guide to Varieties of Standard English*. London: Edward Arnold.

UNESCO. 2012a. Naqqāli, Iranian dramatic storytelling. Paris: United Nations Educational, Scientific and Cultural Organisation. www.unesco .org/culture/ich/en/USL/00535.

2012b. Hezhen Yimakan storytelling. Paris: United Nations Educational, Scientific and Cultural Organisation. www.unesco.org/culture/ich/en/USL/00530.

2013. Internal migrants in India: The millions who cannot exercise their rights. New Delhi: United Nations Educational, Scientific and Cultural Organisation, 16 January. www.unesco.org/new/en/newdelhi/about-this-office/single-view/news/internal_migrants_in_india_the_millions_who_cannot_exercise_their_rights/.

United Nations. 2009. *The Millennium Development Goals Report 2009.* New York, NY: United Nations.

2013a. Deputy UN chief calls for urgent action to tackle global sanitation crisis. *United Nations News Centre,* 21 March. www.un.org/apps/news/story.asp?NewsID=44452#.VGwn8vmUcYE.

2013b. *Millennium Development Goals.* New York, NY: United Nations. www.un.org/millenniumgoals.

United Nations Development Programme. 2009. *Human Development Report 2009: Overcoming Barriers: Human Mobility and Development.* Basingstoke: Palgrave Macmillan.

Valdman, Albert and Arnold Highfield (eds.). 1980. *Theoretical Orientations in Creole Studies.* New York, NY: Academic Press.

Velupillai, Viveka. 2015. *Pidgins and Creoles: An Introduction.* (Creole Language Library 48.) Amsterdam/Philadelphia, PA: John Benjamins.

Vertovec, Steven. 2006. The emergence of super-diversity in Britain. *Centre on Migration, Policy and Society Working Papers* 25. Oxford University.

2010. Towards post-multiculturalism? Changing communities, conditions and contexts of diversity. *International Social Science Journal* 61: 83–95.

Voegelin, C.F., F.M. Voegelin and Noel W. Schutz, Jr. 1967. The language situation in Arizona as part of the Southwest culture area. In Dell Hymes and William E. Bittle (eds.), *Studies in Southwestern Ethnolinguistics: Meaning and History in the Languages of the American Southwest.* The Hague: Mouton, 403–51.

Voorhoeve, Jan. 1961. Le ton et la grammaire dans le Saramaccan. *Word* 17: 146–63.

Wang, Yue. 2013. More people have cell phones than toilets, UN report shows. *Time,* 25 March. http://newsfeed.time.com/2013/03/25/more-people-have-cell-phones-than-toilets-u-n-study-shows.

Wee, Kim Soon Gabriel. 2000. *Intonation of the Babas: An auditory and instrumental approach.* Unpublished BA honours thesis, National University of Singapore.

Wee, Lian-hee. 2008. More or less English? Two phonological patterns in the Englishes of Singapore and Hong Kong. *World Englishes* 27: 480–501.

Wehi, Priscilla M. 2009. Indigenous ancestral sayings contribute to modern conservation partnerships: Examples using Phormium tenax. *Ecological Applications* 19(1): 267–75.

Wehi, Priscilla M., Hemi Whaanga and Tom Roa. 2009. Missing in translation: Maori language and oral traditional in scientific analyses of traditional ecological knowledge (TEK). *Journal of the Royal Society of New Zealand* 39(4): 201–4.

Weinreich, Uriel. 1953. *Languages in Contact: Findings and Problems*. (Publications of the Linguistic Circle of New York 1.) New York, NY: Linguistic Circle of New York.

Wells, John C. 1982. *Accents of English*. 3 volumes. Cambridge: Cambridge University Press.

Whinnom, Keith. 1971. Linguistic hybridisation and the special case of pidgins and creoles. In Dell Hymes (ed.), *Pidginization and Creolization of Languages*. Cambridge: Cambridge University Press, 91–116.

Whorf, Benjamin Lee. 1941. The relation of habitual thought and behavior to language. In Leslie Spier, A. Irving Hallowell and Stanley S. Newman (eds.). *Language, Culture, and Personality: Essays in Memory of Edward Sapir*. Menasha, WI: Sapir Memorial Publication Fund. 75–93. Reprinted in 1956 in John B. Carroll (ed.) *Language, Thought and Reality: Selected Writings of Benjamin Lee Whorf*. Cambridge, MA: MIT Press, 134–59.

Winford, Donald. 2003. *An Introduction to Contact Linguistics*. Oxford: Blackwell.

Wong, Yin-ting. 2009. *The linguistic function of Cantonese discourse particles in the English medium online chat of Cantonese speakers*. Unpublished MA thesis, University of Wollongong.

Woo Yen-yen, Colin Goh [Producers/Directors] and Woffles Wu [Producer]. 2006. *Singapore Dreaming*. [Motion Picture.] Singapore: 5C Films Pte Ltd.

Woodbury, Anthony C. 2005. Ancestral languages and (imagined) creolisation. In Peter K. Austin (ed.), *Language Documentation and Description* 3: 252–62.

Woolard, Kathryn A. 1999. Simultaneity and bivalency as strategies in bilingualism. *Journal of Linguistic Anthropology* 8(1): 3–29.

World Bank. 2012. Mobile phone access reaches three quarters of planet's population. Washington, DC: World Bank. www.worldbank.org/en/ news/press-release/2012/07/17/mobile-phone-access-reaches-three-quarters-planets-population.

World Bank and African Development Bank. 2013. The transformational use of information and communication technologies in Africa. Washington, DC: World Bank. siteresources.worldbank.org/ EXTINFORMATIONANDCOMMUNICATIONANDTECHNOLOGIES/Resour ces/282822-1346223280837/Summary.pdf.

Wright, Claire. 2008. Diglossia and multilingualism: Issues in language contact and language shift in the case of Hong Kong pre- and post-1997. *ARECLS* 5: 263–79.

Wu, Yuncang. 2008. *Language maintenance or shift: The Mongols in Inner Mongolia of China*. Unpublished MA thesis, University of Amsterdam.

Yakpo, Kofi. 2009. *A Grammar of Pichi*. Berlin/Accra: Isimu Media.

Yang, Suyung. 2004. Globalization, tribalization and online communication. In Kwok-kan Tam and Timothy Weiss (eds.), *English and Globalization: Perspectives from Hong Kong and Mainland China*. Hong Kong: The Chinese University Press, 101–13.

Yao Xiaoping. 2011. Wilhelm von Humboldt and the Chinese language. Speech delivered at Humboldt-Kolleg, San Ya, 28 September 2011. www.yaoxiaoping.org/News/news_detail.asp?id=307.

Yip, Virginia and Stephen Matthews. 2007. *The Bilingual Child: Early Development and Language Contact*. (Cambridge Approaches to Language Contact.) Cambridge: Cambridge University Press.

Index

234